Praise for *The Money School*

"If you master your mind—and your money—there's little you can't do. Nicole Lapin has created a comprehensive guide to financial success with *The Money School*. Her straightforward, no-nonsense approach makes this book an essential tool for anyone looking to take control of their financial future."

—JIM KWIK,
New York Times bestselling author
and world's leading brain coach

"A financial guru." —*Forbes*

"Nicole covers trending money topics with the tone of an 'in-the-know' smart girlfriend who will tell you what to do."

—Yahoo Finance

"A financial powerhouse who has turned her expertise into a crusade for financial literacy." —*Adweek*

Praise for Nicole Lapin and Her Books

"A financial diet is like a regular diet: If you allow yourself small indulgences, you won't binge later on. Nicole offers you a plan you can stick to."

—SANJAY GUPTA,
chief medical correspondent at CNN

"Nicole does a fabulous job educating people about money while always keeping it fun and entertaining."

—ALEXIS MAYBANK,
cofounder of Gilt Groupe

"Lapin's unfiltered, energetic advice speaks to anyone taking aim at their own career destiny."

—MIKE PERLIS,
vice chairman and strategic adviser, Forbes Media

"Nicole delivers expert financial advice straight up, no chaser, in a tone that's as lively as it is likable."

—NEIL BLUMENTHAL and DAVE GILBOA,
founders of Warby Parker

"If you're a woman and you like money, you need to read this book. Immediately. You can't afford to miss this one, ladies!"

—ALLI WEBB,
founder and CEO of Drybar

"Nicole brings to life in a highly readable way the real pitfalls and solutions of financial life in a more complex world." —NIGEL TRAVIS,
CEO of Dunkin' Brands

"Whether you want to take over the world or just balance your checkbook, Nicole gives you the tools to save, spend, and succeed."

—RANDI ZUCKERBERG,
technology expert

"I wish I had Nicole's book when I was starting my business. She makes business and finance feel accessible but does it in a sassy, humorous way. It's a must-have for any budding entrepreneur."

—KRISTI YAMAGUCHI,
Olympic gold medalist and entrepreneur

"It's empowering to see an independent, strong woman as the voice of the financial industry. Nicole is truly inspiring and shares essential tips for women who want to take control of not only their bank accounts but also their lives." —JOSIE NATORI,
founder of The Natori Company

"Having the life you want isn't just about managing your career brilliantly. It's about getting control of your finances—starting *right now*. Nicole's sassy, smart, and super-easy-to-digest book will help you do exactly that."   —KATE WHITE,
former editor-in-chief for *Cosmopolitan*

"What I love about Nicole is that you don't need a dictionary to understand her advice. It's crystal clear, straight up, and spot on."
—ALYSSA MILANO,
actress and entrepreneur

"She gives a brash tutorial for women looking to take their share in today's bleak economic climate. Ever astute, Lapin leads the way brilliantly!"   —KAREN FINERMAN,
host of CNBC's *Fast Money*

"Her books should be mandatory reading for every young professional woman who wants to take control of her financial destiny. Lapin provides unfiltered, brilliant advice to a generation of women taking aim at their own success and wealth."   —MINDY GROSSMAN,
CEO of Weight Watchers

"Her books are essential reading for twenty-first century women wanting to rise to the top of the economic ladder. Everything that you need to know is in here, all of it said with the wit and confidence we've come to expect from Nicole."   —REBECCA TAYLOR,
designer

"The role of women in the workforce is changing, and today women are disrupting the workplace—for the better. Ladies, it's time to disrupt your own industry. Nicole will show you how."

—SARA BLAKELY,
founder of Spanx

"Whether you're wanting to branch out with your own startup or just get ahead in your current job, Nicole knows just how to develop those skills to get you where you want to be. She's a perfect role model for young women."

—BRIT MORIN,
founder and CEO of Brit + Co

"Women are underrepresented among entrepreneurs. Nicole is a great guide to help us close that gap."

—DANIEL LUBETZKY,
founder and CEO of KIND Snacks

"Nicole's books are a fun and engaging read to help build your brand and rock your career."

—TONY HSIEH,
CEO of Zappos

"At last! A book that's cool enough for my kick-ass teenage daughters and smart enough for my CEO self!"

—JULIE CLARK,
founder of Baby Einstein

"Taking care of yourself isn't just important for your health—it's crucial to your success in your career. Nicole Lapin understands this firsthand and will help you become your most heroic self."

—JULIA HARTZ,
cofounder and CEO of Eventbrite

"The only way to be of value to anyone else is to be value to yourself first. Nicole's simple twelve steps get you back on track."

—JODI GUBER BRUFSKY,
founder and chief creative officer of Beyond Yoga

"Like a confidence-boosting best friend, Nicole guides you through her own journey."

—PAIGE ADAMS-GELLER,
cofounder of PAIGE

"Read her books to help master the degree of life and achieve more success than you ever thought possible." —ROSIE O'NEILL, cofounder and CEO of Sugarfina

"Nicole's books should be mandatory reading for all women looking to succeed in their careers." —TRACY DINUNZIO, founder and CEO of Tradesy

"Nicole is the real deal. Her influence on women to get their finances and careers in order is unparalleled." —REBECCA MINKOFF, designer

"Nicole reminds us that we can only define success from within, and she helps us to do that without judgement." —PAYAL KADAKIA, founder and CEO of ClassPass

"Nicole's honesty and realness will make you laugh and learn like you're hearing from your smart-ass best friend."

—JASON FEIFER, editor-in-chief of *Entrepreneur* magazine

"Finances can be overwhelming and stressful, but Nicole talks about the human experience, at the same time giving sound financial advice." —DREW BARRYMORE, host of *The Drew Barrymore Show*

"Nicole is the money mentor we've all been waiting for. She guides readers through the benefits of investing, step-by-step. Her encouragement is profound and her passion contagious."

—HOLLY ROBINSON PEETE, actress, philanthropist, and television host

"In order to be truly equal, we need a solution for the masculinity of wealth. We need our own wealth and financial independence. When someone calls you Miss Independent, say 'thank you.'"

—GLORIA STEINEM,
women's rights activist and founder of *Ms.* magazine

"Nicole makes the world of money understandable once and for all. I was blown away with how much I've learned from her."

—TORI SPELLING,
actress and author

"Nicole shows you that taking care of yourself and your finances is not just OK but the only way to succeed."   —BOBBI BROWN,
founder of Bobbi Brown Cosmetics

"Nicole's advice is on point! Her material and delivery is current, real, and entertaining."   —LAVINIA ERRICO,
cofounder of Equinox

"Nicole is a wonderful role model for women today, one that so many of us can relate to. Take her guidance to heart, and it will change your life."

—MARIAM NAFICY,
founder and CEO of Minted

The
Money
School

The
Money
School

12 Simple Lessons
to Master Financial
Markets and Investing

Nicole
Lapin

HARPERCOLLINS
LEADERSHIP

AN IMPRINT OF HARPERCOLLINS

Design by Neuwirth & Associates, Inc.

ISBN 978-1-4002-2967-3 (eBook)
ISBN 978-1-4002-2953-6 (TP)

Library of Congress Control Number: 2024949590

Printed in the United States of America

24 25 26 27 28 LBC 5 4 3 2 1

CONTENTS

INTRODUCTION

How in the world did we not learn about money in school? We learned how to calculate algebra equations we will never have to solve and how to determine when one train meets another, which is a skill I've not once, not ever, used in my life. But we don't learn about how the thing we all need to have to survive works?!

I've been screaming about this for years. I've stood on stages and talked on TV all about the travesty that we can all recite the Pythagorean theorem but so few of us know the basics of investing, like even what a stock or a bond is. I've said it until my blood boiled. I've said it until my throat hurt. I've said it until . . . I decided to do something about it.

The Money School is what I'm doing about it. The fact that we didn't learn money basics in school or likely even in college (that we paid good money for and some of us are saddled with debt for, thankyouverymuch!) should be the perfect excuse for burying your head in the sand. "Hey, it's not *my* fault—no one taught me this stuff." Yeah, and that's true. But even though it's not your fault doesn't fix the fact that it's only hurting you.

And if you're like me, you didn't learn this stuff at home either or get a head start by inheriting a bunch of family money. I mean, I am a first-generation American from a broken home who wanted to be a poetry major. There were no silver spoons around when I was growing up; in fact, there were times that I barely had a spoon of food. I didn't know a single person who had a background in business or finance. I became an autodidact of money out of sheer necessity once I realized that my circumstances were not an excuse for my outcomes. Like, I couldn't tell a creditor that I learned about parallelograms instead of interest rates or a mortgage officer that my father was too busy drinking or doing drugs to read me the *Wall Street Journal*.

By picking up this book, I hope today is the day you also really, truly realize that no one is going to give you a pass for your past and no one is going to care more about your future than you. So, while it sucks and it's not fair, the only way to attain the type of wealth you dream of is by teaching *yourself* everything you *should* have learned but didn't. No, it's not too late. You're never as young as you are today, and as far as I'm concerned, today is as good a day as any to start on your own financial education journey. And I promise: you have figured out much more complicated things in life than what you're about to learn.

Until you picked up this book, you've probably thought the best (and perhaps only) way to grow your money was to make more of it. And don't get me wrong, hustling to make a lot of money is incredible. But the only way to build *real*, lasting, generational wealth is to flip that equation around and make that money hustle for *you*. I mean, you work hard as hell for your money; I think it's time your money returns the favor—don't you?

What the financial industry doesn't want you to know (because they have their own unnecessarily complicated language to keep people intimidated) is that investing is the easiest way to do that. But to do that, you do need to first invest a little time in learning the best practices. At some point, we probably all thought that putting our money in a checking or savings account was how to get wealthy. But by doing that, you're actually *losing* money. The culprit: inflation. Any account—checking, savings, or otherwise—that earns you less than 3 percent interest on your cash will eat into what that money will buy you in the future. Why? Because 3 percent is the historic average of inflation in the US (with post-pandemic rates being painfully higher until recently). So if you earn, say, 1 percent in a basic savings account, you'll be net negative 2 percent. Meaning, you'll be able to buy 2 percent less next year than you can today. So, to at least keep up with inflation and break even with your future buying power, you'll have to grow your money at least 3 percent. Yes, there have been high-yield savings account offers that can bring in about 4 percent interest, which is better than 1 percent; but adjusted for typical inflation rates, that *is* just 1 percent (4 percent gains − 3 percent inflation). That's why it's time to aim higher. It's time to level up your financial market knowledge.

The Money School has four courses, each containing a beginner, interme-diate, and advanced level. The first course teaches you everything you ever need to know about the stock market. The second zooms into debt (the good kind!), where you *own* debt, not owe it, via financial instruments like CDs and bonds. The third course steps it up with more exotic or advanced securities like commodities, currencies, and derivatives. The final part wraps it all up with how you can make a portfolio to help you reach your own financial success as you define it. But this is your book so use it the way that resonates most with you. You can read it straight through or read each of the 101 lessons together before moving on to the next level.

And it's no mistake that there are twelve total lessons. All my books are structured as twelve-step plans primarily because everything financial feels daunting until it's broken down into baby steps. The first step in any journey is always the hardest—and yet, here you are. So, seriously, bravo. I'm really proud of you.

Before we get started, just know that these courses have no prerequisites. If you've never invested, cool; you're in the right place. Even if you've gone to some other (even questionable) class and are dabbling in day trading, you're still in the right place.

I wanted to write this book right now because *everything* changed in the financial world since I wrote my others. And the whole "everything changed" thing has one catalyst: interest rates. When I wrote *Rich Bitch* and *Miss Independent*—two of my books that talk about financial markets (but don't do the full deep dive this book does)—interest rates were super low. Like unnaturally low. Changing interest rates by small percentages or fractions of a percent might not feel like a big deal, but it is the biggest of big deals in the financial world.

To quickly give you some context on this: interest rates were set to nearly 0 percent after the housing crisis of 2008. This was done to try and prop up the economy because it was completely in the dumps. And then during the pandemic—when the dump caught fire—interest rates plummeted again. But in the 1990s, interest rates were hovering around 5 percent and got as high as 10 percent. And the decade before that, in the 1980s, interest rates flirted with 20 percent! Twenty-freakin'-percent! So, if you got used to a world of rock-bottom interest rates, it's time to snap out of it. It was a decision made by the Federal Reserve (the folks who determine interest rates*) to keep us from financial Armageddon. Lowering interest rates is an emergency move, not the norm.

Now, higher interest rates aren't all bad. Sure, if you're a borrower looking to buy a home or get a business loan, higher rates are not ideal because you'll be paying more on your loan in interest over time. But if you're an investor in high-interest-bearing vehicles or a savvy saver, this is excellent news for you because you'll be earning more over time.

Interest rates are the heartbeat in the financial world and help us put our finger on the pulse of the best place for us to put our money. When rates are *low*, as they've been over the last decade, traditional savings accounts and fixed-income investments offer meh returns, nudging us toward finding our high yields in the stock market. This shift has led to a surge in stock market investments over the last ten years, with average returns hovering around 9 percent after adjusting for inflation. But when interest rates *rise*, the allure of investments like bonds and CDs increases. The best investors are on top of interest rate fluctuations because, as rates move, they move their money to the place they can get the most for it.

In *The Money School*, I'll help you understand how the changing interest rates, well, change the game *because rates will change again*. The only constant in life and on Wall Street is change.† So when—not if—it happens again, you'll be ready. While the economy has and will change, solid investing principles haven't and won't. So, no matter who you are or where you are in your investment journey—whether you're on Step 1 or Step 11—success starts with mastering the fundamentals of the system.

My journey to doing that myself wasn't a fun or glamorous one. As a kid growing up in an immigrant family, my parents used only cash; so, instead of having money collect interest in a bank, it collected dust in a safe under the sink. Trying to break the sink cycle by putting my money in an actual

---

* The Federal Reserve is the institution that keeps an eye on banks in the US. They're also the ones who decide the interest rate banks use when lending money to each other. When we talk about the "interest rate," that's what we mean. It's *not* the rate you personally get, but it's what your bank uses to figure out the interest rate you do get on things like credit cards and mortgages.

† Also taxes. But we'll cover those too.

bank wasn't clean or easy. I've been broke. I've been in debt. I've spent too much. I've been intimidated by the stock market and retirement plans. And, perhaps worst of all, I've leaned on people I thought "knew better." Of course, they didn't, but I was too full of guilt and shame to know that at the time.

During my darkest days—when I was elbow-deep in credit card debt or depressed and eating brown rice and beans because it felt fancier than ramen but was the same price—I desperately wanted to find a crash course to learn the practical money lessons to help me, but there wasn't one. I wanted something to help me break my bad money habits once and for all, but there wasn't one in plain English, sans jargon.* *The Money School* is that. It is packed with all the information I wish someone had taught me when I was taking my first steps toward long-lasting wealth by investing in the financial markets. In these pages, I'll be the professor you never had (and honestly, I never expected to be) but always needed.

There's no reason not to succeed here, whether you were a good student in actual school or not. There are no tests that require you to memorize gratuitous information or facts. There are no grades to stress your ego out over. You're doing this for yourself: the smart, whole, extraordinary version that you are now and your even richer future self. You can shout from the social media rooftops that you're doing this or keep it all to yourself, millionaire-next-door style. However you do, it is up to you. It's all on the honor system. If you cheat, you're only cheating that really important person who honestly doesn't deserve that anymore.

Building real wealth not only brings literal riches but the richness of feeling safe and secure. For me, the latter has ultimately proven to be more valuable. But it took me a long time to figure that out because I needed to get the former first.

I wrote this book because I want to help you realize both sooner than I did. I want to you avoid the money mistakes I made (and Lord knows, I've made a lot) by not knowing how the stock market worked earlier. I wrote this book to show you that investing can give you the feeling of always having

---

* I will be defining a lot of the jargon throughout the book, but as with all my other money books, I added a financial dictionary (that you don't need a dictionary to understand) of the most important terms in the back of the book so you can reference it when you need it.

your own back. I hope this book helps you forgive your former self for not knowing this stuff before. And I hope it also helps you give your future self some tough love—that past behaviors that didn't serve you are no longer acceptable.

So, with that, *class is in session* . . . **on mastering financial markets and investing**.

The
Money
School

The Stock Market

STOCKS 101
Walk with Me Down Wall Street

The stock market isn't the only way to make money, but it is an important way the rich get richer. And even though it doesn't always feel accessible, it is. There is no barrier to entry. The stock market is open to anyone no matter where you come from or whom you know. It's a great equalizer—like the subway and the flu. But just because it's available to anyone doesn't mean everyone knows how to navigate it.

In fact, basic personal financial navigation gets mucked up all the time. The wrong order of operations, although most people don't realize it's wrong, is: work for money, have money, spend money. The end. The winning order looks something like: work for money, have money, invest money. Why? The time-value of money. It's simple: a dollar in your hand today is worth more than a dollar you'll receive in the future. That dollar today can be invested and start growing immediately. It's like planting a seed today instead of waiting a year—the sooner you plant it, the sooner you'll see it bloom.

I usually hate clichés but this one is true: money doesn't grow on trees. It doesn't—but money *does* grow in the stock market. In fact, the stock market is some of the most fertile ground for your money seedlings to grow. But again, only if you actually plant them. Whether you want to get super crazy rich or simply grow your money to live a more comfortable lifestyle, in this lesson I'm going to teach you how the stock market is one of your best means to that end.

CHOOSE THE RIGHT PATH

You might be thinking: *The means to an end, really? Well, okay, then let's just skip to the good part!* Not. So. Fast. I get it; get-rich-quick promises are tantalizing and alluring and the rest, but they—from crypto to NFTs to forex scams to drop-shipping or affiliate marketing—aren't real.

It's like trying to bake a complex cake by just glancing at the picture in the cookbook. Sure, you see the end product—a delicious, multilayer cake—but without following the recipe step-by-step or understanding why certain ingredients are needed at specific times, you'll likely end up with a culinary disaster. You might mix the ingredients in the wrong order or, worse, completely miss a crucial element like baking soda and end up with a flat, unappetizing mess. That's what it's like diving into the stock market based on just the superficial gloss without grasping the underlying principles and strategies. The recipe for successful investing requires more than just throwing in what you think might work; it demands understanding, preparation, and following the dang instructions.

So, even if some "expert" on TikTok gives you the "fail-proof" formula for choosing what stocks will be successful, if you don't understand how the stock market works, you're going to flop, just like that poorly baked cake. And I will say: the stakes of failing the stock market are much higher.

FYI — SWEAT YOUR CASH

Every dollar you have has the capacity to earn more, so don't undervalue it. The wealthy understand that there is a "cost of capital," and they use this to their advantage. Imagine your money as a resource with potential. When left in a savings account, its potential is minimally realized, just like being a superstar employee doing a mindless job.

But investing your money—whether in stocks or other securities—is like getting a challenging role to help you make the most of your full potential. The result? Greater impact, greater reward, or in the case of your money, greater returns.

QUESTION EVERYTHING

In every class there's always a contrarian. Someone who sits in the back of the class and pushes back on the teacher because they find everything "sus." While sometimes those students are pains in the teacher's butt, I want to bring them into this class. I can't reiterate enough, it's crucial to think for yourself, use your knowledge of YOU to create the best circumstances for you, and push back when necessary on experts—*including* yours truly.

So, let's say this classroom contrarian asks: *Okay, Prof, you say that investing is a better way to grow your money than stashing it in a savings account—prove it.* Don't get me wrong, savings accounts, especially high-yield ones during times of high interest rates, are better than if your money is earning you nothing under the (hopefully) proverbial mattress or under the literal sink like mine was. If your money isn't invested, here's what you're missing out on:

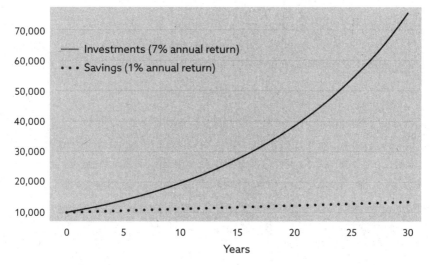

Savings vs. Investing Returns Over Time

That's what a 7 percent inflation-adjusted annual return looks like, compared to a 1 percent annual return. Some of the most common concerns I hear from people who don't want to get started with investing are that they (1) are too old to start, (2) don't have enough money, and (3) aren't "numbers" people. Well, let me show you what your returns look like if you start investing at thirty-five versus twenty-five using just $100 per month:

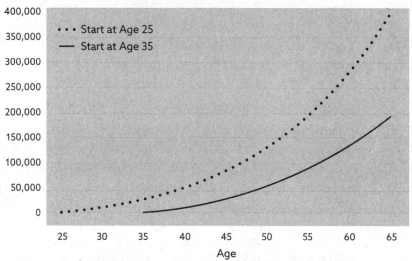

At sixty-five, here's what both have to show for their investment:

- Investor starting at age twenty-five: $389,307

- Investor starting at age thirty-five: $189,476

This significant difference underscores the impact of an extra decade of compound interest. So let's debunk the fears: (1) you are never as young as you are today, (2) you don't need a lot of money to start; you need the most amount of time possible, and (3) once again, I started as a freakin' poetry major.

But I get it. Money has all sorts of deeply ingrained emotional layers. So I also want to take a moment to speak to those in the class who grew up broke, in a financially traumatic or housing-compromised situation like I did. If you come from a background of lack or money anxiety, investing can feel absolutely terrifying. If there have been points in your life when you haven't had any money, signing yourself up for the stock market—where you imagine you can lose everything all over again—is triggering. Your trauma will probably try to take control and tell you that putting your money into the market is the worst financial decision you could make. Trust me, I get it. Not only was I sick at the thought of losing my money, I also had severe impostor syndrome. Who was I, a child of immigrants with zero investing experience, to walk down Wall Street?! I mean, what is ROI anyway? *Isn't that a store that sells camping gear?* (This was an actual thought my former self had. This Cali girl had never been to an actual REI store, to be fair.)

FYI

ROI ON YOU

If you don't already know, ROI stands for "return on investment." I believe the biggest ROI you get in your life comes from the investments—like reading this book and the actions you take from it—you make in yourself. But on Wall Street, ROI refers to just how hard your money will work and grow for you.

To curb your anxieties further, what if I told you that you may already be an investor and not even know it? It's true. Most retirement plans, particularly 401(k)s, which hold trillions of dollars in the US, are intricately linked to the stock market. These plans often include a mix of stocks, mutual funds, and bonds. Plus, pension plans, some of the heaviest hitters in the investment world, are also deeply invested in the market. This means that each paycheck contribution you make to your 401(k) is essentially funneling your money into the market, making you a very willing investor.

Now, instead of remaining a passive player, with your funds being managed and invested without your involvement, let's start acting with intention.

By understanding the stock market and how your existing plans might depend on its performance, you can take a more active role in your own financial show. I mean, no one is going to care more about it than you so you might as well take center stage.

Fools Rush In

Here's the thing—you can't simply empty your savings account and pour it all into the market. Sure, we all want to sign up for that historical 7–10 percent inflation-adjusted return as soon as it finally dawns on us that earning money while you sleep *is* actually possible. But if you make rash, impulsive investing choices, you could see far smaller returns, or even losses. The fact that the internet has further democratized investing is an excellent thing. More people have access to online platforms and investing apps than ever before, and that's freakin' amazing. What's not freakin' amazing is investing willy-nilly and using them like any other app-delivered dopamine drip.

To drive the risk point home, let's talk about these two quotes:

"Risk comes from not knowing what you are doing."

"Hunches will cost you more than they will gain."

What's the difference in sentiment between them? Not much, on the surface. Both quotes speak to the importance of making rational decisions that are backed by real information. The difference between the two quotes is not *what* they say, but *who* said them. The first quote was coined by Warren Buffett, one of the greatest investors of all time. The second quote comes from Stanford Wong, an expert on blackjack.

The more you learn about investing, the more you'll notice the commonalities it shares with gambling. In both worlds, there are winners and losers, and, sure, *sometimes* the difference between the two is pure, dumb luck. But getting savvy on investing strategy is like counting cards . . . legally, of course. The purpose of counting cards is to increase your likelihood of winning; getting educated on investing does just that. Remember, the house always wins—so we're going to learn how to *be* the house.

LET'S START AT
THE VERY BEGINNING

When I say the "stock market," what do you picture? Maybe you think of a green Wall Street street sign. Maybe you think of a serious-looking building with big, imposing marble columns. Maybe you think of Leo in a cocaine frenzy in *The Wolf of Wall Street*. But what is the stock market, actually?

If you're thinking of the stock market as a physical location, you're not actually thinking of the stock market at all; you're thinking about a stock *exchange*. Think of the stock market as more of a system than a physical location. The stock market represents the semimodern idea that you can give money to someone who needs it now with the hope that the money will come back to you, and then some, in the future.

I say semimodern because while dinosaurs weren't investing in start-ups way back when, there is still a rich history to the stock market. It's honestly pretty scandalous. There are pirates, God, love, war, and, of course, money. So, while you may have picked up this book in the Business and Finance section, you could find some of these origin stories in Romance, True Crime, or Religion.

HOW IT STARTED

Not all historians agree, but most pinpoint the start of the investment system as we know it to be the 1600s, long before there was a *Wolf of Wall Street* or even a Wall Street. Can you believe we have had four hundred years to come up with good explanations for the stock market and still need a book like this because most of the aforementioned explanations suck? Anyway, while there are whole books written about the abhorrent ethics (or lack thereof) involved here, what I want you to know is that the Dutch East India Company is considered the very first publicly traded company. They were known for trading spices and for their involvement in the slave trade—hence the abhorrence.

I'll unpack what it means to be a public company at length in the next lesson, but basically a company that is "publicly traded" sells pieces of ownership in the company (and the promise of some future perk) to the public. Back in the old days,* investors would get a certificate saying they owned a little chunk of the company. A little chunk of a company that is sold to investors is called a *share*. When a company lets the public invest in their operations, the company issues a certain number of these shares. Once an investor buys a share in a company, they can call themselves a shareholder. I often see people use *share* and *stock* interchangeably, but they're not exactly the same. Stock is a broad term. You could say you own stock in many different companies. Shares are specific. You could use shares if you wanted to tell someone exactly how many slices of a particular company you've purchased. So you could say, "I own twenty *shares* in XYZ Company, as part of the collection of *stocks* I own."

Now, as in the 1600s, if you buy shares in a public company, you can make money in two ways: (1) You could have an agreement with the company to get a portion of the company's profits, called dividends. Or: (2) You could sell your shares to another interested investor and pocket the profit from that sale. This second moneymaking method gave rise to the first stockbrokers or, more generally, shareholders who sell shares to other investors.

Despite the occasional scam and scandal, this system of investing stuck around for hundreds of years. Why? Simple. Because people were getting paid. The investor got paid, the company got paid, everyone got paid. People of every century like that.

Cut to the 1790s: investing had only grown in popularity. In fact, this system of investing had now made its way to the United States. Even way back then, at the very introduction of investing in the US, Wall Street in New York was a major hub. Men (yes, only men) would get together on Wall Street in the late 1700s and sell shares auction style: They would shout out the prices that certain shares were selling for. Interested investors would gather around and bid on these stocks, and shares would go to the highest bidder.

Investing changed forever when a couple of stockbrokers got together and signed the Buttonwood Agreement right there on Wall Street. These stockbrokers were fed up with this system of auctioning off shares. It had

---

* Okay, not that old. Disney was issuing paper stocks until 2013. In the 1990s, the stock market trade went digital. But it wasn't an overnight transition, as many investors *liked* the paper stocks. They liked them so much, the trade lives on in the hobby of scripophily, or collecting of old paper stocks with no cash value. A 1990 Microsoft stock certificate—just the paper certificate not including the actual stock—sold at auction for $1,305.

led to investment scams, and they worried these scams would become so pervasive that Americans would end up skeptical about the investing system as a whole. So, in order to block out the noise from sketchy sources and garner the public's faith in the system, these stockbrokers decided that they would trade only between themselves behind closed doors. Make no mistake, this move wasn't motivated entirely by the goodness of their hearts. By trading behind closed doors, they also shut out the independent investors who had been taking the DIY approach and investing their money themselves, because before the Buttonwood Agreement, anyone could literally stroll down to Wall Street and buy shares through the auction system. After the agreement, if you wanted to invest, you needed to place your money (and your trust) in the stockbrokers' hands.

Moving stock trading from the streets of New York inside four walls redefined investing as a private system that takes place in a centralized location. This space the Buttonwood boys chose became known as the New York Stock Exchange (NYSE), and it is still the most iconic exchange in the world. The NYSE is so legendary that oftentimes when someone says "*the* stock exchange," they're likely referring to the NYSE, even though there are many stock exchanges all over the world. Essentially, a stock exchange is a space where stocks can be sold and purchased, legitimately. In modern times, you can't create a stock exchange so easily. All reputable American-based stock exchanges are registered with the Securities and Exchange Commission (SEC), which helps ensure exchanges play by a certain set of rules that protect investors.

Next came the advent of the telegraph. The telegraph allowed messages to be sent all over the country practically instantaneously, which was revolutionary in the 1800s. Remember how your life changed when you could suddenly just text and not call? Same feeling, times a million. It wasn't long before the finance industry realized that the innovation would be helpful with relaying stock information. From the telegraph, the stock ticker apparatus was developed. The OG stock ticker was an actual machine that received telegraphic messages conveying what prices stocks were being bought and sold for so that brokers could get real-time pricing from all over the country. The stock ticker would print out stock prices on what was appropriately called "ticker tape." Before this, if you wanted to invest in a company based on the West Coast and you lived on the East Coast, you would have to rely on sluggish channels, which might make you the very last person to hear updated information on a stock. As we'll soon talk about, being behind on stock trends may cause you to also fall behind on investment gains. Same situation (just way slower) back then.

Of course, much later, the internet made the ticker contraption look like absolute child's play, but even so, we still use the term *ticker* today to mean a few different things. When you hear someone referring to a ticker, they could be referring to the same collection of information that used to be broadcast on ticker tape: stock symbol, stock price, and whether the price is up or down. Or, more commonly, they could be using ticker interchangeably with "stock symbol." When a company goes public, they get a stock symbol, which is the abbreviation for their company name that will be the primary nickname used to refer to the company at the stock exchange. For example, AT&T's ticker symbol is T. When you want to buy stock in AT&T, you're investing in the company AT&T, but on paper, you will be buying T shares. Occasionally, tickers can be clever, in the case of Harley-Davidson (HOG) or the Cheesecake Factory (CAKE).

HOW IT'S GOING

The NYSE is still, of course, alive and well. While a lot has obviously changed since 1792, the principle of stock exchanges is still the same: to provide a safe, legitimate space for people to buy and sell shares of companies. But the system has gotten much more sophisticated compared to the days of street auctions and paper certificates. Instead of the handful of meet-up zones to rendezvous and sell shares that were around in the 1800s, there are many, many different stock exchanges today. The NYSE is still the biggie that trades shares of major companies like General Electric (GE), JPMorgan Chase (JPM), Johnson & Johnson (JNJ), Visa (V), Verizon (VZ), IBM (IBM), and so on. There are some other exchanges that you may have never heard of before, like the New York Mercantile Exchange (NYMEX), which trades commodities like crude oil, gold, and other metals. There are exchanges like the Intercontinental Exchange (ICE), which trades options on sugar, coffee, even orange juice. All of these exchanges *together* make up the stock market.

You may be wondering if you need separate accounts to invest with different exchanges. Thankfully, the answer to that is no. Which stock exchange a company is associated with typically means more to the company than to investors like me and you. When a company decides to trade on a certain exchange, the lingo is that they're "listed" on the exchange. Here's how to use it in a sentence:

Wall Street Bro: "Yeah, my company is about to go public."

You, an A+ Money School Student: "Oh really? Where will it be listed?"

Wall Street Bro: "Well, I'm a tech guy at heart so the company will be on the NASDAQ."

You, an A+ Money School Student: "Cool, cool. Love the faux bell-ringing vibe there."*

One of my great joys in life is putting a Wall Street bro in his place. Anyway, since he brought it up, the NASDAQ (pronounced Naz-dak) was the first completely online stock exchange. In other words, the NASDAQ was remote before it was cool (or mandated). With NASDAQ, there was never a pit or big imposing columns or a street address for that matter. And keeping very much on brand with the whole digital thing, the NASDAQ mostly lists tech companies. Some notable players are Apple (AAPL), Amazon (AMZN), Microsoft (MSFT), Facebook (FB), and Tesla (TSLA).

Basically, the NYSE is like your wise uncle who has a lot of good adventure stories and "lived many lives" while the NASDAQ is your younger cousin who just went backpacking in Europe and won't shut up about it. But, in all seriousness, the NYSE and the NASDAQ are two of the most prestigious exchanges, so investors tend to take note when a new company starts trading on one of the exchanges.

---

* The NASDAQ "bell" isn't an actual bell like it is at the NYSE; it's more like a green screen.

US EXCHANGES AND THEIR SPECIALTY

NYSE (The New York Stock Exchange): Large, established industrial and financial companies.

NASDAQ (National Association of Securities Dealers Automated Quotations): Technology and internet-related stocks, growth-oriented companies.

CBOE (Chicago Board Options Exchange): Options and futures on stocks, indices, and interest rates.

OTC Markets Group: Over-the-counter (OTC) securities, including small and foreign stocks.

CME (Chicago Mercantile Exchange): Futures and options across multiple asset classes, mostly commodities.

NYMEX (New York Mercantile Exchange): Energy, commodities, and environmental futures and options.

Which exchange a stock is listed on typically doesn't make a big difference to us investors because, like I mentioned, no one is walking into an actual stock exchange to buy shares anymore. Brokerages, or companies that facilitate the purchase and sale of stocks (aka, where brokers are employed), compile the stocks across most heavy-hitting stock exchanges, so by investing through a brokerage (like E*Trade, Schwab, Fidelity, Vanguard, and so on, but more on that in Stocks 201), you can buy stocks across all exchanges in the exact same way.

Let's Go Shopping

So far, we've covered a lot of verbal ground: we've thrown out terms like stock market, brokerage, shares, stocks. How, you might ask, do they all relate to each other? Well, the stock market operates pretty similarly to grocery shopping. In the modern-day stock market, a brokerage is like the supermarket, a stock exchange is like the aisles within the grocery store, and the companies are the products. Hear me out.

When you go food shopping, pretty much anything that would be on your grocery list you can find at your local supermarket. Say you need broccoli and milk. It would be a huge drag if you needed to go to the Dairy Store for milk and the Produce Store for broccoli, right? But instead, you can go to one location and within that store, go to the produce aisle, the dairy aisle, the baking aisle, all the aisles. That's basically how a brokerage functions.

Now let's double-click on stock exchanges being like the different aisles in the grocery store. Even if your grocery list is a mile long and practically tallies up to one of everything, you have a sense of which product will be in which aisle. For example, if you're looking for ice cream and toaster waffles, you're probably headed toward the frozen foods aisle. Similarly, certain exchanges are known for listing particular types of companies, or companies within a particular industry. I just mentioned that General Electric (GE) trades on the NYSE. If the NYSE were an aisle in the grocery store, it would be the Large Venerable Companies Aisle, because it's known for trading, well, large and venerable companies that have been around the block. Whereas, Apple (AAPL) is a tech company, an industry that is much younger, and will be found on the NASDAQ, the exchange most known for trading tech companies (and promoting the wearing of black turtlenecks).

Plus, each aisle doesn't only have one product, right? It's not like in the produce aisle there are only apples. Within the produce aisle, there are many different fruits and veggies you can choose from. That's exactly how companies fit into this metaphor. Within a stock exchange, there are many different companies listed, and all of those companies are available through your brokerage. Just like how within an aisle there are many different types of products, all of which you can buy at the grocery store.

The grocery store (brokerage) is set up in aisles (exchanges) that compile products (stocks, bonds, funds, and so on) from different industries and vendors and present them to you in a centralized, literal one-stop shop. When you invest, your brokerage is like your financial local grocery store: it's your one-stop shop for any company you're interested in investing in.

You might be wondering, "*Wait a New York minute. If companies are all available through brokerages anyway and aren't bought or sold any differently . . . why does it matter which exchange they list on?*"

With that question, you're basically asking: *If you're a farmer selling your apples to a grocery store, what do you care which aisle you're in? Your apples are still in the grocery store, which should mean people will buy them, right?* Well, kind of. Without getting too in the weeds, different stock exchanges have different requirements to be listed and different perceived perks of membership. So, if you're the farmer whose apples are being sold in the grocery store, and your apples end up in the frozen food aisle, well, that doesn't really work for your product. If a shopper is looking for apples, they'll probably choose whatever apples are in the produce aisle and skip your weird frozen apples. It's the same idea with stock exchanges. Some exchanges have rules and regulations that are a better fit for certain companies' needs. To be a savvy investor, you don't need to know why each stock ended up on an exchange any more than a shopper needs to know why each type of apple ended up on the apple display.

Now if you want to buy Apple *stock*, you can just type AAPL into the search bar of your brokerage account and you're set. Also, please don't go to the actual Apple store to buy Apple stock.* This is a real story and while it might sound crazy if you (now) know that stocks are bought through brokerages, it's understandable to think someone could assume the Apple store would sell Apple stock. Remember: forgiveness of our former selves for what they didn't know at the time but tough love for our future selves because now that we know better, we should do better.

---

* If you can buy an iPhone, you most certainly can buy AAPL stock. At the time I'm writing this, you could buy five shares for about the price of the newest phone. And only one of those purchases has an impressive ROI over time.

WOLFETTE OF WALL STREET

At eighteen, I lied to get a job.

I needed a job and the job I was offered was in business news. I said I knew about business and finance, but I did not. *I have figured out harder things in life*, I thought. And I had. But the finance School of Hard Knocks still required some damn hard knocking.

Reporting from the floor of the Chicago Mercantile Exchange was an incredible opportunity . . . in hindsight. At the time, it felt like a prison sentence. I felt like a fraud, especially because I was one of the youngest journalists to ever report from the floor of a stock exchange, so I wore my inexperience on my face. That and I knew nothing about money except that I never had enough of it.

Before I started working there, I'd never seen a trading floor. The energy there was unlike any other: a combination of a raging nightclub, a horse auction, and a Middle Eastern bazaar. It reeked of AXE Body Spray, testosterone, and Adderall.

The idea of talking about finance—for a living—scared me to death. It was a topic I viscerally hated but one I was determined (and needed) to learn ASAP. My job was to write scripts about the latest business happenings based on the wire reports that came out every morning, like the day that Google released Gmail, or when the first iPod came out. I read the scripts from atop a crate perched over the roar of the trading pit so that the camera would actually see my face (there was a height restriction on the heels women were allowed to wear on the floor . . . seriously). It. Was. Chaos. I once was picked up by a man on the floor of the pit. No, I don't mean "picked up," like asked out, although that happened too. I mean I was physically lifted and moved out of the way by a very aggressive, drugged-out stockbroker. Again: chaos.

Back then, buyers and sellers communicated through a system called open outcry, which is perhaps the most spot-on description in the history of the English language. Sellers would yell out the price they wanted to get for their shares, and buyers would try to get the sellers down to a price that would work for them. To cut through the ruckus, traders developed a type of sign language to communicate across the trading floor. If you check out a video of this, it may look like some sort of caveman primitive language with people beating their chests and flexing, but it is an actual language, called arbitrage (or "arb").*

In order to make this language effective, brokers and traders needed to find a way to get the attention of the buyers selling and filling orders. Brokers would wear the most ridiculous jackets—I'm talking sequins, highlighter-neon colors, and every pattern you could imagine: checkers, lots of four-leaf clovers, the works. Many people thought that MTV was the place to go for outlandish style in the aughts, but no, my friends, the real trendsetters were on the trading floors of America's stock exchanges.

This is the image of the stock market that we romanticize today. It's a pretty wild picture; I can understand why it's stuck around and why Hollywood keeps perpetuating it. But—and I hate to break it to you—this is no longer the reality of the stock exchanges today. Some people are actually surprised to hear this, but it's true: there are no more wolves howling on Wall Street. As it turns out, all that yelling, open outcry, and the special hand signals? Well, computers can have those conversations more quickly and quietly, without all the hullabaloo. In the '90s, the open outcry's heyday, the NYSE had five thousand employees working on the floor. Now, there are about five hundred and you can barely smell the AXE.

---

* I'll teach you a sign: Ball your hand into a fist and put the back of your hand against your forehead. Then, keeping your fist tight, swoop your hand outward away from your head . . . and, thank you! You just offered me one hundred bucks. If your palm is toward you, you're indicating that you're buying. If your palm is toward the room, you're indicating that you're selling.

SHOPPING IS ALWAYS BETTER WITH A FRIEND

The road to recovery is much better with someone in the passenger seat, so seriously think about finding a study buddy as we get further along this investing journey. Pick someone you can talk with about the concepts you learn here. A trusted person can not only be your sounding board but also ideally your accountability partner as you make your way through *The Money School.** We can be so hard on ourselves about money, but beating ourselves up never leads to positive, productive change. Some accountability, though, from a BFF, spouse, or sibling might.

Teaming up with someone will also help us all fight back against the frustrating reality that we (society, the world at large) are not talking about money enough. Ever notice that we will talk about *everything* before we talk about money? You know what you chat about with your besties, especially after a couple of glasses of wine. Sex? No problem. Politics? Bring it on. Money? Totally taboo. But it doesn't have to be that way.

For most of our big life decisions, we crowdsource advice from friends and family. If you were buying a car, wouldn't you call up your pal who just bought a car and ask them what tips they can share? If so, then why wouldn't you call up that friend to ask them what investments they have (if they're investing at all)? Keeping our financial lives secret from our support systems does nothing other than hold us back from bettering ourselves . . . *together*.

---

* I know these conversations can be tricky, so I added some starters as study group questions in the back of the book.

STOCKS 201

Blocking and Tackling

When it comes to economics, the traditional first-year college classes are macroeconomics and microeconomics. Macroeconomics is the study of the big picture; it's all about how large economic systems work. Microeconomics is about the little stuff and how economics affects the behaviors of small groups or systems.[*]

We're going to do our own quickie (practical) version of macro- and microeconomics right here. I'm going to teach you all the macro stuff—what the alphabet soup of acronyms means and how the stock market works. All the big stuff you need to know about. We'll also dig into the micro side as well, which is your own personal economy. The stuff you can control, how to pick a brokerage, and how much to invest. It can feel overwhelming to be presented with a long list of new terms to learn. But this isn't about shutting you out. Rather, the financial world is full of very specific concepts that require precise language to describe. Try not to feel intimidated even though

---

[*] Mind you there were no classes on personal finance or investing at my school . . . just these esoteric classes with big words and term papers on old economists. Knowing who John Maynard Keynes is has never helped me know that I should have invested any extra dollar I had in Apple or Google when I was reporting on the invention of the iPod and Gmail at eighteen.

that's what it's intended to do. I'll have you decoding the *Wall Street Journal**
in no time.

There's probably some other part of your life where you're the expert.
Maybe it's baseball or maybe it's houseplants or even the Marvel extended
universe. Whatever it is, I bet you spent a lot of time learning it. In *The Money
School*, we'll be doing the same thing. Remember, Malcolm Gladwell says it
takes ten thousand hours to become a pro in something. Well, being a pro in
money *makes you money*, so if that isn't motivation enough to start clocking
those numbers, I don't know what is.

BLOCKING

Before we go forth and block,† I want to make sure you're understanding
some top-level truths of the stock market. Here are the five golden rules of
investing that you'll need to remember as we move through the rest of this
book:

1. Gains of 7–10 percent in the stock market are trends, not prom-
    ises. Other investors and I tout those returns for the stock market
    because we think it's important for you to know the data and the
    likelihood of positive outcomes. But past performance does not
    guarantee future returns. (You'll start hearing that phrase more
    as you get into this world.)

2. You are not protected from bad decisions. The stock market is not
    your understanding parent and does not cover your mistakes or
    lapses in judgment. If you put your money in a sketchy company
    and the company fails, you will lose whatever you put in it.

3. You have not *made* money on a stock until you've sold it. If you own
    a stock that has doubled in value, you haven't made any money

---

* Just don't name a newsletter "Decoding the *Wall Street Journal*" because they will come
after you as they did my twenty-seven-year-old self.

† I am no sports guru but in this "blocking and tackling" metaphor, we will "block" jargon
and conventional wisdom so we can then "tackle" specific investment strategies to get us
toward our financial goals.

on it yet. Dividends are the exception, which I'll explain in a sec, but overall, think of this as the hard-and-fast rule. This is a very common misconception that drives me absolutely nuts. Someone will tell me that if they bought a stock for five dollars and now it's ten dollars that their profit is double their investment. No! That is wrong. You can only really "profit" on an investment when you sell the investment. Your brokerage account is not your bank account. You can't buy groceries with your AAPL shares. The money in your brokerage account is only yours to spend once you cash out an investment.

4. You have not *lost* money on a stock until you've sold it. Similar to rule 3, you haven't officially lost money on a stock until you sell the stock at a lower price than what you bought it for, or if the stock goes to zero. The stock market goes up and down; that's what it does. If the company you're invested in is only down and not out, you're not SOL. Don't fall into the trap of panic selling because you're mourning "paper losses."

5. Buy low, sell high.

It's obviously so exciting to talk about all of the ways you can make money, but you shouldn't lose sight of the fact that you can also lose money; investing isn't a magic trick where you put your wallet into a hat and it comes out 7–10 percent fatter. I promise you there were folks who decided to finally make the leap into investing on Friday, October 16, 1987, only to have a really bad day on October 19, 1987, otherwise known as Black Monday.* There will be other Black Mondays, recessions, and maybe even depressions. Keeping that top of mind will make you a better investor, one who is hopefully divorced from emotional whims that happen with novices who are surprised by tough times

---

* On Black Monday the Dow Jones Industrial Average plunged 22.6 percent in one day. It's still the biggest one-day drop in the Dow's history. It was kind of a fluke. Mostly, it was due to technical issues like popular hedges, new technology, and trades closing out of order. Investor panic was only a small part of the problem. Within a few days the market was halfway back to normal and the crash wasn't followed by a recession.

in the financial markets. The good news is: *we have never not recovered from a single one in history*. And if for some reason we don't in the future, we will all have more important things to think about than our TSLA stock . . . like zombies and apocalypse vibes.

THE FIRST $100K IS THE HARDEST

Let's assume an 8 percent annual rate of return and that you invest $1,000 per month.

To reach your first $100K: it takes approximately seventy-seven months or about 6.4 years.

Then to go from $200K to $300K: it takes an additional thirty-eight months or 3.2 years.

But to go from $900K to $1 million: it takes only fourteen months or 1.2 years.

I know the initial slog can feel like the power of compounding isn't working for you, but once you get over the $100K mark it really does start picking up quickly.

SETTING YOURSELF UP

Believe it or not, purchasing shares of a stock is the easiest part of this whole thing.* Buying a stock, like ordering food on your phone, can be as simple as clicking a button on an app. When it comes to exactly what app or where online you're clicking, you have a *lot* of choices.

In order for me to give you a recommendation, you'll need to decide whether you want to be hands off or hands on with your investments. If you're the hands-on kind of investor, that means that you can see yourself picking investments on your own and will check the value of your stocks and portfolio on the reg. If you're a hands-off kind of person, you're probably

---

* To demonstrate just how easy it is, I put a step-by-step guide to buying a stock in the study guide if you need it.

leaning toward outsourcing some of those decisions to an investment professional.*

To get started, pick a brokerage. If you know you want to do it for cheap and go it totally alone, there are brokerages like Robinhood, Interactive Brokers, Webull, or Acorns. Be warned that they often put stock research behind a paywall even for account holders, if they offer it at all. Some, like Firsttrade, offer unique perks like extensive offerings in Cantonese and Mandarin. Another, Public, offers rebates on options trading. If you want a little more support or you think you may in the future, many legacy brokers like Fidelity, Charles Schwab, Vanguard, and E*Trade offer free trades, access to research, and the option to get professional guidance if you ever need it as do some of the newbie brokerages like Ally Invest and SoFi Invest. If you want to let the AI take the wheel, there are plenty of options—some of the big firms like Fidelity offer robo-advisors, but there are also AI-forward robo-investment brokerages like Wealthfront and Betterment.

FYI — MACHINE EARNING

Robo-investors were first defined as automated investment systems and are now AI run; a robo-advisor will do 100 percent of the stock picking and portfolio management for low fees. Robo-advisors use a mix of index funds and careful tax strategies to help you capture the returns of the market or attempt to beat it if you choose an aggressive track.

People constantly ask me which brokerage I prefer, and I always say the same thing: honestly, they are all pretty similar. It really comes down to a matter of preference—truly whichever one you like and will actually stick to is the right one for you. Here are some features to check to find your perfect match:

---

* It's also worth getting a sense of your risk tolerance now. I put a pop quiz you can't fail in the study guide as well so that you can assess how much stock spice your stomach can handle.

- account minimum / minimum balance (usually zero for most no frills accounts)

- commissions on trades (they should have none)

- promotions (these can be no fees for the first few months or a small amount of freebie cash—usually $50 to $100)

- web/mobile interface (make sure you like it and it has the features you need)

If you have enough money to pay for Amazon Prime, you have enough money to buy stocks. Heck, if you have enough money to buy Chinese food delivery for dinner, you have enough money to buy stocks. In fact, you don't even need to buy a whole stock. Fun fact: fractional investing was invented by a short-lived brokerage called buyandhold.com in the 1990s. But it didn't take off until it was offered by Schwab in 2019. Fractional investing makes it possible for anyone to own a part of even the most expensive stocks like a piece of Berkshire Hathaway Class A shares, which currently trade in the mid-six figures. Really.

For you hands-off folks, you'll want to go with a full-service brokerage. Examples of those would be: Merrill Lynch, Goldman Sachs, CitiFinancial, UBS, Morgan Stanley, Wells Fargo. The advantages of a full-service broker-age include having extensively researched, personalized recommendations for you and your goals, updates on market trends and tax laws, and access to IPOs. Of course, you'll have to pay for these perks, and there are much higher minimum balance requirements. Some of the features to look for here include:

- Cost per trade (usually free* but can get pricey—like thirty dollars a trade!—if broker assisted)

---

* There's no free lunch. While trades no longer cost the investor money, the brokerage usually makes money off payment for order flow (PFOF). This is a practice where the brokerage is paid by a "market maker" or middleman, who is usually a big investment bank, for routing a trade through them. The practice has been banned in the EU but remains legal in the US.

- Annual service charge and maintenance fees (usually free, but some charge hundreds for inactivity)

- Research (sometimes free, sometimes up to thirty dollars a month)

- Exclusive investment access (this can require a minimum balance of tens of thousands of dollars or more and may be charged as a percentage of the account balance)

TO BROKER OR NOT TO BROKER

The most common mistake I encounter is seeing people hand the financial reins completely to a financial advisor (or worse a stockbroker) who claims to "know better." If you're in a meeting with an advisor and you smile and nod when they ask you something that was not a yes or no question, they're going to take you for a ride, and it could be hard to get off that ride once you realize it's not what's best for your money. Never, ever forget: *no one cares more about your financial life than you do.* When push comes to shove, they will do what's best for *their* bottom line, not yours.

I'm sorry to give you trust issues, but it's true. The financial world has done an excellent job making folks believe that the only people qualified to make big investment decisions are the guys who went to business school and work on Wall Street. This misconception has led people to hand over the decision-making power, ultimately becoming too hands off with what's going on with their own money. That unchecked power on a more macro level is what leads to crises like the FTX debacle, the Madoff investment scandal, the 2008 subprime mortgage crisis, and sadly so on. Of course, we have no control over macro issues or the macro economy, but we do have full control over our own little micro economy (and issues).

So let's decide together that we don't need a *broker* to help us actually execute investments, but we might look at a financial advisor who is a fiduciary,* someone who has a duty to look out for your best interest. There is an important difference:

	BROKER	FINANCIAL ADVISOR (FIDUCIARY)
Primary Role	Facilitates buying and selling of financial products.	Provides holistic financial planning and investment advice.
Duty	Operates under a suitability standard. Must recommend suitable investments but not necessarily in the client's best interest.	Operates under a fiduciary standard. Must act in the best interests of the client.
Compensation	Often compensated through commissions on products sold.	Typically compensated through a fee-based model (for example, a percentage of assets under management, fixed fees, or hourly rates).
Fee Structure	Fees can be transaction based (per trade) or commission based on products sold.	Fees are often more transparent and can be asset based (a percentage of the assets managed), flat fees, or hourly rates.

* And does not have their series 7 licenses (which allows them to buy/sell securities) so be sure to ask. Some brokers can also be fiduciaries so that's not the only thing you need to make sure of. If you're stumped on how to have a conversation about this, I've put a sample script in the last lesson of the book.

	BROKER	FINANCIAL ADVISOR (FIDUCIARY)
Typical Services	Focuses on executing trades and selling financial products.	Offers comprehensive financial planning, including investment management, retirement planning, tax planning, and estate planning.
Objective	May prioritize products that offer higher commissions.	Prioritizes the client's financial goals and interests.
Relationship	Transactional focus, centered on specific investments and trades.	Long-term relationship, focusing on the client's overall financial health.

Even if you opt for a fiduciary, you still need to have the foundation of knowledge to be able to check and understand what your advisor is doing. This isn't a full outsourcing situation; it's an opportunity to level up. Just like if you hire a personal trainer to step up your fitness game, they can't do all the moves for you, nor do you have to do all the recommendations they give if something hurts or feels like too much for you. Ultimately, like a trainer, a great financial advisor would assess your whole health picture to help you get and stay in tip-top fighting shape. Start by looking at the CFP website for recommendations or reputable RIA (Registered Investment Advisor) firms like Creative Planning, Zoe Financial, or Facet. These companies, and others like them, offer different services, from in-house financial services to playing matchmaker to helping you find your perfect advisor.

POP QUIZ

How many times can you spend money? If you said once, you'd be right if you're thinking about cash. But if you have an asset like a stock portfolio* you can borrow against it over and over and over. You can turn it into cash in hand without selling. After all, you can only sell once and when you do, you have to pay taxes on the sale. Of course, if you take out a loan you do have to pay interest but this is one of the tricks the wealthy use to create generational wealth. Rather than spending their cash, they create a stockpile of assets like property and stocks to borrow against, using those assets as collateral for the loan.

HOW MUCH SHOULD I INVEST?

I know all of this stock talk is very exciting, but just like you shouldn't live beyond your means, you also shouldn't invest beyond your means either. In order to figure out how much you can comfortably afford to invest, you should make sure you have a solid spending plan that you're comfortable with. As I've discussed in depth in my other books, my advice for creating a spending plan boils down to separating your budget into the three Es:

- Essentials: what you probably have to pay every month like rent or mortgage, utilities, food, transportation, bills, insurances, loan payments. The basics.

- Extras: the fun stuff, the eating out, or ordering in, getting the pricier shoes because they're pretty and you want them.

- Endgame: savings for your dreams, your future, like having a sweet retirement or buying a home or supporting a child or parent, ideally through investment accounts.

---

* You can borrow against your stock portfolio with a margin loan through your brokerage or a securities-based line of credit from your bank. These can be risky because if the value of your stocks drops, you could need to deposit more cash or pledge more stocks to avoid the sale of the stock that has been pledged as collateral.

The percentage of your endgame allotment that you should invest really depends on your future goals. I mean, obviously, the more, the merrier. But if you know that you'll need to buy a new car in two years, you won't want to tie up a big chunk of your "endgame" allotment in investments that you want to hold on to for decades. So this question of how much to invest is really personal. But here are two things you should be able to say "hell yes!" to before putting a big chunk of your money in the market:

1. Is your emergency fund in check? The pandemic is the perfect example of how unpredictable life can be. For these unexpected challenges that life inevitably throws our way, you need some cash squirreled away. A doomsday fund, a treasure chest, an "oh, crap" fund, a "break in case of emergency" fund; whatever you want to call it—you need one now. My recommendation for how much you should put in your emergency fund differs depending on your job and which industry you work in, but generally, I suggest you have enough reserves to cover the monthly expenses in your bare-bones budget for six to nine months.

2. Have you paid off high interest–bearing debt? If you have outstanding debt, you'll want to crunch the numbers to see whether it makes more financial sense for you to wait to invest until you've paid off the entirety of your debt. If you have credit card debt with an interest rate of 15 percent and are making 7 percent returns in the market, you're accumulating debt faster than you're earning returns in the market. For example, if you have $10,000 invested for ten years with compounding interest at 7 percent annually, you'll have more than $19,000. Not bad, right? But what if you had $5,000 in credit card debt with 15 percent interest? After ten years you would *owe more than $20,000. Even if you owe half as much as you are investing, you will erase all your gains and still end up in debt.*

If you're twenty-two years old and owe $160,000 in private student loans, plus an additional $5,000 in high interest credit card debt, your budget will look different than if you're sixty-six with a low-interest almost-paid-off mortgage and $2 million in retirement savings. But, broadly speaking, you want your essentials to be no more than 70 percent of your budget.

That leaves at least 30 percent for paying down debt, investing, and extras. When it comes to debt, you want to pay off the highest interest rate debt first. At 20 percent, not an uncommon credit card interest rate, *it takes about three and a half years for the debt to double if you make no payments.* Making the minimum payment can also result in a revolving debt storm, even though you've paid more than the original amount you borrowed several times over.

If you have a high interest rate debt, consider a breakdown that is 20 percent debt repayment, 5 percent investing, and 5 percent extras. Once the debt is paid off, you can switch to allocating 25 percent to that endgame and 5 percent to extras. But toward the end of your career, if you are well funded through retirement and have no outstanding high interest rate debts, your breakdown may be more like 5 percent endgame and 25 percent extras. Once you've considered how much cash you need for immediate or short-term projects, your emergency fund is in good shape, *and* that debt monkey is off your back, you should have a good sense of what you have available to invest.

TACKLING

As we tackle the market, we'll want to understand what it means when someone says "the *market* is up." Usually, this refers to the performance of an index. An index is a collection of different stocks, grouped by a certain set of parameters. So when you hear stock market reporters saying, "the Dow is up blah-blah," "the S&P 500 is down XYZ," and "the NASDAQ is at la-di-da," they're talking about the three main indexes investors use to track the stock market as a whole. Similarly, when reporters say things like "the market is down" or see the market "trend" in a certain direction, they're likely making those observations by tracking one of those three indexes. While many feel that the S&P 500 is the most reliable index to track, most publications will also refer to the Dow as a gauge of what is happening in the overall market.* Let's unpack these three biggies:

- The Dow Jones Industrial Average (or just "the Dow") tracks the thirty biggest stocks in the US, including Apple, Microsoft, and Disney. They are considered "blue chip" companies, which has nothing to do with snacks or gambling but rather refers to their high quality.

- The S&P 500 is made up of five hundred large companies, each with a value of over $15.8 billion, as of the start of 2024. The S&P 500, which includes all of the companies on the Dow, makes up more than 80 percent of the US stock market by value.

- The NASDAQ is an index that tracks mostly technology and digital-related companies that trade on the NASDAQ (yes, the NASDAQ is both a stock exchange *and* the name of the index that tracks the stocks listed on the stock exchange . . . which is both a little helpful and a little confusing). There are more than thirty-three hundred companies in the NASDAQ including Meta, Alphabet (parent company of Google), and Amazon.

Some days the market will be up, and some days it will be down. Some years the market will be up and other years it will be down. What matters is how long you stay invested, because big picture: the market trend line goes up over time even though there will be days and years where it doesn't.

Time in the market > Timing the market

---

* While these indexes can tell you a lot about what is happening in the market, you can't actually purchase a share of them, but you can buy into what they are doing. That is where index *funds* come into the picture. When you buy into an index fund, you are basically buying a little bit of all of the companies within that index, without ponying up for individual shares in the individual companies. Course IV level 101 goes into this more.

WHAT DO I INVEST IN?

Well, *what do you want?* Are you looking for a bigger nest egg for retirement? To fund a project you foresee happening ten years down the line? To buy your first home? Are you looking to turn investing into an income stream? Your answers to these questions can, and should, change, but they will affect your investing strategy: specifically, how you decide to invest in companies (or funds made up of mostly companies) known as "value stocks" versus companies (or funds made up of mostly companies) known as "growth stocks."

Growth stocks are companies that investors believe have a lot of promise to, well, grow. But because of that, growth companies may not be making a lot of money . . . yet. Typically, when a company is on a growth trajectory, it may not be earning much money now—but investors aren't buying the company for what it is *now*; investors are buying the company for what they think it *will be*. Growth stocks tend to be new companies and/or companies that are inventing new tech or services. They are more likely to experience big ups and downs than value stocks.

Don't forget major companies once started as growth stocks. Tesla IPOed at $17/share and has grown to many, many times that. Growth companies may not have proven themselves to be uber profitable at the time of investment, so they tend to be considered higher risk, higher reward: if investors are right and the company "grows" into a big player, they'll reap the rewards. Look at TSLA—a $10K investment in 2010 would be worth around $2 million today. But if investors are wrong and the company crumbles, they could lose it all (hello, Pets.com and your sock puppet of shame that crashed and burned during the dot-com bubble).

But for every Apple, there are multiple rotten growth stocks that would turn an initial investment of $10,000 to zero today. The dot-com crash of the early 2000s saw many once-promising internet companies, often referred to as "dot-coms," go into the pooper with several eventually being delisted or removed from stock exchanges. This period was marked by a rapid rise in internet-related stocks, followed by a steep fall as the bubble burst.

Value stocks, on the other hand, are companies that do show consistent earnings and have shown themselves to be profitable. In contrast to growth stocks, value stocks tend to be older companies and/or companies that exist in really stable markets. But stability is a double-edged sword: although it means lower risk of dramatic losses (yay!), it also means lower chance of dramatic gains (boo!). These stocks are concentrated in sectors that are moneymakers but not explosive growth areas, (boring) sectors like the financial industry, health care, energy, telecommunications, utilities, industrial sectors, and legacy sectors of consumer goods. The companies are usually well-known too. So think Bank of America, Pfizer, Exxon, and Coca-Cola.

A $10,000 INVESTMENT IN APPLE'S IPO

Before value stocks were value stocks, they were growth stocks. Yes, even Apple. If you were lucky enough to have $10,000 to invest when the company IPOed, it would be worth upward of $15 million now.

I'll show my work:

Apple's IPO was on December 12, 1980, at a price of $22 per share. But Apple has had multiple stock splits since its IPO. These splits have occurred on the following dates and ratios:

June 16, 1987	2-for-1 split
June 21, 2000	2-for-1 split
February 28, 2005	2-for-1 split
June 9, 2014	7-for-1 split
August 31, 2020	4-for-1 split

Each stock split increases the number of shares owned while decreasing the price per share proportionally. To calculate the total number of shares you would now own, you multiply the number of shares purchased at IPO by the split ratios.

Initial Purchase: $10,000 / $22 = approximately 454 shares (ignoring fractional shares for simplicity)

After first split (1987)	454 shares x 2	=	908 shares
After second split (2000)	908 shares x 2	=	1,816 shares
After third split (2005)	1,816 shares x 2	=	3,632 shares
After fourth split (2014)	3,632 shares x 7	=	25,424 shares
After fifth split (2020)	25,424 shares x 4	=	101,696 shares

As of this writing, Apple's stock price is around $150 per share so the current value would be approximately 101,696 shares x $150 (current approximate share price) = $15,254,400.

"But, Prof," you might be asking, "why would I invest in a value stock if it isn't going to grow that much? I mean is 3M, a 'value stock,' ever really going to experience a boom in the demand for Post-it Notes!?"

Well, the short answer is that while these stocks may not experience a lot of growth, they have rock-solid fundamentals—and most value stocks pay a consistent dividend, which are essentially monetary "thank-you" gifts to shareholders.* Let's double-click on this "thank-you" gift, and talk about the ways investors make money from their investments.

THE WAYS TO MAKE MONEY

There are essentially two ways to earn money from stocks: earning dividends and selling shares. Let's talk dividends first. Most dividends are paid quarterly, but some companies may pay out dividends at a monthly or annual cadence. Stocks that pay dividends are known as **income stocks**. There are a few different types of dividends. The three biggies are:

1. *Cash dividends:* some companies will give investors dividends in the form of cash. The investor will likely receive the money via a deposit into their brokerage account.

---

* The classification of a stock as a "value stock" can change over time based on market conditions, company performance, and investor perception. Remember Nokia? If you were born before 1995, they probably made your first cell phone. For years they were considered a value stock with reliable dividends until they fell out of favor. The opposite is also true. Companies making computer chips used to be considered undervalued reliable performers until they blew up over the last few years.

2. *Stock dividends:* instead of cash, some companies will give investors additional shares in their company or a partner company.

3. *Dividend Reinvestment Programs (DRIPs):* this is the true "everybody wins" option. DRIPs are usually opt in. If an investor chooses to receive DRIPs, any cash dividend issued by the company is automatically reinvested in the company's stock. The company wins because they get more money to play with. The investors win because they get more stake in the company and therefore a greater opportunity to reap more dividends later on. When an investor increases their investment in a company, you might hear them say they're taking a "larger position."

How much can you make off dividends? Well, it really depends on how big a slice of the pie a company can afford to give shareholders and how many shareholders are splitting that slice. Let's make up an example: Let's say The Money School Company (MSKL) had a blowout year and raked in a lot of money, because of course we did. Because we're good leaders who want to make our shareholders happy (and want to encourage them to keep investing in us), we decide to give out dividends.

Let's say, for easy math, we have $1 million that we want to pass off as dividends. If there are only ten shares and one of them has your name on it? You, my friend, are getting a $100,000 thank-you gift. A-mazing. But if there are a million shares and only one of them has your name on it? Well, you'll be depositing a not-so-exciting $1 dividend payout. The number of shares issued by a company is called "shares outstanding." You can see why you would want to know the details on the company's shares outstanding, because that can really affect your payout as an investor. Shares outstanding will tell you if you're a big sunfish in a kiddie pool or a teeny sardine in the Atlantic Ocean.

The amount investors get from dividends varies widely. But so you have some sort of reference, I will say that, historically, big companies will pay dividends that are around 2 percent of the stock price. In other words, if you buy shares in a company that is trading at $100/share, assuming a 2 percent dividend, you'll be getting $2.

The second way to make money from a stock is to sell it. Say you buy three shares of a stock for $50 each, or, in other words, you make a total investment of $150 to buy three shares. After five years, let's imagine that the stock is now worth $100/share. You can sell all three of your shares and have $300 to play with. That would mean after five years, you doubled your investment! Major kudos.

Alternatively, at that five-year mark, you could say to yourself: *Wait a minute, the value of this stock has doubled in the last five years. Maybe it will double again . . . if that's the case, I definitely want to keep some of my shares.* So you decide to do a mix of selling and holding. You could sell just one of your shares for the market price of $100 and then keep the remaining two shares in the hopes that the stock price will keep going up and up. In that scenario, you still own two shares of the stock *and* $100 that is now free and sitting in your brokerage account to either move into your bank account or reinvest in something new.

I'll keep reminding you: you don't lose money until you sell your shares (so don't weep too much over those paper losses), and you do not make a profit until you sell your shares either (so don't rejoice too hard over those paper gains). This is the same concept as if you own your house. I don't care what the "Zestimate" says, your house is only worth what someone else will pay for it. The most important days for investments are (1) the day you buy and (2) the day you sell. Everything else is just noise. So when you hear someone say, "OMG, my portfolio lost so much money today!" I hope you wonder, "Did you actually lose money or did the value just go down on paper (or on the screen)?"

BUY LOW, SELL HIGH

I already told you that buying a stock is the easy part. But choosing a stock? That hits different. I would say that it's simple (once you learn the mechanics) but not easy. There are a lot of different factors that go into choosing a stock, but to start, let's drive home the golden rule: buy low, sell high. In other words: buy a stock when it hits a low price per share, and then sell it once it reaches a higher price. It's like buying something on sale and then reselling it for a premium. It works. The problem is: no one knows exactly what the lowest low will be, and no one knows what the highest high will be.

When you decide to buy a stock, you may be plagued with analysis paralysis: *What if I buy the stock today and the price goes down tomorrow? Then I will have essentially missed out on a better deal and paid a higher price than I would have paid if I just held on a liiiittle bit longer. But what if I wait to buy the stock and the price goes up tomorrow? Then I will have essentially missed out on a better deal and paid a higher price than I would have paid if I just acted a liiiittle bit more quickly.* You can have the same internal dialogue when it comes time to sell: *What if I sell the stock today and the price goes up tomorrow? Then I will have missed out on the chance to earn more money by selling my shares when the price was higher. But what if I wait until tomorrow and the stock price goes down? Then I will have missed out on a better gain. Gah!*

You can drive yourself crazy spinning around on a merry-go-round of doubt and "what ifs." The truth is: you'll never know with absolute certainty when it is the right time to buy or sell. But there are some insights and tricks you can use to maximize the chance that you'll get it right. I recommend you 1) opt for dollar-cost averaging and 2) diversify.

Dollar-Cost Averaging

Dollar-cost averaging is a strategy for protecting yourself (in finance-speak, we call this "hedging") against the unknown fluctuations in the stock market as in not knowing where lows and highs are going to happen. Dollar-cost averaging (DCA) basically is when investors take the total sum of money they want to invest in a company or fund and invest little chunks of that total in the company at different times, instead of all at once.

For easy math, let's say you have $12,000 that you want to invest in The Money School Company (MSKL). Because you don't know if today's market price of MSKL shares is going to be the lowest point ever, or if you'll get a better deal later on, you hold off on putting all $12,000 in on the same day. Instead, you put in $1,000 every month for a year. This will improve your chances of investing in the company at points when the share price is on the lower side (see next table). I'm not promising you that it will definitely work, but, short of having a crystal ball or psychic abilities, it will give you the best shot at success—and that's all we can really ask for in anything we do on Wall Street. The zillions of variables will do their thing; you are never going to have total control. The most successful investors know that, which is why they DCA.

$12,000 INVESTED AT ONCE

	JAN	FEB	MAR	APR	MAY	JUN	JUL	AUG	SEP	OCT	NOV	DEC	TOTAL
Investment	12,000	0	0	0	0	0	0	0	0	0	0	0	12,000
MKSL Stock Price	100	150	100	100	50	75	50	100	125	150	150	100	
# of Shares	120	120	120	120	120	120	120	120	120	120	120	120	120

$1,000 INVESTED EACH MONTH

	JAN	FEB	MAR	APR	MAY	JUN	JUL	AUG	SEP	OCT	NOV	DEC	TOTAL
Investment	1,000	1,000	1,000	1,000	1,000	1,000	1,000	1,000	1,000	1,000	1,000	1,000	12,000
MKSL Stock Price	100	105	100	85	90	105	90	100	110	90	100	100	
# of Shares	10	9.52	10	11.76	11.11	9.52	11.11	10	9.09	11.11	10	10	123.22

Automating dollar-cost averaging can really help mitigate the impact of market volatility and can lead to a lower average cost per share over time. Many online brokers and robo-advisors provide tools to automate your investment process. All you have to do is decide on the fixed amount of money you want to invest regularly and what interval you want—this could be weekly, biweekly, monthly, whatever. Then you just arrange for automatic transfers of the determined amount from your high-yield savings account (so you're still earning interest on the money waiting in the wings) to your investment account at those chosen intervals. This is typically done through a standing order or direct debit setup with your bank. Then, in your brokerage account, set up an automatic investment plan to purchase your chosen stocks or funds whenever your money is transferred. Some investment platforms offer the option to automatically reinvest dividends. This way, your money gets invested automatically without you having to worry about it. Set it up once and then it's a seamless part of your financial routine.* And, the best part: by automating this process, you remove the *emotional* aspect of trying to time the market and avoid the spin cycle.

Diversify and Chill

Whenever I open social media I always see videos of stock "experts" saying things like, "Such-and-such stock is so hot right now! This new <insert weird industry> company is the next big thing!" I am especially tickled when they get super excited about their assessment that's going to "blow up." Excuse me, guys, but when is it a good thing if something "blows up"? When I reported on the trading floor, if a company "blew up" it was actually a bad thing.

Anyway, let's debunk that kind of thinking right now. If you're interested in long-term growth, you don't want your investing strategy to rest entirely on one so-called "hot stock." Again, the stock market relies on way too many constantly changing factors for us to be able to predict with absolute confidence which stock will "blow up"—for better or for worse.

The best strategy is not to find the perfect, dreamy stock but to build a diverse portfolio.

Diversification is the investing principle telling you not to put your eggs all in one basket. The economist who applied this logic to finance won a Nobel Prize, which is absolutely bonkers to me because it's a phrase we all grow up with. It's like winning a Nobel Prize for the advice "if you lost something, check the last place you had it." But even though diversification is an idea that is colloquial, it is a prizeworthy idea when applied to your investments because it protects you from losing everything. It's sort of like dollar-cost averaging; but instead of spreading out the *pacing* of your investments in order to increase the likelihood of buying at a good time, you're spreading out *what* you're investing in to decrease the likelihood of a devastating loss.

Here's how it works: Say you have $100 to invest and you're going back and forth between investing in a proven company or investing in a "hot stock." If you throw all $100 into one hot stock, let's call it GameStop (GME),

---

* While dollar-cost averaging is a relatively hands-off strategy, it's still important to periodically review your setup, which we will talk about in the last lesson.

in a perfect world, you'll make a great ROI. Let's say your investment in GME takes off and your investment grows 50 percent after one year, and that $100 investment turns into $150. But what about a less-than-perfect world? If you put $100 in GME and the stock crumbles (as it did in 2021), poof! You may have less than the $100 you invested, and you'll have FOMO over not picking a stock that performed better. Or worse, if the stock goes to zero, so does your investment: you would lose every penny of your $100 investment.

Here's how diversification would save you in that scenario: If you're super bullish (finance speak for "confident") on video games and put $50 in GME and $50 in a more established company in the space like Electronic Arts (EA), then you increase the chances that you've picked a winner. If that perfect-world scenario comes to be and your GME investment does earn 50 percent, you've still earned a stellar ROI on your $50 investment, plus whatever return your investment in EA made. That's great; we can be happy with that. But what we can be even happier about is that we've lessened our exposure to risk, because if the worst-case scenario comes true and that GME investment turns out to be a dud, you haven't lost it all. You still have your $50 in EA (plus whatever they hopefully grew) to keep you afloat.

As this example shows, the payout can sometimes be better if you hitch your entire ride to a good investment, but oftentimes the risk is much higher than the reward. Remember: in the last example, you risked $100 to gain $50. See what I mean? Higher risk, relatively lower reward. In that scenario, I choose medium risk, medium diversified reward, every time.

I didn't pick GME for that example by accident. I think it's fair to say that one of the biggest stock market headlines in the last decade was the Game-Stop meme stock craze, where an online flash mob of Redditors virtually came out of nowhere and changed the financial game. Lots of people asked me why the financial world was so upset during the GameStop debacle. And, first, I have a correction: the financial world wasn't upset; *finance bros* were upset because they are sore losers, and they lost at their own game.

CONFESSIONS OF A PROFESSOR

EVEN WHEN YOU WIN, YOU CAN LOSE

"Stay away from all that stuff," my guest, who chose to remain anonymous, told me.

"But you made almost two million bucks!" I said, shocked.

"And I'm incredibly lucky to have done that. For every Game-Stop situation that happens, there are just as many that stay trading in that $12 range or go lower," he said as a cautionary tale to our listeners.

On my daily podcast *Money Rehab*, I talked to a Redditor who "made" almost $2 million (he spent almost half of that on short-term capital gains taxes) on GameStop. But even among the winners, stories like that were exceptions, not the rule. Many people got caught up in the frenzy, holding the stock too long and losing their investment. These were novice investors who jumped on a fast-moving Roaring Kitty train without understanding how or when to get off. The Redditor I talked to on *Money Rehab* said that, even though he took home seven figures on the stock, the volatility was so deeply stressful that he's not sure the panic attacks and sleepless nights were worth it.

His advice after emerging from the GameStop war: "Start with index funds. Be conservative. You're not going to hit a home run in six months and quadruple your money."

The hardest part of investing isn't managing your money; it's managing your emotions. And listen—I get it. I don't come from money, and so the idea that as soon as the clock strikes 9:30 a.m. ET (opening bell on Wall Street) I could be losing money freaks me out too. There will be times when you doubt yourself, but try not to let that stop you. You are smarter than you think and more capable than you give yourself credit for.

If you do have an overwhelming amount of investment anxiety, playing around with a free stock simulator is a way to dip your toe in the investing waters without actually spending any money. It allows you to basically play house with the stock market; you get to experiment and see what would happen if you were to invest a couple hundred dollars in a stock. If the money grows in the simulator, you're not actually going to be getting any returns . . . but you're also not losing anything, and you're not spending any money, while still learning a lot.

The day you start investing for real is the first day of the rest of your wealthy life. Momentum begets momentum. As soon as you see some green arrows, you'll be hooked. I was. Of course, not all days will be easy green arrows kinds of days; some will be hard and triggering as hell. Money has a weird way of shaking up some old personal demons. But I believe that change happens when the discomfort of the present outweighs the fear of the unknown. So, as soon as you are ready, investing—your money and in yourself—will be there. And if you really think about it, the stock market is predicated on the hope that the future will be better than it is today, and I think that's a beautiful mindset to lean into.

STOCKS 301

Fundamental and Technical Analysis

A iming for expertise in stock picking is a bit like the story of Socrates and the Oracle of Delphi (I promise this will be my one reference to Greek philosophy in this course). As the story goes, the Oracle of Delphi—a prophet that was a big, big deal in Greek life in the 420s BCE—proclaimed that Socrates, a revered philosopher, was the smartest person in Athens. That's a pretty big compliment coming from a reputable source.

Very few people at the time questioned anything the Oracle said, but Socrates himself did. He became determined to go around Greece and find the person who was *truly* the smartest of them all. He tracked down poets, politicians, priests—anyone who had smart-cookie street cred. But every time Socrates approached a so-called smarty pants, they gave him a BS answer to *sound* important and all-knowing. (Haven't we all met these guys at parties?) Socrates sought out these people thinking they were sources of great wisdom, but every person he talked to ended up just being the proverbial wise guy. After talking to enough of them, Socrates thought to himself, *You know what, perhaps I am the smartest person in Athens because I am aware of the fact that I don't know everything.*

When it comes to investing, be like Socrates: be wary of the anyone whose answers are wordy nonsense spewed to help them look like the smartest person in the room. And let me tell you, the financial world is full of these types who will tell you that they are the wisest of them all and can beat the market with both hands tied behind their backs. These clowns are even more ridiculous than the early Athenian scholars because not only do they claim that they know everything, but they also claim they can predict the future . . . and sometimes use that false claim to try and take your hard-earned money. In this lesson I am going to help you know everything in investing that's *actually* knowable.

THE FUNDAMENTALS

There are two kinds of analysis for assessing investments: fundamental analysis and technical analysis. *Fundamental analysis* looks at easily accessible information like news reports and financial statements. It is what long-term investors look to in order to assess the general health of an investment over time. *Technical analysis*, on the other hand, looks at the company's share price and volumes to try and pick out trading patterns. This kind of analysis is predominantly for short-term trading. Basically, fundamental analysis is mostly the study of words and technical analysis is the study of numbers.

	FUNDAMENTAL ANALYSIS	TECHNICAL ANALYSIS
Focus	Evaluating a company's intrinsic value based on financial performance and industry position	Forecasting future price trends based on historical market data and price patterns
Key Elements	Financial statements, earnings, growth potential, profit margins, management quality	Price movements, volume, patterns, and trends in stock charts
Time Horizon	Long-term investment decisions	Short-term trading decisions

	FUNDAMENTAL ANALYSIS	TECHNICAL ANALYSIS
Analysis Type	Qualitative and Quantitative: Financial ratios, management evaluation, industry analysis	Statistical and Pattern Based: Chart patterns, moving averages, technical indicators
Use Cases	Used by long-term investors, value investors	Used by traders, short-term investors

THE NEWS

The movement of the stock market is greatly influenced by current events. Some of these events are predictable, like elections, while others are less so, like natural disasters or pandemics. After seeing the way that travel companies tanked and companies producing sanitizing products skyrocketed during the pandemic, I can't help but roll my eyes even harder when some Wall Street bro suggests that they are the "smartest" investor or at the "smartest" firm out there.

There are two kinds of news you should be tracking as an investor: (1) news about the company individually and (2) general economic news.

On the individual company level, here are the types of headlines to look out for:

- Has the company announced any big plans that could lead to major earnings down the line?

- Have they announced product launches?

- Are there mergers or acquisitions rumblings?

- Is there any talk of expansion into new markets (domestic or abroad)?

Don't be fooled by good marketing and overused buzzwords like *innovation*. If a company has an innovative product, they probably don't need to tell you it's innovative. Just like if someone is *really* powerful, they don't need to tell you they are powerful. (Same goes for rich.)

Another thing to keep an eye out for is who is in the boardroom. Has the company recently replaced a CEO? Is the leadership of the company clued in to their customer's demographic? (Spoiler alert: This is basically the series arc of the show *Succession*.) For example, since its inception, the cosmetics industry was run by men who were targeting their products to women. Later, these executives realized it made a whole heck of a lot more sense to have women, that is, people who could speak to the perspective of the target customer, in the boardroom. (Spoiler alert: This is basically the series arc of *Mad Men*.)

We all have cultural and social blind spots, but if the leadership team of a company you're invested in are demographic clones of one another, then they probably have the same blind spots. It's important to have a team that includes the perspective of their key consumer demographics to make sure that they have their finger on the pulse of important trends within said customer base. Plus, obviously, we want to support companies that are in line with our values. Don't forget that with investing, just like any other financial exchange, a dollar is a vote on those values.

MONEY TIP

STAY ALERT

You can find updates like these on the company's website under the Investor Relations tab. Or you can set up your own custom RSS feed for the news you need or Google alerts for the companies and/or their executives so you're the first to know.

On the macroeconomic front, you want to generally be up to speed with what's happening in the world at large, not just the business world. The general sentiment or vibe check around the globe will affect markets. Think about it: at the start of the pandemic, markets crashed. The stock market is very responsive to the big headlines around the world. When Silicon Valley Bank crashed in 2023, the whole banking sector of the stock market plummeted. But financial headlines aren't the only pieces of news that affect the market. If conflict is worsening in the Middle East, normally the price of oil is affected, which, in turn, affects the stock market as a whole. It is all interconnected, so it will help your portfolio if you're up on the latest news.

FYI

BLACK SWAN

The term *black swan* comes from a colorful, metaphorical feather in the cap of Nassim Taleb, a finance professor, former Wall Street trader, and author. In his cult classic 2007 book, *The Black Swan*, Taleb describes these unexpected, rare, and impactful events based on an old saying. Historically, it was believed that all swans were white because all the swans that people had encountered were white. This belief was upended when black swans were discovered in Australia. The term became a metaphor for any theory that seemed true but could be demolished by a single unexpected event like, say, the total meltdown of the housing market in 2008 or the COVID-19 pandemic.

In addition to staying on top of headlines and global events, you might also want to start getting comfortable with some key economic reports and indicators. They may sound intimidating, and trust me, I felt the same way when I first sifted through them, but markets seriously move on these numbers. Pro investors analyze and overanalyze these reports for gems and nuggets to get a leg up on the competition.

ECONOMIC INDICATOR	FUNCTION	RELEASE FREQUENCY
Gross Domestic Product (GDP)	Measures the economic activity (goods and services) for the country during a set time frame	Quarterly and annually
Unemployment Rate	Measures the percentage of the population that is actively seeking a job	Monthly, seasonally, and annually
Consumer Price Index (CPI)	Measures the average price that consumers are paying for goods and services	Monthly
Producer Price Index (PPI)	Measures the average price that producers are asking for goods	Monthly
Consumer Confidence Index	Measures how consumers are feeling about the economy both at that moment and what they expect in the future	Monthly
Retail Sales	Measures the change in activity in the retail sector—not the price movement, just if people are buying more or less stuff	Monthly
Industrial Production	Measures the change in the output of manufacturing, mining, and energy production	Monthly
Housing Market Indicators	Various reports that track the change in the number of homes started, built, or sold as well as reports that track the price movement	Monthly and Quarterly

When you're trying to project how a company might grow, it is very important to consider how the industry at large is going to change within the window of time you're planning on investing. Let's say, for example, that the year is 1960 and you think a Cuban-based cigar company is about to take off. You pour all your money into that investment and then two years later a little thing called the Cuban Missile Crisis happens and all of a sudden, the US bans products from Cuba.

To try and prevent a situation like this from happening to you, look at trends in that company's industry: Is legislation going to change how the company can operate? Does the company sell a technology that is at risk of becoming obsolete? Here's a biggie: Will this industry be affected by which political party is in office?

Politics always moves markets. Investors watch to see what the candidates say on fiscal and monetary policy. Yes, fiscal policy and monetary policy sound the same . . . but they are different. *Fiscal policy* refers to financial moves made by the government using tools like taxes and spending, while *monetary policy* results from moves by a central bank to stabilize the economy and control inflation, using tools like interest rates and the money supply.

Fed Watch

It's about time I introduce you to your new frenemy: the Federal Reserve. The Fed is led by a chair, who is appointed by the president of the United States. Using monetary policy, the Fed tries to keep our economy in balance. It does that while also keeping a sharp eye on what banks are doing. And let's not forget: the feds are the ones printing our money. That's a biggie.

Eight times a year, they meet to decide whether to switch up the interest rate. The Fed controls the interest rate at which banks lend money to each other overnight, aka the federal funds rate. Why does this matter? Because it's like the master volume knob for the economy. When the Fed tweaks this rate, it influences *everything* from inflation to employment, and it affects all types of loans—whether you're a gigantic business or an individual consumer. And all of that ultimately affects the markets.

The prime rate is what banks charge their best customers, like big corporations. Essentially, banks use the federal funds rate as a starting point and then add a bit extra. The prime rate is slightly higher than the federal funds rate because, well, banks gotta make their profit too. This rate is super important because it ultimately affects consumer loans like mortgages and credit cards.

Now, central banks aren't unique to the US. Globally, there are others like the European Central Bank (ECB), the Bank of England (BoE), the Bank of Japan (BoJ), and the People's Bank of China (PBoC). Each of these central banks run the show in their respective economies, setting their monetary policies, supervising banks, and working to keep their financial systems in check.

THE FINANCIALS

I'm going to save you the embarrassment and tell you right away what a P&L is. P&L is an abbreviation for the spreadsheet that companies use to track their profits and losses. If you're ever walking around a corporate office, you may hear someone say this really fast, and it might come out like "P 'n' L." Well, I told you I would save you some embarrassment, because the embarrassment has already been covered by someone else . . . me. Early in my career, when I heard all these people talking about P 'n' Ls, it was just gibberish to me, and I was desperately trying to make sense of it. My initials are N. L. So, in my non-jargon-y brain, I rationalized this nonsense as "pee, N. L." So . . . yeah. I thought people were periodically asking if I had to pee before heading to the studio. Big yikes. While P&Ls have nothing to do with *that*, a P&L *can* tell you whether a company is going down the toilet.

At the most basic level, a P&L aims to show you the net profit of the company—or, in other words, how much the company is *actually* making after accounting for expenses. The formula to solve for this yourself is:

MONEY COMING IN (sales, subscribers, users)	−	MONEY GOING OUT (office space rent, payroll, equipment, travel expenses, manufacturing costs)	=	NET PROFIT

The simplest way to think about it is that you want to invest in companies that have impressive net profit numbers and are reporting increases in profit year over year. According to some experts, you can be impressed by a company if they are pulling off 10 percent profit growth. Even though it's generally assumed that the simplest answer is normally the best one, I wouldn't necessarily agree here. I would actually opt for the more complex answer that factors in *why* net profit may not be growing year over year.

Let's imagine that you are deciding between investing in The Money School Company (MSKL) and a competitor—let's call them the ICK Company (ICK). To decide which company you should invest in, you look at both of their P&Ls, and they look like this:

	MSKL NET PROFIT	ICK NET PROFIT
2023	$1,000,000	$1,000,000
2024	$1,000,000	$1,100,000

According to this data, ICK is showing signs of year-over-year growth while MSKL is staying stagnant; and in the stock market, standing still means falling behind. Plus, increasing profits tend to increase the perceived value of a stock—so this could signal to you that ICK shares will be more beneficial to you in the near future. But what if you asked me for the full P&L and I showed you this:

MSKL P&L

	MSKL GROSS PROFIT	MSKL EXPENSES	MSKL NET PROFIT
2023	$1,500,000	Payroll: $350,000 Office Space: $150,000 **Total Expenses: $500,000**	Gross Profit $1,500,000 – Expenses $500,000 **= Net Profit $1,000,000**

	MSKL GROSS PROFIT	MSKL EXPENSES	MSKL NET PROFIT
2024	$2,500,000	Payroll: $700,000 Office Space: $300,000 R&D: $500,000 **Total Expenses:** **$1,500,000**	Gross Profit $2,500,000 – Expenses $1,500,000 **= Net Profit $1,000,000**

ICK P&L

	ICK GROSS PROFIT	ICK EXPENSES	ICK NET PROFIT
2023	$1,500,000	Payroll: $350,000 Office Space: $150,000 **Total Expenses:** **$500,000**	Gross Profit $1,500,000 – Expenses $500,000 **= Net Profit** **$1,000,000**
2024	$1,400,000	Payroll: $200,000 Office Space: $100,000 **Total Expenses:** **$300,000**	Gross Profit $1,400,000 – Expenses $300,000 **= Net Profit** **$1,100,000**

All of these details paint a very different picture than looking at net profit alone. While the MSKL net profit stayed the same, there was growth in both expenses and *gross* profit. From the Expenses column, we see that the spending on payroll and office space doubled, implying that the company is growing. Furthermore, there's a big new expense for R&D. R&D stands for research and development, or the financial shorthand for the expenses associated with iterating new products. In some cases, high expenses are not a good sign, but when expenses represent the company investing in itself, that can be a great sign.

On the flip side, the ICK P&L is not telling the best story. Yes, the net profit increased, but gross profit *decreased*: immediate red flag. In order for a company to show increasing net profit in the face of decreasing gross profit, the expenses need to be slashed. In the case of ICK, in 2024, we see that the company cut payroll and office space costs—which likely means that employees were laid off and branches were closed. These are both bad signs.

I'm not saying that high expenses are always a good thing. These are just two examples to get you thinking. High expenses need to be justified. Like, if you invest in a winter jacket company and see that they have $500,000 of new travel expenses, sure, it could be legit. But then you're seeing the CEO post glamour shots of their business trip to Barbados. What business is a winter jacket company doing in Barbados? Probably funny business.

Balance Sheets

Another document you'll want to track down is a company's balance sheet, where you can get a sense of a company's equity. While profit shows you how much the company is making in a given time frame, equity shows you how much the company is *worth*. You can calculate the equity of a company by taking what they own (their assets) and subtracting what they owe (their liabilities). It's the same formula that you would (and should) use to calculate your own personal net worth. Here's the same information, but pretty:

$$\text{ASSETS} - \underset{\text{(debt)}}{\text{LIABILITIES}} = \underset{\text{(equity)}}{\text{NET WORTH}}$$

Ah yes, owing versus owning: who knew one little letter could make such a big difference in the meaning! In a balance sheet, a company should be able to show you the breakdown of the assets they have: financial, tangible, and intangible.

- A financial asset is something like a stock, bond, or actual cold, hard cash.

- A tangible asset is something that has value but would need to be sold in order to gain monetary value like a building or product.

- An intangible asset is something that has value but would need to be sold in order to gain the monetary value *and* is not something that you can physically tap with your hand: like intellectual property or patents.

The balance sheet is typically a little bit more clear cut than a P&L statement. While it's not necessarily a warning sign if a company's net profit decreases, it is a big, honking red flag if a company's equity decreases. That likely means the company's debt is increasing and it doesn't have the assets to cover it, and that can sometimes lead to bankruptcy. As always, you'll want to look at these things holistically. Maybe a company's equity looks pretty good on paper because they have $1 billion in assets. Sweet! But then we take a closer look and see that 100 percent of those assets are shares in a sketchy cryptocurrency called Fyre Festival Coin 420 or something less obviously sketchy but sketchy nonetheless.

The 10-K and 10-Q

The final set of important docs is a company's 10-K and 10-Q. Both reports detail similar financial updates (which is why they tend to be grouped together), but the timing is different; 10-Ks come out annually, while 10-Qs come out quarterly.

While P&Ls and balance sheets are important sources of information, they can be fluffed or even fibbed a little. But 10-Ks and 10-Qs are overseen by the SEC, so that data has less room for added pizzazz from a company's chief financial officer. Pretty much every financial expert makes the joke that running a 10K is easier than reading one, and even as someone who considers negotiation cardio, I happen to agree. 10-Ks and 10-Qs are jargon-filled mazes that make it difficult to find the information you're looking for. If you have the time and energy to sift through a whole 10-K and a 10-Q, A+!

More realistically, these will be there for analysts to dig into, and you can read the analysts' reports. But any digging you can do into the company's data yourself—especially if you're thinking of making a big bet—the better off you'll be. A company's headlines may be telling you how much they could make *if* they sold their products. But are they *actually* selling them?

Any investigation you can do to see if the story that a company is projecting really adds up will, well, really add up for you.

There are a lot of financial analysts and punditry out there but not all of them are created equal. Morningstar, Bloomberg, and the *Wall Street Journal* are all reputable sources for analysis. All three companies also offer many of their newsletters for free to nonsubscribers. Try to get in the habit of reading one business news story or newsletter a day. If you play Wordle every day on the *New York Times* app, get in the habit of looking at a business story too. Just getting regular exposure to the language and the big players is a great place to start.

FYI THE BEST OF THE BEST FOR FREE

The New York City Public Library has actual Bloomberg terminals, the fanciest financial data you can get, available to the public in Midtown Manhattan. This is what the pros use. They cost about $25,000 per use, *per year*.

THE TECHNICALS

Let's review the more technical components of investment analysis, even if we only reference it as needed. These markers will help you to gauge whether a stock is investment worthy or to check how a stock you've invested in is performing. Maybe you've seen abbreviations like Div, Vol, Yld, P/E on the rolling scroll at the bottom of TV business news. Or if you're on an app, it may look something like this:

SYMBOL	MSKL
Price	20
Open	19
High	20

SYMBOL	MSKL
Low	18.5
Vol	1,000
52W H	20
52W L	10
Beta	1*
Div.	2
Dividend Yield	0%
EPS	10
PE	2
Mkt Cap	20M

I've seen Egyptian hieroglyphics that are easier to decipher. As I walk you through these metrics,[†] I'm going to reference the data above to help demystify the meaning of these terms. When I was teaching myself this info, it was super helpful for me to think about these terms in real-life examples rather than trying to decipher obscure financial terms with zero context.

While a whole financial markets dictionary (that you don't need a dictionary to understand because I've definitely needed one for other financial definitions out there) is in the back of this book for you to reference as you go or anytime you ever need it, here are the main terms you need to know to get through this section:

SYMBOL (aka the ticker) is a nickname that references a particular public company. For The Money School Company example I've been using, the ticker is MSKL.

PRICE is the current price investors would need to pay to buy one share of MSKL stock. So, if you look at the table above, you see that

---

* Calculated based on the Russell 2000 index at time of writing.

† Stats can come in different orders depending on where you look. For this lesson, I'll decode the terms in the order of the chart above.

if someone wanted to invest in us (they have great taste), they would need to cough up $20 to buy one share.

OPEN is the price of one share at the time the market opened that day. So, based on our trusty table, at 9:30 a.m. ET when the opening bell rang, MSKL was trading at $19/share. Already from these first two pieces of information, we know we had a good day. Why? Because the price of the stock is climbing. At the beginning of the day, the stock was at $19, but it has jumped up to $20/share.

HIGH will tell you the highest price the stock reached that day. For MSKL, the highest price point the stock reached was $20/share.

LOW is the opposite. On the day we're checking our stock, MSKL hit a low point of $18.50/share.

VOL stands for the volume of shares traded within a time frame, typically one day. So, in my example, MSKL volume is 1,000, meaning 1,000 shares were traded today. Volume is usually in millions, denoted with an "M." Understanding what volume means for your investment is a bit tricky. High volume indicates a strong interest in a stock, either because people want to buy it or they want to dump it. Pro investors don't make investment decisions based on volume alone, so I'd recommend we don't either (we are pros in the making, or pre-pros, after all).

52-WEEK HIGH is the highest price the stock has reached in the last year. This year, our high is also our current price of $20/share. In other words, MSKL is currently hitting what has been the company's high.

52-WEEK LOW is the opposite. That's the lowest price the stock has been valued at within the last year.

Investors tend to see what story the 52-week high, 52-week low, and current price tell when analyzed together (these are my favorite metrics to watch before buying). If the 52-week high is much larger than the 52-week low, *and* the current stock price is closer to the record high than record low—investors may evaluate that stock as one that is growing in value. But hitting the 52-week low isn't always a signal to avoid the stock; it could mean that the stock is "on sale" and you *should* buy.

The reason the current price is important to this story is because the current price helps show the trajectory of the stock. For example, if you looked at another company with the same exact high ($20/share) and low ($10/share) but the stock was currently priced at $15/share, the investor may wonder if the $20 high was a fluke—a random bump that's not indicative of real value—and if the current price will go lower still and fall back to the $10/share low point. But because MSKL is currently priced at the all-time high, the investor may summarize that the stock is on an upward trajectory, or that it has peaked.

It's kind of like a dating profile. You might match with someone who looks absolutely jaw-dropping, heart-thumpingly gorgeous in one picture, but in the next pic, they look a bit meh. You scroll back and forth trying to figure out which one is more representative of what they actually look like, but there's no way to discern; you need more data. You decide to invite your match to go to coffee because the only way you'll figure out what they really look like IRL . . . is to see them IRL. The current price serves the same function: it helps investors guess whether the record high or low is more representative of its value, and whether the stock is hot or . . . not.

Alternatively, investors may think that if there's a big difference between the high and the low, the stock could be volatile—meaning, the value of the stock jumps around a lot. You don't need to be an investor to know that volatility is an unappealing thing. Think of anyone in your life you'd describe as volatile. Do you want to keep those people around? Probably not. Most investors (or at least most conservative investors) feel the same way about volatile stocks.

FYI **CHECK THE VIBE**

The VIX, often called the "fear gauge" or "fear index" on Wall Street, stands for the Volatility Index (and is pronounced "vicks," not V-I-X). It's like the pulse monitor of the stock market's anxiety levels.

Here's why it matters:

MARKET SENTIMENT INDICATOR: The VIX is a real-time market index. Think of it like a thermometer, measuring how crazy people think the market will get. A high VIX reading suggests that the market is pretty hot, and people think prices will change a lot. A low VIX means everyone is feeling pretty chill and looking forward to a calm, confident market.

RISK MANAGEMENT TOOL: If the VIX is high, it's like a warning sign that the stock market might get wild, and for some investors, that means it's time to rotate out into unrelated assets like bonds. Other investors may see it as a time to find good deals on stocks.

CONTRARIAN INDICATOR: Sometimes the VIX is used the opposite way. A very high VIX can mean the worst is over because fear is peaking. But when it's really low, it might mean people are too chill, which could mean the market is at its peak.

Volatility on its own isn't bad or good for the markets: it's a bit like chili peppers. A little bit can add flavor, but too much can be overwhelming. Volatility can present opportunities for profit, especially for those who thrive on short-term trading and try to capitalize on quick price movements. But for the average investor, especially for those with a long-term view, high volatility can increase the risk of losses. High volatility is a double-edged sword—offering potential for high returns but also higher risk. The key is understanding your tolerance for spice in your financial diet.

Beta is a measure of a stock's volatility within the context of the overall stock market's volatility. In technical analysis, the volatility (or beta) of the entire stock market is assigned the value of "1," so if the beta of a given stock is between –1 and 1, it is considered to be less volatile than the stock market. If the beta is above 1, or below –1, it means that the stock is more volatile than the stock market. For example, a beta of 0.50 would mean that the stock is 50 percent less volatile than the stock market at large, while a beta of 1.5 would mean that the stock is 50 percent more volatile than the market.

A company that falls into a pretty steady industry, like the "consumer goods" category (groceries, cleaning products), is going to have a low beta. Verizon, a go-to example for a value stock, has a beta of 0.45. That means Verizon is less volatile than the stock market overall. But a company within a more variable industry, like energy, is going to have a high beta. EOG Resources, an American energy company (at the time I'm writing this), has a beta of 2. That means it is twice as volatile as the overall stock market.

There are also negative beta values. A negative beta means that the company's stock has an inverse relationship with the stock market's movement. In other words, in moments when the stock market dips down, companies with negative beta values tend to perform well. An example of a security with a negative beta is gold. When the stock market declines, gold prices tend to rise, like a seesaw. Investors tend to look at stocks with negative beta values as possible hedges against the market—or, in other words, investments that will add some diversification to their portfolio so that if the market crashes, these negative-beta hedges will rise in value and hopefully cancel out some losses. A high or low beta isn't bad or good. It can change depending on the volatility of the market. (Hi again, VIX.)

FYI — SOUNDS LIKE GREEK

If there's beta, you better believe there's going to be alpha. Alpha measures how profitable an asset is compared to similar assets. It is sometimes used to measure an asset's "edge," which is why there is a popular investing site called

"Seeking Alpha." So why doesn't everyone just invest based on alpha? Well, because it is a trailing indicator. So it doesn't tell you as much about the future as it tells you about the past.

DIV, or dividend, shows the dollar amount shareholders will get from the company annually in dividends.

DIVIDEND YIELD is typically the representation of the return you'll get on your investment via dividends, shown as a percentage of the stock price. It's calculated as:

$$\text{DIV YIELD} = \left(\frac{\text{ANNUAL DIVIDEND TOTAL}}{\text{STOCK PRICE}} \right) \times 100$$

If you see a "-" or an empty value in the Yield column, that doesn't necessarily mean a company had crummy profit and, therefore, a crummy dividend return; it could mean simply that the company does not issue dividends.

EPS, or earnings per share, is a measure of the company's profitability, with respect to the number of shares available to investors. Sadly it isn't a measurement of how much money investors will make when they buy a share. If only companies were cutting EPS checks to investors . . . but alas, that's not what's going on here. EPS is calculated by dividing net profit by the number of shares outstanding:

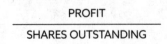

$$\frac{\text{PROFIT}}{\text{SHARES OUTSTANDING}}$$

Let's say MSKL has $10,000,000 in profit and one million shares outstanding.

$$\text{MSKL'S EARNINGS PER SHARE IS:} \left(\frac{\$10,000,000}{1,000,000 \text{ SHARES}} \right) = 10$$

Compare that to our other example company, ICK. Let's say that ICK also has an EPS of 10. Same as MSKL, right? Yes . . . but what if I told you ICK's profit is $100, and the number of shares outstanding is 10 ($100 / 10 shares = 10). Of course, this is a really dramatic example, but you can see that even though ICK and MSKL have the same exact EPS, MSKL is a heck of a lot more profitable.

P/E RATIO represents the relationship between the stock price and earnings per share (EPS). This is a big metric when it comes to the stock market. It is one of the top considerations when evaluating a stock's performance and potential. P/E ratio is calculated by dividing the stock price by EPS:

$$\text{P/E RATIO} = \frac{\text{STOCK PRICE}}{\text{EARNINGS PER SHARE}}$$

Let's fill in the equation with MSKL's data. Let's use the 10 we got for our EPS:

$$\text{MSKL'S P/E RATIO} = \frac{\$20 \text{ (STOCK PRICE)}}{10 \text{ (EPS)}} = 2$$

Typically, (conservative) investors say: the lower the P/E ratio, the better— |an EPS of 15 is generally considered good value. But let me break this nice, neat rule: at the time I'm writing this, the Walt Disney Company, one of the largest media organizations in the world, has a P/E ratio of 70.24. You might be thinking: *Whoa, Prof! You told us a P/E ratio of 15 is considered a good value. Walt Disney is one of the biggest companies in the world! Are you telling me that it's not valuable?!*

No, I'm not, because here's the catch: a high P/E ratio means that the share price is high compared to how much profit a company is making. But here's the thing: low profit—even zero profit (and, therefore, zero EPS)—isn't always a bad thing.

There are two reasons a company might not be profitable: first, they suck and they're not making any money. That's what we may have assumed and now are seriously stumped because we know that the Walt Disney Company certainly does not suck. The second reason a company might not be profitable is because they're taking all of the money that they're making and putting it back into the company, which is the situation with Disney. At the time I'm writing this, Disney is shoveling all of their money into building out their streaming service. For a media company, that's probably a good use of all their money. But it makes for a painful-looking balance sheet.

Let's circle back to a group of stocks we've talked about before: growth stocks and value stocks. Growth stocks tend to have high P/E ratios, while value stocks tend to have lower P/E ratios. An important thing to remember about growth stocks, though, is that investors are typically actively looking for evidence that a growing stock really is going to prove its worth and not go bust. We can do this with Disney by looking at the profits it's raking in despite its spending blitz. Another sign investors will look for is whether growth companies are reporting increasing profit year over year, which would mean the number of the P/E ratio would fall over time. Investors do want to see that potential for profitability.

MKT CAP is the abbreviation for "market capitalization," a number that represents the value of a company, specifically from an investing perspective. To find the market cap, you take the number of shares outstanding and multiply that by the share price.

PRICE   **×**   SHARES OUTSTANDING   **=**   MKT CAP

In our table, we were given market cap, but we could have solved for it. If MSKL has 1,000,000 shares outstanding, the market cap would be:

$$\underset{\text{(the stock price)}}{\$20} \quad \times \quad \underset{\text{(number of shares outstanding)}}{1,000,000} \quad = \quad 20,000,000$$

Conventional wisdom is that risk decreases as the "cap" gets larger. In other words, a mega cap company like Apple is too big to fail. On the flip side, it's generally suggested that smaller cap companies are riskier but have the most room for growth.

CONFESSIONS OF A PROFESSOR

THE BIG FAIL TOO

"I think we can probably grab the noon shuttle downtown," my freshman year roommate said as she grabbed a beanie and "Hot Paws" to brave the lakefront chill.

"Urgh I think this Cali girl is going to freeze her butt off," I said putting an unnecessary amount of layers on. "Maybe I can ask Kelsey to use one of those face shield things her family got her."

My roommate stopped and stared at me.

"Whatever! She's from Texas and gets me. I know you're a pro at this winter stuff, Miss Milwaukee," I said sassily assuming she was going to make fun of me again for knowing absolutely nothing about how to dress for a Chicago winter.

"No, Nicole . . . didn't you hear?" she said in a softer tone than I expected.

"Hear what?" I said still not totally sure if this was going to be part of a bit.

"Kelsey had to go home all of a sudden."

"Is she okay?" I asked.

"She's okay but her grandpa is on SW," she said in a way I now knew was serious.

"Oh no, that's terrible . . . Wait, what's SW?"

"You know, a 5150," she said almost as a whisper.

"That sounds awful—is that a sickness?" I said trying to read her cues to understand what exactly she meant. I had certainly had my fair share of mental health struggles, but these abbreviations were foreign to me at the time.

"Her grandpa is on suicide watch . . . everyone is really worried about him. It's not like him but he worked at Enron and the whole company went under and everyone was let go," she said.

"Oh gosh, that's horrible . . . So you mean the layoff led to him being . . ."

"I only talked to her roommate about it for a minute but it sounds like he was less than a year away from retiring and he had hundreds of thousands of dollars in their retirement program but now it's worth nothing."

Enron went under in December 2001. At the time its market cap was $65 billion. It was an energy company based in Houston that grew into a big player in the mid-eighties. It continued to be the picture of a successful, stable company until the very end. Just before disaster struck, Enron was trading at $90 per share so it came as a shock to everyone—reporters, bankers, investors, employees, the world—when Enron filed for bankruptcy in 2001 and the share price plummeted to under $1.

How could this company have failed so hard? Well, for starters, Enron measured its value based on *projected* revenue from a given project rather than the actual revenue. Essentially, their book-keepers were like, "Hey, we're probably going to make X amount of dollars from this project . . . let's just write that down for now for funsies." But these projects did not always make X amount of dollars. In fact, sometimes the projects would *lose* them money. But Enron's bookkeepers did some zhuzhing again and shuffled numbers around, most significantly assigning these losses to companies that Enron owned but weren't on Enron's books so that Enron could keep losses off their P&L.

In the fallout, experts estimate that investors lost a total of $74 billion, and thousands of former Enron employees lost not only their jobs but much of their retirement nest egg. Enron recommended that employees put their 401(k)s into Enron stock (probably because Enron needed the money), and so many employees lost everything, like Kelsey's grandpa. It's a reminder of the importance of diversification and keeping a watchful eye even over those companies deemed "too big to fail." But it's also just heartbreaking for the people involved—maddening and traumatizing to those who lived it and everyone around them. I haven't checked in with Kelsey in a bit, but I am sure she has been skeptical of all jobs and retirement options from that day on.

All of these analyses are important to know and use . . . regularly. All of these metrics take the temperature of a stock for *one moment in time.* You'll need to look at these numbers across several quarters, or even several years, to get the most accurate picture.

Enron is the perfect example of the issue with these metrics: they don't tell the whole story of a company. That's my issue with people making big investment decisions based on the handful of statistics that show up on the investing apps. You can't determine whether a company is growing by looking at its stats as a snapshot.

Plus, companies can manipulate these metrics to make their stock look more valuable than it is. For example, companies can buy back shares, which essentially takes them off the market and shrinks the number of shares outstanding. With a small number of shares outstanding, the EPS value will go up. Let me show you the math.

Say that a company made $10,000,000 two years ago and had 1,000,000 shares outstanding. Their EPS would be:

$$\text{EPS} \quad = \quad \frac{\$10{,}000{,}000 \text{ (profit)}}{1{,}000{,}000} \quad = \quad 10$$

Now, let's say that last year was really rough on the company, and their profit went down to $5,000,000—around half the cash they brought in the year prior. That would mean that their EPS would now be 5:

$$\text{EPS} \quad = \quad \frac{\$5{,}000{,}000 \text{ (profit)}}{1{,}000{,}000 \text{ (shares outstanding)}} \quad = \quad 5$$

So, their EPS went down 50 percent, which would be a red flag for investors. But if the company buys back 500,000 shares outstanding, their EPS would now be calculated as:

$$\text{EPS} \quad = \quad \frac{\$5{,}000{,}000 \text{ (profit)}}{500{,}000 \text{ (shares outstanding)}} \quad = \quad 10$$

Meaning, the company would be back to its steady 10 EPS, which looks like business as usual to the outside world, but profit has actually dropped. Make no mistake: technical analysis at any given point in time is still useful in understanding the value of a stock, and it is an important dialect in the language of investing. But those who are fluent in it have practiced and built up that fluency over time by revisiting the individual metrics habitually. The more you learn about investment analysis (or anything, for that matter), the more you realize there's so much more to know, Socrates. But, as the science of habit teaches us, the most surefire way to stick to something is to get a reward from it. In this case, the reward is money . . . so it's easy to see how you can get hooked.

POP QUIZ

Let's take what we've learned so far and apply it to a real-life example with actual data from a real company. But this time, I'm going to keep the ticker a secret for dramatic effect.

NAME (SYMBOL)	????
Price	347.51
Open	354.83
High	380.00
Low	249.00
Vol	2.201M
52W H	380.00
52W L	2.57
Beta	−2.08
Div.	—
Div.	2
Dividend Yield	—
EPS	−1.78
PE	−199.34
Mkt Cap	24.24B

Well, what do you think? If are you thinking *danger, danger, red alert*? You're correctamundo. This is what GameStop (GME) stock looked like about eight months after the GameStop hullabaloo went down (or, rather, up).

What tipped you off to this being a risky stock? If you were looking only at the stock price, you'd maybe think to yourself: *Huh, that's a pricey stock . . . it must be valuable*. But nope! There are three red flags I hope you picked up on:

---

* That was a crazy day! Trading was halted several times and there's a lot of debate about what actually happened so historical stock data is in short supply. This chart goes off several screenshots.

The EPS is negative. Some finance folks will call this "negative earnings," but let's just say it how it is, guys: it's a loss. A negative EPS means that the company is losing money.

Beta is -2.08. That means that the GameStop stock has an inverse relationship with the market, which isn't always bad if you're looking to add a hedge into your portfolio. What is no bueno is the 2.08 of it all—that means this is *double* the volatility of the stock market. It's giving big chaotic energy. If you don't have a high risk tolerance, this number probably made you nervous.

It's trading below the day's high and the 52-week high, which are both the same.

Cutting Losses Isn't Losing

Even if you pore over balance sheets and crunch the technical analysis numbers, there will be times when the value of your investments goes down. Mine certainly have. And yes, it is a bummer. Everyone loses money in the stock market. I can't promise you much when it comes to investing, but I can promise you that. So it's not losing money that differentiates great and new investors; it's how you handle your losses.

If the stock market is down, novice investors will be incredibly quick to cash out their investments out of fear that the market will continue to crash. But here's the thing: since its inception, the stock market has never not recovered from every dip and blip in its history. In our lifetime, there will be many more dips and blips, and maybe even recessions and depressions. But I expect us to recover from them all. I don't know how long those recoveries might take—but we will recover if you zoom out on history, nonetheless.

When people are surprised that the market is down, I am, well, surprised. The market is a roller coaster; that is what you're signing up for when you invest. Maybe more financial experts should spend time spelling that out explicitly. Maybe the stock market should come with a warning label. Until that day, here's a pill you're going to have to swallow: chill. Don't try and jump off the ride in the middle. Roller coasters can be scary, invigorating, topsy-turvy, just like the market. In the thick of the 2008 financial crisis, the Dow fell from a pre-recession high of $14,000 to around $6,500—that's a 50 percent drop. But at the time I'm writing this, the Dow is at $39,754, more than double what it was in pre-2008 recession times. My point is: the market fluctuates. Don't watch it too obsessively or you'll get nauseated. Just like any major decisions, do not make any investment decisions when you're panicked (or inebriated). Believe it or not, the most seasoned investors do not liquidate their investments when the market is down. Instead, they often buy more. Pro investors "buy on dips" because, from their perspective, fundamentally sound companies are on sale. If you're looking to find a time to really "buy low," a recession is actually the best time.

But you also need to know when to cut your losses; and sometimes that will mean selling a stock for less than you bought it for. I know I told you not to get too emotional and that time in the markets beats timing the markets. That's true. But holding on to a stock is only the right move if you are sure that you've made a good investment.

Here's the key: the *market* plummeting means something entirely different from an *individual stock* price plummeting. As I just said, the *market* is very good at rebounding; but the stock value of a failing company won't rebound; it will just . . . fail. Don't be that person who follows the individual stock all the way down to the bottom.

If the market crashes, it could be due to a multitude of reasons—a war, an election, a pandemic, something that makes investors feel that the future is uncertain. A market dip doesn't necessarily mean that the stock market is broken but more likely indicates a rough financial time across the board. A dip in a specific stock price, on the other hand, could be due to fundamental problems with the company you invested in. There are bad times and bad investments. Please don't confuse the two.

When exactly you cut your loss is up to you and your risk tolerance. Just don't fall for the break-even fallacy. This is a common mistake new investors make: if they've invested in a company and that stock price has dropped, they will assume the price will recover a bit (which, to be fair, does happen). So they say they'll wait until the stock gets back to the price they bought it for, and *then* they'll sell their shares.

The problem with this mindset is that people don't do the math correctly when thinking this over. They think: *My stock has gone down 30 percent—ugh. So it needs to rebound 30 percent in order for me to break even . . . not great, but stranger things have happened?* Wrong-o. The stock price will need to rise more than 30 percent to break even. I know it doesn't immediately make intuitive sense, but let's double-click on an example.

For easy math, let's say you invested $100 in a stock that went down 30 percent to a stock price of $70. Now say the value *did* rebound 30 percent. When you do the math, you'll find that a 30 percent growth of $70 is $91 . . . and $91 is not your original investment of $100. Nope, it's just a little short. If you lost 30 percent of an investment, the stock price would actually need to rise *43 percent* before you broke even.

Think of it this way: falling down takes a whole lot less effort than climbing up, and the same is true for stock prices. The farther the price of a stock falls, the harder it's going to have to work to climb back up to the point where it fell. Let's look at an example with a bigger drop: If a stock falls 50 percent, how much does the price have to rise from that point before you break even? One hundred percent! If you lose 50 percent on the value of a stock, the stock price is going to need to double in order for you to break even.

To help visualize this, here's a little look into the future of what happens when a stock drops after Year 1. In the table on the following page, I'm comparing five scenarios. In bold, I show the year that these stocks "break even" with your original $100 investment:

As you can see, the more you lose in an initial dip, the longer it takes to break even. In the example of the 50 percent loss, it takes *ten years* to get back your initial investment. That's why I suggest that any student in *The Money School* at least considers selling an investment if the price is dropping faster than the overall market, without reason to believe that it will reverse its fortunes anytime soon.

Because deep down I'm a hopeful romantic and an optimist of financial markets, the way I motivate myself to see a dud is to remind myself that there is an opportunity cost for holding on to this loser. This happened to me recently when I was thinking about selling some REITs (which are real estate investments that we will talk about in the last course). I bought them when I was having remorse that I wasn't flexing the same real estate portfolio that

AFTER $100 INVESTMENT...	STARTING POINT	YEAR 1	YEAR 2	YEAR 3	YEAR 5	YEAR 10
10% Loss	$90	$97.20	**$104.98**	113.37	132.24	194.30
20% Loss	$80	86.40	93.31	**$100.78**	117.55	$172.71
30% Loss	$70	$75.60	81.65	88.18	**$102.85**	$151.12
50% Loss	$50	$54	58.32	62.99	73.47	**$107.95**
8% Gain	$108	$116.84	125.97	136.05	158.69	$233.16

some of my peers were. Long story less long, they were commercial projects that all went in the pooper. I held on to them for too long (just like we do with some relationships) hoping they would turn around. But then, finally, one day I was like, "Screw this! I could have these thousands of dollars growing in Nvidia instead." Sometimes seeing what you're missing is what really motivates you to finally leave a toxic relationship—in investing or otherwise.

FYI   BULLS, BEARS, AND BUBBLES, OH MY!

Bull and *bear markets* are terms used to describe how the stock market or a particular stock is trending overall. If the stock market is in a period of decline, it's considered a bear market. On the flip side, when the market is trending upward, it's considered to be a bull market. An easy way to remember it is that bulls charge forward and bears go down to hibernate.

When a specific market has been in full bull mode for a while, people begin to worry it's a bubble. In finance, a "bubble" is a scenario in which a particular investment is overvalued; meaning the stock price does not reflect the fundamentals of the company—the balance sheet, P&L, and 10-K. And, like any bubble, financial ones pop.

Stock picking has long been the focus of investing classes. Sometimes it's even synonymous with the term *investing* itself. Don't get me wrong, a working understanding of the stock market is an incredibly valuable tool for anyone looking to gain some financial know-how, and that's why we hit that first. But putting your money into individual stocks is actually not the only—or even best—way to invest. Even the most famous, badass investor types won't pick the right individual stocks 100 percent of the time. And I sure as heck know I won't, which is why I typically do not focus the bulk of my investment strategy around specific companies to invest in but rather funds that include a smattering of different securities (more on that soon).

I think a healthy approach to investing is what I call "the chocolate chip cookie" method. Seriously. Everyone knows that chocolate chips (tantalizing individual stocks) go into the mix, but they're not the *only* ingredient. If you just stick chocolate chips into the oven and expect that you're going to have chocolate chip cookies in ten minutes, well, you're in for a real surprise (and probably an unhappy smoke alarm). It's the same with your investing mix. The recipe for a satisfying (and dare I say delicious) portfolio needs more than stocks. It needs a variety of securities, just like a chocolate chip cookie recipe needs more than chocolate. But I do love an upside-down dinner, so we just got the sweets in first.

The Fixed-Income Market

FIXED INCOME 101
When Debt Is a Good Thing

Most of us (me included) have a lot of financial trauma around the word *debt*. Debt is such a stressful word that we don't think there's any way it can be a good thing, let alone profitable. An important thing to remember is that when you're *investing* in debt, you're not getting into debt. That's because you're not the one borrowing money; you're the one *lending* to someone borrowing money.

On Wall Street, debt is known as "paper." (Unlike in rap songs, where "paper" means money.) To someone in the investing world, all those song lyrics about "getting paper" means getting into debt. But owning "paper" means owning *someone else's* debt, which—abracadabra!—turns it into an asset for you.

Throughout this course on fixed income, I'll help you transform your narrative around debt from one of fear and stress to seeing it as a strategic investment tool and an avenue for growth. I'll walk you through the two main ways to buy this type of asset. The first way is through your bank with debt vehicles like CDs, which I will cover in this lesson. Yes, you can turn the tables and profit from lending your bank money rather than the traditional other way around. And the second way to invest in debt markets is with bonds—the government variety, as we will talk about in 201, and the corporate kind, which we will talk about in 301.

BUYING CDS

Certificates of deposit, commonly known as CDs (I'll spare you the compact disc joke), are basic types of fixed-income investments offered by banks and credit unions. When you purchase a CD, you agree to leave a lump sum deposit untouched for a predetermined period, which can range from a few months to several years. In exchange for this commitment, the bank pays you interest at a specified rate, which is usually higher than that of regular savings accounts.

CDs are considered a pretty vanilla investment because once purchased they offer a *guaranteed* return with a fixed interest rate, no matter what the market is doing. This makes them the perfect match for investors looking to tuck some money away in a safe spot while still earning income from the interest on it. CDs also are insured by the FDIC (Federal Deposit Insurance Corporation).

POP QUIZ

How much of your money can you protect with FDIC insurance?

If you said up to $250,000, you're correct. The FDIC protects deposits up to $250,000 *per* depositor, *per* FDIC-insured bank, for *each* account ownership category. CDs are classified with other single accounts like checking accounts and savings accounts. So, if you have a checking account and a savings account, you're covered for $250,000 on the total of both accounts combined. But if you have a personal savings account and checking account with your spouse, you're covered for $250,000 on each account. FDIC insurance only covers losses in the event of a bank failure. It does not cover losses due to theft or fraud.

In years past, mentioning FDIC insurance would be a throwaway point because banks "didn't fail." But then, they did. As a result of the 2008 financial crisis, banks that no one ever thought could possibly fail did, including

Lehman Brothers, Bear Stearns, and Washington Mutual, while other heavy hitters were sold off in a fire sale to save themselves, including Wachovia and Merrill Lynch, while a slew of others like Citigroup got huge government bailouts. Cut to fifteen years later when another bank collapse came seemingly out of nowhere after Silicon Valley Bank, Signature Bank, and First Republic Bank all went under. So now, FDIC insurance is far from an afterthought. It's something very real to consider in a world where no bank is too big or mighty to fail.

HOW BANKS USE YOUR MONEY

I know you might think when you put your money in a bank, it's sitting there behind a cinematic bronze vault in perfect little bundles right there next to shiny gold bars. Hate to break it to you but it's not. It's being put to work making more money for the bank. Don't panic! Your bank does keep a fraction of your money on hand for when you need it, under a system known as fractional reserve banking. But banks are trying to live up to their names and make bank here, which means putting your money to work. They lend out your money and invest it in bonds and the stock market to try and get a big fat return from it.

Ever notice how banks charge you more to borrow money from them (like with a mortgage) than they do to lend to them (like with CDs)? This difference in interest rates is known as the bank's "spread" and is a bank's bread and butter. By leveraging your money in this way, banks can use your money to make money while also funding everyone's loans.

STEP INTO ONE YOURSELF

When you're picking a CD, it's important to make sure you and your CD are aligned so that it can meet your needs and help you achieve your goals. You're looking to be compatible on term length, interest rate, and minimum deposit requirement. This is a commitment. If you may need your money in a year, and you're looking at a two-year CD with a penalty for early withdrawal, that's not the CD for you. There's a better fit out there—maybe it's a shorter CD or one that allows you to take your money out early.

To find your match, start by checking with different banks and credit unions to see who's offering the best rates. Don't worry about banking monogamy here: if a bank other than your current one has the best rates, it's okay to have your CD in one place and your checking account somewhere else. Depending on your net worth, it may even be a good idea in order to ensure you'll be fully protected by FDIC insurance. Sites like Bankrate, NerdWallet, and The Motley Fool can help you compare and contrast the latest rates while also showing you any promotional offers. But they won't show your local matches. The credit union down the street may beat all the big names, so don't forget to search community branches. Big banks have shareholders and profits to worry about because they are run as a business (often publicly traded). Credit unions are essentially owned by the clients and don't have to worry about profit margins, just paying their employees and operating costs. They can pass on that savings to you. Here's an example of what you could have been offered at the end of 2022:*

BANK NAME	6-MONTH CD RATE (%)	1-YEAR CD RATE (%)	2-YEAR CD RATE (%)	5-YEAR CD RATE (%)
Bank A	1.50	2.00	2.50	3.00
Bank B	1.60	2.10	2.60	3.10
Bank C	1.40	1.90	2.40	2.90
Online Bank D	1.70	2.30	2.80	3.30
Credit Union E	1.65	2.25	2.75	3.25

The CD rates offered by different banks and credit unions are shown as annual percentages. You can use a CD interest calculator online to see the

---

* CD rates dramatically increased during 2022 after a rough pandemic, but in January 2023 they inverted, leaving early 2022 the last year we have normalish data for. Since 1980, this has only happened one other time, and that was for four months. This offers some unusually juicy returns on short-term CDs right now, so check those out at whatever time you're reading this.

gold you'll get at the other side of this fixed-income rainbow. This is an easy way to compare CDs and see if you are getting the best deal.

What determines the returns on CDs? Again, it's a combination of macro and micro factors. The macro influences are all the big-picture stuff, like the central bank's monetary policy and the current interest rate environment. This means that if interest rates are high, then mortgage rates and CDs would be too; if they are low, both debt instruments and others would be low too. On the micro side, it comes down to the local scene, such as just how much a bank can afford to pay you. Low overhead is why online banks and credit unions will often be your CD soulmate even if you bank somewhere else.

Next, consider your cash flow needs and when you'll need access to your money. CD terms can range from a few months to several years. Longer terms generally offer higher interest rates but require you to lock in your money for longer. There have been times, particularly post-COVID, where the CD yields for short-term CDs have been higher than those of long-term CDs. Remember how I said that the central bank's monetary policy influences CD rates? This is how that plays out. As I'm writing this, short-term CDs are offering a rate that reflects the interest rate set by the Fed. But everyone expects the Fed to lower rates, and so banks don't want to be locked into higher rates on their long-term CDs. So they've kept long-term rates lower than short-term rates in anticipation of the Fed lowering the interest rate. This is a very unusual situation and one that will likely change in the future, so it's always good to consistently reevaluate the timeline of your financial goals and which CD terms are offering the best rates.

Finally, review all the terms of the CD, including the interest rate, term length, withdrawal penalties, and renewal policies. Once you've purchased your CD, you'll receive confirmation and documentation. Keep these records in a safe place for future reference. Also keep an eye on your CD's maturity date (calendar reminder!). As it approaches, you should decide whether you want to withdraw your funds or roll them over into a new CD. Some institutions automatically renew CDs at maturity, so know their policy and notify them if you have different plans.

The Inflation Risk

One of the only risks associated with CDs is inflation. Longer-term CDs traditionally offer better rates, but if inflation spikes they could become a liability. If the rate of inflation is higher than the interest rate you're earning on your CD, then the real value—or the purchasing power—of your money decreases. This means that when the CD matures, although you'll receive your principal plus the promised interest, the total amount you can buy with that money will be less than it would have been when you first made the investment.*

Let's say you invest in a CD with an interest rate of 2 percent per year. If inflation is running at 3 percent per year, your investment is actually losing value in terms of real purchasing power. After one year, your investment

---

* There are CDs that have built-in inflation protection. We'll talk about those in a bit.

has grown in nominal terms, but when you adjust for inflation, it has less buying power than when you started. This is a particular concern in periods of economic uncertainty or when inflation rates are volatile and trending upward. The early 1980s CDs had interest rates as big as the hair that was in style. We're talking as high as 17 percent returns here. This looks amazing until you factor in that for the same year the inflation rate was 14.5 percent. All of a sudden those returns don't look nearly as impressive once inflation takes a bite out of your profits.

WTF is inflation anyway? I'm so glad you asked. Inflation is basically the increase in prices over time for the things we buy, from lattes to laptops. It's why movie tickets were five bucks when I was growing up and they are twenty bucks* now. It's essentially the world slowly turning up the cost-of-living dial. Conversely, deflation is what happens when stuff costs less than it used to. Yes, that can happen; it did during the Great Depression and even a little in the Great Recession.

And *why* does inflation happen? Well, it actually comes in three flavors:

- *Demand-pull inflation:* This occurs when demand for products is higher than the supply, causing prices to rise. Think of the latest smartphone launch—everyone wants one, but there aren't enough to go around, so the price goes up.

- *Cost-push inflation:* When the costs of production increase (like wages or materials), companies often pass these costs onto consumers. Think of a hurricane disrupting oil supply, making gas—and, in turn, stuff transported by trucks—more expensive. Or if that hurricane messed up massive amounts of orange groves, that would increase the price of OJ at the market or at a restaurant for you because those stores need to pass the higher cost onto us.

- *Built-in inflation:* Sometimes this is called the wage-price spiral. This is a bit of a self-fulfilling prophecy. If workers expect prices to rise, they demand higher wages. Businesses then increase prices to pay these wages, leading to more inflation.

---

* $19.75 to be exact.

Now, inflation isn't always bad. A little bit of inflation is normal and even good for a healthy economy. It encourages people to buy now rather than later, which keeps businesses bustling and the economy moving. But too much inflation? That's like the latte suddenly costing ten dollars—it starts to hurt our wallets and can slow down economic growth. In that case, it would likely be time to step away from CDs.

How do we know if the inflation monster is coming? The Consumer Price Index, or CPI (one of the key economic reports I told you to keep an eye out for in the last course). CPI looks at a smorgasbord of different staple goods (think transportation, food, medical care) and tracks their prices over time to determine the rate of inflation. Inflation and interest rates tend to move together. When we are in inflationary times, interest rates usually go up. In times of crisis or stagnation, the Fed will lower rates in an effort to stimulate or stabilize the economy; prices also fall during those rare deflationary periods. You can peep the CPI and PPI (Producer Price Index) on the Bureau of Labor Statistics website if you want it raw; otherwise, major financial news outlets will report on the gist.

Climb the CD Ladder

If you're looking to escape inflation, one of the easiest ways is to climb above it all by creating a CD ladder. To build this ladder, you invest in CDs with different maturity dates. As each CD matures, you can reinvest in a new CD at the current interest rate, which may be higher if inflation has risen. This ladder gives you a hedge against inflation, since if inflation rises, your interest rate will as well.

But that's not the only reason to climb a CD ladder. Because you regularly have CDs coming to maturity, you can get the benefits of investing in debt without all your money being locked up or taking the financial hit of cashing out early. This strategy can be a great way to earn a little extra income on money you know you will need access to soon and don't intend to take on too much risk, like a down payment on your first house.

Here is an example of a CD ladder using interest rates from 2022. It assumes you have $10,000 to invest, which will be evenly distributed across five different CDs, each with a different term length and corresponding interest rate. Here's how the first cycle of investing would look:

One-year CD at 2.5 percent:
- Amount invested: $2,000
- Maturity value: $2,050

Two-year CD at 2.75 percent:
- Amount invested: $2,000
- Maturity value: $2,111

Three-year CD at 3.0 percent:
- Amount invested: $2,000
- Maturity value: $2,185

Four-year CD at 3.25 percent:
- Amount invested: $2,000
- Maturity value: $2,272

Five-year CD at 3.5 percent:
- Amount invested: $2,000
- Maturity value: $2,375

In a CD ladder, each CD matures at a different time, providing you with cash at regular intervals, which gets reinvested in CDs of a different length to repeat the cycle. The idea is that you will always have access to cash. For instance, once the one-year CD matures, you can reinvest the proceeds into a new five-year CD, maintaining the ladder, and when the five-year CD matures, you can reinvest it in a one-year CD. Let's look at the numbers for that second round of investments.

New five-year CD at 3.5 percent:
- Amount invested: $2,050 (the amount earned from the first-year CD at maturity)
- New Maturity value: $2,434

Four-year CD at 3.25 percent:
- Amount invested: $2,111
- Maturity value: $2,399

Three-year CD at 3 percent:
- Amount invested: $2,185
- Maturity value: $2,387

Two-year CD at 2.75 percent:
- Amount invested: $2,272
- Maturity value: $2,398

One-year CD at 2.5 percent:
- Amounted invested: $2,375
- Maturity value: $2,434

After ten years, your $10,000 has a guaranteed return of $2,079, all while delivering you an annual payday if you need some cash on hand. If that sounds like something you might want to try, banks make it easy-peasy to do because CDs are a good deal for them too. But here's a quick step-by-step guide:

1. *Determine your investment amount:* Decide the total amount you're willing to invest in CDs. This total will be split across several CDs with varying terms.

2. *Decide on the ladder structure:* Choose how many "rungs" your ladder will have. Each rung represents a CD with a different maturity term. Common structures include ladders with terms like one, two, three, four, and five years.

3. *Divide your investment:* Split your total investment evenly across the chosen number of CDs. For example, if you have $10,000 and want a five-rung ladder, you'd allocate $2,000 to each CD.

4. *Shop for rates and buy:* Use the same strategies we talked about earlier to find the best interest rates for each term length. Open each CD with the respective term and amount and set maturity instructions. Decide what happens when each CD matures. You can choose to have the funds automatically reinvested in a new CD with a similar term, which is usually the default, or you might

want to change the duration or transfer the money to a different account or even bank.

5. *Monitor and maintain your ladder:* Keep track of maturity dates and interest rates. As each CD matures, and you decide you want to keep the ladder going strong, just reinvest the recently matured money into the new longest term of your ladder (e.g., a new five-year CD) to maintain the structure. Periodically review your CD ladder in light of changing interest rates, your financial goals, and liquidity needs. Adjust your strategy as necessary.

Remember, the key to a successful CD ladder is diversification (our fav) across different maturity dates, which allows you to benefit from higher interest rates of longer-term CDs while still having periodic access to part of your investment. This strategy also helps mitigate the risk of reinvesting all your money at a time when interest rates might be low.

FANCY CDS

To recap: we started out with traditional, straightforward CDs, which we expanded into the CD ladder. But there's more! There are "fancy" types of CDs that offer upgrades from the basic CD, complete with special features and unique benefits that can be appealing to new investors looking to diversify their strategies and potentially enhance returns. While traditional CDs are akin to a classic, reliable sedan, these advanced versions are more like sophisticated sports cars—offering a range of options and experiences, each tailored to different investment needs and appetites for speed (investment risk).

BROKERED CDS

I know I said this lesson would all be about the kinds of fixed income you can buy at a bank, but brokered CDs, as the name implies, are typically purchased through a brokerage firm, not directly from a bank. They are called CDs, so I left them here, but unlike traditional bank CDs, where you go to a bank and open a CD account, brokered CDs are bought and sold much like stocks or bonds through a brokerage account.

Brokered CDs are part of a larger pool of CDs from various banks, brought together under the umbrella of a brokerage. Most major brokerage firms have a range of brokered CDs from different banks, offering you a bunch of rates and terms to choose from. This variety is a key difference from regular CDs. While your local bank only offers their CDs, a brokerage can provide access to a diverse array of CDs from banks across the country, sometimes even globally.*

One of my friends recently sold her fashion company for a nice, juicy exit. She was looking to invest some of her newfound earnings but was terrified about picking wrong and losing her money. After I spent weeks giving her all the arguments I've been giving you, she begrudgingly agreed to invest $25,000 in a CD. Off she went to her Merrill Lynch account and looked up CDs. Buying one made her so nervous she actually held her breath when hitting the BUY button. When she called me up to share the good news, I explained to her that she didn't actually buy a CD like we talked about through her Bank of America account. She freaked! Then launched into a diatribe about how she knew she should just leave it all in her BofA checking account. She claimed she wasn't fit to be an investor and didn't want to lose any of her hard-earned money. (Money that she earned as a founder/CEO of a huge company, mind you. Money trauma is for real.) I told her, "No, no, no, you're totally fine, it's basically the same thing. Just a little, well, fancier variety." She exhaled and said, "Okay, phew, well, that's definitely my style."

I will say that while you can't buy brokered CDs directly from a bank, the CDs themselves are still bank products. Just like the traditional ones, most brokered CDs are FDIC-insured up to the legal limit, so your principal is generally safe. The brokerage acts as an intermediary, giving you access to CDs from various banks. Because they come from a reseller, they have slightly different perks and risks compared to traditional bank CDs. For instance, they may offer the flexibility to sell on the secondary market before maturity.

---

* It's absolutely crucial to research the creditworthiness of issuing banks because at the end of the day paper issued by a bank is only as good as the bank itself.

Don't get me wrong, being able to sell early is a huge perk with this type of CD. But it's not all rainbows and butterflies. The secondary market for brokered CDs can be fickle. There's no guarantee you'll find a buyer if you need to sell before the CD matures, meaning it may be tricky to get your cash out early. Or you may be able to sell it but for less than your original investment, which is not the outcome anyone wants.

So these fancy CDs have all the interest rate risk of traditional CDs but with added complexity. For traditional CDs, interest rate risk primarily involves the opportunity cost. If you lock in a CD at a certain rate and interest rates rise afterward, you miss out on potentially higher rates. But your investment is secure until the CD matures, and you will receive the agreed-upon interest rate regardless of changes in the market. This is true of brokered CDs as well, but there's an added dimension of possibly selling the CD on the secondary market before maturity. The value of a brokered CD on the secondary market is influenced by current interest rates too. If you bought a CD paying 3 percent interest and rates rise so that current CDs are paying 5 percent interest, then your 3 percent CD is as unwanted as an actual CD of internet novelty songs. So if you need to access funds before the CD matures, but new CDs on the market are earning higher rates, this would most certainly mean you'd sell your less desirable CD at a loss. When it comes to brokered CDs, be sure to read the fine print because they often come with more intricate terms and conditions than what you'd find at a standard bank. Some brokered CDs may be callable. But we'll talk about these in more detail in a bit.

JUMBO CDS

These are similar to traditional CDs but require a larger minimum deposit, often $100,000 or more. Jumbo CDs typically offer higher interest rates than standard CDs because of the larger investment. You can't necessarily cold-call your bank and ask for these. As you can imagine, CDs with this high of a minimum deposit are more of a boutique offering. While they are usually offered by large and online banks, some small or regional banks specifically cater to the type of client that is looking to sock away $100K in a nice, safe CD. At the time of writing, the difference in rate of return on jumbo CDs versus regular CDs is fairly small, and so in some cases you would be better off with a traditional CD. Even in a less favorable market, however, these can have a role in financial planning if you have a very large sum of money you want to protect while earning a modest return. Remember, FDIC insurance only covers you for up to $250,000. So if you have $100,000 you are planning to use for a down payment on a house in five years, a jumbo CD at a bank different from the one where you have your checking and savings accounts could be a great way to keep your money safe, insured, and invested without having to think about it too hard.

- Traditional CDs: Suppose a traditional CD offers an interest rate of 2.5 percent APY (annual percentage yield) for a twelve-month term.

- Jumbo CDs: A jumbo CD for the same term might offer an interest rate of 3 percent APY or higher.*

The difference in rates can be more pronounced when interest rates are high and banks are actively seeking to increase their deposits. Banks make a lot of their money from the interest on loans and mortgages. So when interest rates are high, banks want to loan out as much money as possible. To do that they need more money in the bank, literally. By attracting larger deposits through jumbo CDs, banks can increase their capital reserves, having more funds to lend (and profit from).

BUMP-UP CDS

Bump-up CDs offer a unique blend of security and flexibility in the world of fixed-term investing. Unlike traditional CDs, where the interest rate is locked in for the entire term, bump-up CDs allow you the option to increase your rate of return if the bank's rates for new CDs go up. This comes in handy when interest rates are on the rise and makes this the perfect CD for investors with a case of FOMO. Bump-up CDs offer that "have your cake and eat

---

* These examples reflect general 2022 rates. The difference might be smaller, especially in low-interest-rate environments or when the demand for deposits is low.

it too" feeling. They're a hedge against rising rates, while maintaining the core benefits of a CD.

Sounds too good to be true? It's not, but there is a catch. These CDs often start with a lower interest rate compared to their traditional counterparts, balancing out the flexibility they provide. Generally, the opportunity to bump up the rate isn't unlimited. Most only allow you to trade up once or twice during the CD's term. As with any investment, be sure to read that fine print and know the rules of the bump.

STEP-UP CDS

Bump-up CDs aren't the only fixed investment choice for the commitment phobic. Let me introduce you to step-up CDs. With these, the interest rate increases at predetermined intervals throughout the term of the CD. This makes it the perfect CD for when you want to invest in CDs but you're sure that interest rates will rise before your CD matures.

If you lock in a step-up CD, over its term, the interest rate automatically climbs at specific points, like climbing a staircase. Each step represents a higher interest rate, giving you the potential for greater returns as time goes on. It's a bit like a long-term bet on rising rates. The initial interest rate on a step-up CD might be lower than a traditional CD's rate, but as the steps kick in, you could end up with a better overall return.

LIQUID CDS

What if your fear of commitment isn't about rising interest rates? What if it's locking up all your money that gives you cold feet? Then allow me to introduce you to a super flexible CD, one that flows (sorry, had to) to fit just that situation. A liquid CD sets itself apart from standard CDs by allowing you to withdraw some or all of your money before the maturity date without facing any penalties. Obviously this isn't a free-for-all, and there will be rules about how much and how often you can withdraw funds

If you're squirreling away part of your future baby fund or other cash you may need sooner than expected in CDs, this can be a great choice to give yourself a little more flexibility. But the trade-off for this convenience is typically a lower interest rate compared to traditional CDs; with liquid CDs you're paying (with potential future earnings) for easier access to your money. Like several of the more unusual CDs discussed here, these can require a little shopping around to find. Just a heads-up, depending on the bank, the money may not be immediately available for withdrawal. So liquid CDs are for money that you may need earlier than expected but with some notice—not for your emergency fund.

CALLABLE CDS

We've talked about the commitment-phobic investor, but what if you like a little more risk in your investments? If you're an adrenaline junkie looking to maximize your return and don't mind a little more risk, then the callable CD may be your perfect match. This is a CD that offers a top-tier interest rate, but that comes with a price. The bank can say "mine now, give it back" at any point and call the CD back from you before it fully matures. You get all your money back plus whatever interest you've made so far, but you miss out on any potential future returns. This feature typically comes into play when interest rates fall significantly after the CD is issued. Lower interest rates mean that the bank can—and probably will—refinance its debt at a better rate.

Banks love these CDs, especially when they think the interest rate is going to fall because this gives them an escape hatch to a lower rate. It's important to note that not all banks offer callable CDs, and the terms can vary significantly between those that do. If you're considering one, make sure you understand the specific call terms, including how soon the CD can be called after being issued.

ADD-ON CD

Okay, so now we've talked about commitment phobia on your end and on the bank's end. But what if you're a CD stan? You just can't get enough of them, and you want to take your relationship to the next level. But maybe right now isn't a good time for you to tie up a big chunk of your money. In that situation, what can you do? This is where an add-on CD can come in handy. There are some limits here, and it varies from institution to institution and even CD to CD, but generally with add-on CDs, the interest rate is fixed, and you will be able to add funds on the account up to a limit or a set number of times over the life of the CD. So, say you have $100 now to invest, and you know you're going to be getting $1,200 back from your tax refund in a few weeks—but you really want to lock in an awesome rate on a CD. In that scenario, you could try to snag a CD with the $100 you have now and add on the $1,200 later. "What are the drawbacks?" you might ask. Good question and I'm glad you've picked up on the basic fact that all investments have downsides. The drawback is that add-on CDs offer interest rates that are often lower than those of traditional CDs. Give and take. Rinse and repeat.

FYI BANKS GET CREDIT RATINGS TOO

Just like credit ratings for individuals, credit ratings for banks assess their financial health and creditworthiness. Before giving any bank a loan, peep their credit rating. It's like *their* financial report card and can help you understand the risk involved in investing in or doing business with a bank. Rating agencies such as Standard & Poor's (S&P), Moody's, and Fitch Ratings provide credit ratings for banks.

In a world with high interest rates, CDs aren't the only way to earn a good rate of return on your money in the bank. High-yield savings accounts can also offer alluring interest rates while keeping the perk of easy access to your money. They can be a great choice for your emergency fund. But after that's covered, I do like how the inaccessibility of CDs can help keep you invested by simply removing the temptation to withdraw money early.

Remember: there's just one letter but a world of difference between owing debt and owning debt. Owing debt brings up all sorts of connotations. But hopefully after you finish this course, you'll have new associations with being on the other side of debt.

And owning debt from the bank? You guessed it. Makes *you* the bank.

The Fixed-Income Market

FIXED INCOME 201
Government Bonds

When someone says, "My word is my bond," they mean that what they're promising you, you can depend on. It's the idea that someone's spoken vow becomes their sacred commitment. In the 1500s, this concept allowed merchant traders to make legally binding verbal contracts. In 1923, the London Stock Exchange made its motto *Dictum Meum Pactum* (My word is my bond). And, of course, that line was famously used by Michelle Obama during the 2008 Democratic National Convention. This concept also plays into the meaning of *bond* in our modern-day financial world.

Let's say you buy a bond from me; I'm giving you my word that I'll give you your money back with a certain interest* rate after a certain period. For certain. A bond is essentially a glorified IOU. When you buy a bond, you are promised the return of your initial investment, plus a rate of return (the bonus money from the interest rate).

There are three general types of bonds that we'll cover in the rest of this course: (1) government bonds (federal government bonds are called US

---

* A note about taxes. Interest earned is taxed as income. So it will be taxed at whatever the top end of your tax bracket is. It can even bump you up to the next level and be taxed at a higher rate than your income.

Treasuries and local ones are called municipal bonds), which we will cover in this lesson, (2) corporate bonds, and (3) international bonds, both of which we will cover in Fixed Income 301.

GOVERNMENT BONDS

If you buy a government bond, you're basically letting the government use your money—say, to finance a road—and, in exchange, as is the case with all bonds, you will get your money back with a little something extra. The history of bonds in the US goes back to day one. Literally. Even before the founding of the Department of the Treasury, the Founders were using bonds as part of their efforts to raise money for the Revolutionary War. In "thank you, Professor Obvious" news, war is extremely expensive, and so using bonds in wartime is an economic through line across global history. For example, bonds were vital during the First and Second World Wars. During World War I, the US government ran a major advertising blitz to encourage Americans to purchase Liberty Bonds. The Liberty Bond program was a smash hit. The media campaign was run by volunteers who really felt like it was their patriotic duty in the least corny way possible. Owning Liberty Bonds got you more than just sweet investment income; it also got you lots of freebies like pins and signs you could put in your window. It was more than an investment; it was a mission statement and a way to show that you were a patriot who supported the war effort.

Almost everybody participated. During the first public offering, one in every six households had a family member that bought Liberty Bonds. About half of the war bonds sold during that initial offering were in the smallest amount available, fifty dollars, which would have been equal to two weeks' wages for someone working in manufacturing. By the end of the war, the sale of bonds had raised $17 billion and twenty million people had purchased them. To make that number even more eye popping, there were twenty-four million households at that time. That would be approximately $342 billion today. The final tally ended up being very impressive: of the total amount of money raised for the war, two-thirds came from the sale of war bonds.

Because of the Liberty Bond's success, the government sought to finance World War II the same way. This campaign had all the glitz of a Super

Bowl commercial combined with a viral influencer campaign. Big Hollywood celebrities at the time, like Carole Lombard, Red Skelton, and Marlene Dietrich (fun fact: when I was twelve years old and in a school play, I was kinda "discovered" by acclaimed director Louis Malle for the role of Dietrich's daughter in a new film he was doing*), helped encourage Americans to buy war bonds. In one campaign that would never fly today, Hedy Lamarr (an actress who also invented the technology that would be the basis for Wi-Fi . . . for real) offered to kiss anyone who bought more than $25,000 worth of war bonds. The government told her to get out of the lab and into the kissing booth to sell those bonds. Through her efforts, which was diversified beyond kissing strangers, she sold around $25 million worth of war bonds, and that's face value, not adjusted for inflation. Defense bonds, created in April 1941, were popular to begin with, but after the attack on Pearl Harbor, they were relabeled war bonds and interest skyrocketed. War bonds have a uniquely high profile and special place in American history.

Of course, bonds are not exclusively used to fund war efforts; tons of important national projects were made possible through bonds. The Golden Gate Bridge, the Louisiana Purchase, the transcontinental railroad, Route 66, JFK Airport, the Panama Canal, and the purchase of Alaska were all made possible with some fundraising through bonds.

Bonds have been an important way for the American government to finance infrastructure development; but bonds have also provided for the development of some intangible infrastructure as well. Funding projects through government bonds meant that the government did not need to rely on funding from banks or other private institutions. The government has a responsibility to the people first and foremost. But when the government gets too snuggly with big banks, the public (whether it's justified or not) worries that the government will start having to answer to the big banks ahead of the people. Receiving funding from the public, however, is an excellent system to keep the needs of the public aligned with the government's activities. Plus, owning bonds makes Americans financially and spiritually invested in the US. Not to get all in your feels, but there is a special element of pride involved

---

* Malle died before the film could get off the ground but it was set to star Uma Thurman. So here we are talking bonds instead of me being a Bond girl.

when you're driving over the Golden Gate Bridge and can say that you were a part of making it possible.

LET BONDS LEAD THE WAY

The bond market in general is considered a "leading" indicator for the economy, meaning that it's a good predictor of what's going to happen in the future. If the markets are flying high and the economic outlook is bright, people dump their money into stocks. In order to compete, bonds often have to offer a higher rate of interest. But in times of uncertainty, people start looking for a safe place to stash their money. If people are just looking for safety and don't mind a lower rate of return, bonds don't need to pay out as much. Layer into this the fact that in bad economic times the Federal Reserve, the body that sets the interest rates for the entire country, will lower interest rates. That's to incentivize investors to take on riskier investments (and for people to buy cars and homes) and therefore stimulate the economy.

By contrast, "lagging" indicators point to a trend that has already been happening, like unemployment rates, which typically reflect pains in the economy in the preceding months. That's why leading indicators give us the best clue into what's going to happen next. So understanding how bonds work will help you understand—and even predict—major moves in the economy. That's why I hope your eyes don't glaze over when we talk about interest rates or inflation. Paying attention to how those indicators are moving will give you the power to make informed decisions about the timing of your goals. For example, in the low interest rate environment of 2022, you'd likely have gotten a better mortgage but less ideal returns on bonds or savings accounts.

RIDING THE YIELD CURVE

The trick to understanding how bonds function is to use what's known as the "yield curve" to gauge where the market is going. The yield curve is simply a chart with all the different rates of return on all the lengths of maturities on bonds. The rates of bonds change every day, so the shape of the curve changes accordingly.

Example of a Yield Curve

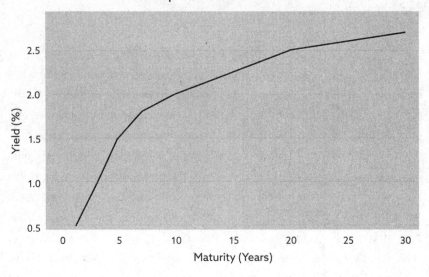

In this example, the maturities of the bonds range from one to thirty years, and their corresponding yields are plotted on the graph. The yield curve can take different shapes, but this one shows a typical upward slope—indicating that longer-term bonds have higher yields compared to shorter-term bonds—which signals a healthier economic future.

Example of an Inverted Bond Yield Curve

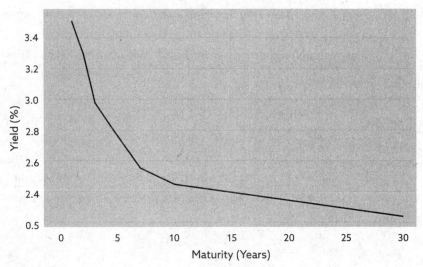

Right before a recession, people are often putting a lot of their money into the stock market but aren't very optimistic about the longer-term future. This means that there is a willingness to invest in longer-term bonds but a reluctance to invest in the short-term ones because of the opportunity cost of not being able to invest in the stock market short term. This creates the economic conditions for an "inverted yield curve."

For decades the yield curve was one of the most reliable indicators of a recession. But the yield curve inverted in 2022 and stayed that way through 2023, all while the market had a good year. While that didn't technically result in a recession in the market, it is worth noting that plenty of people spent 2023 feeling like they were in a recession. So perhaps that's what it predicted.

To grow your wealth for the long term in a healthy, sustainable, and successful way, you need not only think about investing in bonds yourself but also to understand how the bond market functions. Once I did, I felt like a real player in the game. And once you do, I think you will feel like you're playing for keeps too. You have my word. And you know what my word is.

HOW DO BONDS WORK?

We understand how borrowing money works from the other areas of our life, right? When we buy a house, we typically take out an IOU—aka a mortgage—from a bank. If you have a crummy credit score, your lender will view you as risky. In other words, they have reason to doubt that you'll make your payments on time, or at all. If you are seen as a risk, your lender will hit you with a higher interest rate, which gives them a little bonus for taking on the risk. With bonds, however, you are not the "I" that owes but the "U" that is owed. When the roles are reversed and you are a bond buyer, you get the benefits of this system: if there's more risk involved, you—the lender—will earn a higher interest rate. Remember how we talked about the house always winning and that I would teach you to become the house? Being the lender, instead of the borrower, is a great way to become the house.

In many ways, as a bond buyer, you have more of a predictable rate of return than banks do with their credit card or mortgage loans. With a mortgage, you might not necessarily sit down with the bank and say explicitly, "At a 7 percent mortgage, you'll be making $X from me in interest, and get to deposit $Y in total in profit at the end of my mortgage term."* But a key part of the bond-buying process is getting a clear return on investment and the terms. You won't see all of these listed when you're buying a bond, and depending on what kind you are looking at, and what site you're shopping on, you'll see a different combination. But here are the biggies:

PAR VALUE: Also known as "face value," this is the amount the bond is worth when it's issued. Most bonds have a par value of $1,000.

MATURITY VALUE: The amount your bond is worth when it has "matured," as in when all is said and done.

TERM: How long you're going to hold on to this thing.

PRICE: This is how much your bond would be worth on a secondary market at any point in time.

COUPON: The interest rate paid by the bond, which won't change over the course of the bond. To determine what you're taking home, you'll multiply the face value by the coupon.

YIELD: This is a measurement of how much the bond is paying when it takes into consideration the current value of the bond. Bonds trade from investor to investor as well as from issuer to investor. The yield matters when buying or selling the bond before maturity. It tells you how much you'll get based on the market value of the bond and the remaining time.

DISCOUNT RATE: This is exclusively for Treasury bills. Instead of a coupon you'll buy them at a discount rate to the face value and then get the full value when it matures.

---

* You can always pay off your mortgage early and stop accruing interest. As a result, the bank will make less than if you paid off the loan on their terms, rather than *your* terms. This is why I always recommend at least trying to make biweekly payments instead of monthly.

When a bond is issued, it's like an open call asking to borrow money. The bond itself represents a promise that the bond buyer will be paid back, plus interest, by a certain date. Bonds are considered fixed-income investments because you get a fixed rate of return (that is, interest after a fixed period).

I want to say loud and clear: *bonds are really hard to calculate and explain.* The equations and rationales get so wild that my head hurts when I dig super deep into the math. I've tried my best to give you what you really need to know here but also show you some basic equations so you know conceptually what's up. But when you are ready to buy something, please just use a bond calculator.*

POP QUIZ

How much will you get with these two lovely bonds?

Bond A

Face Value	$1,000
Coupon	8%
Term	1 year

If you said $80, you would be right! You multiply the coupon by the face value.

Bond B

Price	$800
Yield	10%
Term	1 year

If you said $80 here as well, you'd be right again. If you don't know the coupon, you can solve for what you'd get as one by multiplying the yield by the price.

Pro-tip: Make sure you understand payment frequency. If the payments are semiannual, then you would divide by two and you'd get forty bucks twice a year.

---

* You can use mine at TheMoneySchool.com "tools" section.

RISKY BUSINESS

Typically, to incentivize investors to take on risk, riskier bonds offer more money back. In contrast, the less risky a bond is, the less you'll earn on your investment. The best way to assess the risk level of the issuers of the bond is by looking at their credit rating. The credit rating agencies I mentioned in the last lesson—Standard & Poor's and Moody's—also score a bond's creditworthiness.

It's like the credit check you get when you apply for a credit card or mortgage but for the government or major corporations and using a different scale. Credit scores for us range from 300 at the lowest to 850 at the highest. For bonds, credit ratings range from D at the lowest (meaning the government or corporation is in default) to AAA at the highest (meaning the country or company is economically rock solid). The lower the rating, the more interest you'll be promised in exchange for your investment. Anything lower than BBB is considered "sub investment grade" or "junk bonds." Sometimes they are referred to as "high-yield bonds," which sounds awesome—but remember the yield (interest) is high because it's super risky.

US TREASURIES

Bonds (more specifically, government bonds) are generally considered one of the safest investments you can make. That doesn't mean there is zero risk, but it's pretty low. Many of the smartest, richest investors out there swear that the safest bonds ever are US Treasury bonds because they are backed by the US government. And while, sure, there's a chance the US government is going to default, there will be way bigger problems than not getting the principal back on one of your bonds if that happens. So, for that reason, investing in Treasuries is a good way to make your overall portfolio more secure.

During times of economic uncertainty, you'll hear business news talking heads going on about a "flight to safety." That basically means a ton of people are flocking to buy bonds because other stuff is too risky. There are different kinds of Treasuries—not all Treasuries are the same, and not all of them are even called bonds. The major types of Treasuries are Treasury bills, Treasury notes, Treasury bonds, and Treasury Inflation-Protected Securities.

When I was first digging into the world of bonds, I remember thinking: *Dear Lord, why are there so many different types of Treasury bonds? Why couldn't the government say, "These are all called Treasury bonds." The end. Is that so hard?* While that would have been nice, the reason there are different names for different Treasury bonds is to denote the length of the bond term. That is helpful to keep straight because the length of term affects the purchase price.

> **MONEY TIP**
>
> **RAISING THE ROOF**
>
> You've probably heard rumblings about the "debt ceiling." This hits the headlines every few years and it's basically a fake fight in Washington about whether or not to pay their bills. It sounds apocalyptic on the news, but it's always (so far) a false alarm. Regardless, short-term bond yields rise on the perceived threat that the government won't pay its bills, so it's a good time to try and act opposite of the hysteria (usually a winning investment strategy) and buy some extra T-bills because the return will have just popped on them.

There are a couple ways to purchase Treasuries. I'm not going to lie; it can be annoying. The most annoying way is through a noncompetitive auction process on TreasuryDirect.gov. By the way, it's called an auction, but the T-bills are pretty much offered at a fixed price, and there are no paddles involved. But it's confusing, and the UX/UI on a government site is . . . lacking.

You can also usually buy them through your brokerage but it's sometimes not mobile friendly. My favorite and I think the easiest way to buy Treasuries is through the trading app Public.* I will say that there's not a lot of variety in duration on the platform, but it's never been easier to buy Treasuries.

---

* I have a small investment in Public through an SPV, or Special Purpose Vehicle, I invested in.

T-BILLS

The Treasuries with the shortest term are technically called Treasury bills but are more commonly referred to as "T-bills." They come in increments of weeks: four, eight, thirteen, twenty-six, or fifty-two. (That's one, two, three-ish months, six-ish months, and a year for those of you who haven't had kids and don't speak in weeks.) There are also super short-term T-bills that pay out in just a few days, called Cash Management Bills. T-bills pay out slightly differently than other bonds because they are shorties but goodies. With T-bills you pay a discount rate and get the face value back at the end of the term.

So, let's say a fifty-two-week T-bill has a face value of $100 and a discount rate of 2 percent. That means you would pay $98 up front and then at the end of the term you get the full $100 par value back. You're getting a profit in the end, of course, but there aren't coupon payments like there would be with bonds with longer terms. With shorter terms also come lower entry points. T-bills are sold in increments of $100. So, if you just have $100 to play around with, you're going to get more back with a T-bill than in a savings account for not much more risk.

T-NOTES

Treasury notes (T-notes) are the intermediate term of the T-crew (and no, that's not a technical phrase; I made it up all of five minutes ago), and you can buy them in increments of two, three, five, seven, and ten years. They offer interest payments every six months until maturity (so no discount rate situation here). In times of high interest rates (which usually go along with a sluggish stock market), T-notes are actually really good investments because they pay a higher yield than many other investments but don't lock you in for too long.

T-BONDS

Again, technically, all of the investment vehicles we're discussing in this section are bonds, but the Treasury only calls the ones that mature from ten to thirty years "T-bonds." Like T-notes, T-bonds pay interest every six months. T-bonds have the highest rate of interest of all the T-crew because of the risk you are taking, not that the country might go under but that there will be higher interest rate bonds available later on, meaning that you've missed out on the opportunity to make a little more from your investment. You have to hold on to a T-bond for forty-five days at a minimum, but after that you can sell it on a secondary market. I'll unpack that option at the end of this lesson.

TREASURY INFLATION-PROTECTED SECURITIES (TIPS)

TIPS are mainly used to protect your money against fluctuations in inflation. Similar to T-notes and T-bonds, you get semiannual interest payments. But here's the great thing about TIPS: when you buy TIPS, the par value rises and falls according to the consumer price index (CPI), which tracks inflation. For example, if you buy $1,000 in TIPS and the interest rate is 1 percent, you get $10 in interest payments. If inflation stays the same then nothing happens. But—this is my favorite part—when inflation goes up, say, 5 percent, your bond adjusts: so, your bond would then be worth $1,050 and your payment would go up to $10.50. I know fifty cents doesn't sound like a lot, but if you own more TIPS and inflation gets nutso, then that's *real* money.

Investors who think we are headed for inflationary times will typically buy a lot of TIPS to take advantage of the increase in inflation and the corresponding increase in their return. But, just as TIPS can adjust up with inflation, they can adjust down during deflationary times—and we don't want that. It's tricky to predict inflation, even with all the charts and curves and analyses in the world. So the best way to balance these forces is to balance the amount of TIPS you buy with traditional Treasuries (T-bills, T-notes, and T-bonds).

SERIES I BONDS

When inflation was going bananas in 2021–23, I beat the Series I bond drum really hard on my podcast *Money Rehab*. The interest rates of I bonds also rise with inflation, so if you snagged one between November 2021 and October 2022, the interest rate climbed as high as 9.62 percent. The rates adjust along with the CPI and are basically designed to ensure your investment keeps pace with inflation. You can cash in your I bond after a year but they technically mature after thirty years. You should try to hold on to it for five years because if you don't you'll lose three months of interest. For example, if you sold it at twenty-four months, you would only get twenty-one months' worth of interest.

In times of cuckoo crazy inflation, it's possible to earn more with I bonds than with TIPS. But, unlike TIPS, there is a purchase limit for Series I bonds. Honestly the big downside is that you can't buy many of them. The limit is $10,000 in electronic bonds via TreasuryDirect.gov (our least favorite site) and an additional $5,000 in paper bonds using your federal income tax refund. One way to potentially increase your purchase limit is to buy bonds both individually and through entities you control, such as trusts or businesses, as these purchases are counted separately. Also, there is no I in "bond," so couples can each purchase up to the individual limit, effectively doubling their family's annual investment.

CONFESSIONS OF A PROFESSOR

I HEART THE IRS

"So I think you'd be really proud of me this year. I'm crushing it with investments," I said to my accountant, wearing sweat shields under my armpits, like I do for any occasions that make me nervous and will likely cause my hyperhidrosis to act up.

"That's great, Nicole. You definitely had a good year," she said in her casual but no-nonsense tone. I am still always freaked out by anything tax-related thanks to some poor tax habits I saw growing up, so she could be singing and I'd still be scared.

"Well, thank you . . . but maybe some of these investments will help me with capital gains," I said flipping through the extra organized collection of records for the year on my lap. My coping method for any tax trauma I've had is to be overly cautious and by the book with everything, so while I know it's completely irrational to be scared, I would be lying if I said the remnants of fear weren't still there.

"Awesome, so you sold some stocks after a year?" she asked.

"Oh no, I still have stocks invested for the long haul but some of my Treasuries came up so we have those," I said, proud of my new foray into big-girl bonds.

"Treasuries are excellent investments, but those don't have the same tax advantages. They are still taxed at ordinary income levels, not the more beneficial 'long-term capital gains' levels that you might see if you held on to a stock for more than a year and sold it," she explained calmly.

"Wait, so that's just like I earned that money at work?"

"Basically, yes, but a cool perk of Treasuries is that you don't have to pay state and local taxes on the money you make. But, yes, you do have to pay federal taxes at ordinary income rates and you should be proud of how high you're getting even though that means you have to pay more to Uncle Sam," she said, taking notes and smiling.

I was silent, vacillating through nonsensical thoughts that I'm going to go to jail and embarrassment for not knowing that this money move wasn't going to help my taxes in the ways I anticipated.

"But it's all good! These are great problems to have . . . You're making more, you always do the right thing, the IRS loves you, it's all good . . ." she said, knowing by now that I have completely nonsensical freak-outs.

I looked up from my color-coded folders and half-smiled.

"Can I get you some water or maybe turn the air on?" she said in as non-judgey a tone a person could have after noticing my huge pit stains on my blue button-down. Yes, that was with the sweat shields.

MUNICIPAL BONDS

Just as the federal government issues bonds when it needs money to build stuff, so do states, cities, and counties. When a city or state needs to build, say, a big park or a mass transit system, it may issue municipal bonds, or "munis" for short, to pay for it. The interest it pays back is usually exempt from federal taxes, unlike Treasuries. Most are also still not taxed by the state that issued them, which is another added hook-up for hooking your state up. But if you buy a bond from a different state, your state will tax you. So if you're in a higher tax bracket, a lower-paying, tax-free bond of, say, 4 percent might have the same benefit as a taxable bond at 7 percent. The math probably won't be quite that straightforward, but that's roughly how it will look. The tax benefits alone make munis worthy of a closer look, my accountant agrees.

But they are not without their drawbacks. Munis typically offer lower interest rates compared to taxable bonds to make up for their tax-exempt status and lower risk. They can be sensitive to interest rate changes; rising rates can decrease the market value of the bonds. This only matters if you're trading munis; if you hold them to maturity, you will almost always get your investment back plus interest. While defaults are rare, they can occur, especially in municipalities with financial struggles. I did a whole series about this at CNBC called "States of Pain" (clever, I know) showing some US cities and states on the verge of bankruptcy.

Remember how the riskier the bond is, the more interest you get back? Munis are no exception. Some US cities—like Detroit or Chicago—are more at risk fiscally than others. The ones in the worst financial straits offer more interest in exchange for lending them money. Some US cities have gone bankrupt, like Detroit in 2013. When that happens, muni bondholders get screwed. Again, that's unusual. Cities often have the ability to tax their way out of trouble (by taxing their constituents, not the bondholders themselves) and ultimately pay back their debt.

There are two main kinds of muni bonds:

- General Obligation (GO) Bonds, which are for projects that won't make money, like public schools. These are paid back with tax dollars.

- Revenue Bonds are for projects that will make revenue, like toll roads. These are paid back by the revenue from the projects.

Some investors prefer individual muni bonds, choosing those with the best balance of yield, credit risk, and tax benefits. Others might opt for municipal bond mutual funds or ETFs, which we will talk more about in the last course for diversification and professional management. A ladder strategy, just like we did with CDs in the last lesson, where you buy munis (or any of the bonds we talked about for that matter) with different maturities, can provide a steady income stream while managing interest rate risk.

SELLING BONDS

Let's recap what we know so far about buying and selling bonds: You can buy government bonds at TreasuryDirect.gov or on the secondary market. You can also *sell* some government bonds on TreasuryDirect or on the secondary market. If you're looking to purchase a different type of bond, usually you can sell them on the same platform you bought them. The "secondary market" is a fancy finance term to describe the exchange from investors to investors, rather than from issuer to investor. The latter exchange—issuer to investor—is the primary market.

For most of us, the secondary market is where we do most of our investing. Participants in the primary market are typically governments and big financial institutions because when a security is first issued, it is normally purchased by a financial institution first. I find that the difference between primary and secondary markets is actually a bit easier to understand when talking about equity securities like stocks rather than debt securities. So, in the interest of making this concept easier to understand, I'm going to give you the equity securities example.

When an organization is transitioning from being a private company to a publicly traded company with shares that can be bought and sold on the stock market, it goes through what's called the initial public offering (IPO) process. Before investors like you and I can buy the shares, an underwriter (typically an investment bank) works with the company going public to set the initial stock price. Then the investment bank buys all of the shares of the stock. Only then can the shares be sold on the market. That exchange between the company going public and the investment bank—when the security is first issued, the price is set, and then it is purchased for the very first time—is an exchange on the *primary* market. If you buy on the primary market, it means you are the first party to own that particular security. Once the investment bank starts selling shares on the public market, and then brokers and investors sell their shares to each other, the stock is considered to be trading on the *secondary* market.

This creates an important distinction between the primary and secondary markets: security prices on the secondary market are subject to supply and demand, whereas the primary market operates on a set price. This makes sense in the IPO example we just examined, right? The underwriter and the company are partners; the underwriter agrees to buy all of the shares of the company's stock when it goes public at—and this is important—a price agreed upon by the underwriter and the company. In the stock market, however, buyers and sellers are not partners. Sellers are trying to sell their shares at the highest price possible, and buyers are trying to buy at the lowest price possible. That's why there is a bid and an ask typically listed. The bid is the highest price a buyer is willing to pay for something and the ask is the lowest price a seller is willing to accept. So they're more like frenemies. Where the market price ends up falling depends on whether demand is high—and therefore sellers can get buyers to fork over a big sum in exchange for their popular shares—or if demand is low, and buyers can scoop shares at a low, enticing price.

Remember, just like with equity securities, bond prices fluctuate on the secondary market. We talked about this earlier, but let's dig a little deeper into the secondary market. Think of it this way, if you were presented with two options:

Option 1: Bond A, which has a par value of $100 and a coupon of 10 percent

Option 2: Bond B, which has a par value of $100 and a coupon of 50 percent

Which one do you choose? I mean, would you rather have 10 percent of $100 or 50 percent of $100? If you said, "Uh, the higher one? Obviously?" you're right! There's no catch here—anyone in that position would choose the bond with the higher interest rate.

Here's where the supply and demand forces come in: because investors will consider it a no-brainer to buy the bond with a higher interest rate, the unpopular option (the bond with the lower interest rate) will become less desirable. With less demand for this bond (in our example, Bond A with the 10 percent interest rate), the market price will drop. It's possible that the market price will actually drop below the par value ($100); when this happens, the bond is described as being sold "at discount." On the other hand, say Bond B is such a hot ticket that people are willing to pay more than $100 for that sweet 50 percent interest rate. If a bond is being sold above the par price, it's being sold "at a premium."

I want to make something super clear, though, because this point often gets lost in translation: when I say the "market price" will drop, that does not mean that amount you're earning on your bond drops. If you have purchased a bond with a fixed interest rate, it is exactly that: "fixed." If interest rates fluctuate, it doesn't mean that your returns will change. While the value of your bond on the secondary market may be falling, you still have the same bond you bought. If you end up keeping it, at maturity you will get whatever you expected to get; it may be a bummer, but you still have cash in hand at the end of the term. It's like buying an iPhone and then the very next day a brand-new iPhone with a bunch of new features comes out and is being sold at the very same price you paid for your now outdated iPhone. You could sell yours at a loss if you must have the new one or you could just keep and use the phone you got in the first place. In the bond world, it's somewhat similar: if you buy a bond and then interest rates rise, you have a less profitable investment than the other bonds that will be issued after yours. *Le sigh.*

Bonds of any kind are built on trust with a little dash of blind faith. In our relationships we (hopefully) get rewarded the more trust we have. In the finance world, it's actually the opposite. We get rewarded less if we have more trust in the other side. But in both worlds, if you have no trust at all, you have no bond.

The Fixed-Income Market

FIXED INCOME 301
Corporate and International Bonds

My first love was words. Long before I found my passion for helping people understand financial planning, before I even made any money myself, I loved the language of money. If being a "financial linguist" were a thing, I would be that. Despite it being intimidating at the start, deep down I find it so curious. Like, if I told you that I had a "high-yield" bond to sell you, you would be stoked, I presume? High yields as in high interest rates? Sign. Me. Up.

Then, what if I said I had a "junk bond" to sell you? You might be saying, "*Junk?!* Hell-to-the-no. Mama didn't raise me to buy junk."

But . . . what if I told you that they were exactly the same? Because they are. Remember, in the bond world, the less you trust the other side, the more you can ask for in interest. Not trustworthy = lower grade = junk. That means that if you take on more risk lending to someone, whether it's a country or state or city or company, you want more reward back for that risk. More reward = more interest = high yield. And if it works out and the other side doesn't fail or go under, then you win big for loaning money to someone you so-so trust. We've talked about Socrates, and the WWII bond shenanigans. But in this lesson we're moving on to movies and cocaine. It's time to speculate about some wilder assets and times.

CORPORATE BONDS

Did you see the movie *Wall Street* or the sequel *Wall Street: Money Never Sleeps*? If you haven't, get out there and watch it! Consider this move homework. The film, about the corruption on Wall Street, was based on a bunch of high-profile scandals and ended up foreshadowing the conviction of Michael Milken.

Milken is the famous and rather infamous "junk bond king" (TL;DR—he was charged with conspiracy and fraud, went to prison, started the Milken Conference, which is like the nerd Oscars, and Trump pardoned him). The movie takes us back to the wild Wall Street days of the 1980s with wide lapels and piles of cocaine. Milken realized that lending money to risky companies netted him way more money than lending to safe companies. Milken marketed these junk bonds to investors while also offering them to a whole range of companies. Some of these companies were making wild, newfangled products that traditional finance guys didn't think would ever take off—you know, like cable companies and cell phone makers. A phone you could take everywhere with you? Who would even want such a thing? So people flocked to him because they were getting a higher return for the perceived higher risk that really wasn't.

Milken discovered this undervalued niche market and got crazy rich. The inevitable rise, fall, and rise again—followed. At the time, more pedigreed Wall Street guys looked down on this type of investment. Some of that is due to its poor reputation as the bond of choice for businesses like casinos. But by creating a lucrative market for junk bonds, Milken made them profitable for everyone.

Despite the serious charges he faced and pleaded guilty to, in my years covering Wall Street, major players believe that Milken is a genius for revolutionizing Wall Street by creating a whole new market and that the charges were unmerited. I tell you this origin story because it's a perfect scene setter to this kind of investment lesson, if not an analog. Corporate bonds aren't vanilla, but if you have the stomach for them, the rewards can be quite satisfying.

WHAT ARE CORPORATE BONDS?

Corporate bonds get issued when a company needs more money for some reason—to expand, to hire more people, or to rebuild from a setback. Corporate bonds have been issued by a ton of companies including Amazon, Apple, Anheuser-Busch, AT&T, Comcast, Bank of America, Citi Bank, FedEx, McDonald's, Microsoft, and many more.

Just like government bonds, when you buy a corporate bond, you are helping a company in exchange for your money back and a little something extra (interest). Some investors might decide to buy a corporate bond rather than shares of the company because the risk of owning a bond is likely smaller than the risk of owning the stock outright. Stocks can go up or down. But bonds almost always pay out more than you put in. If the company does go bankrupt, bondholders can often (eventually) get their investment back. Stocks in a bankrupt company are typically worthless. Other investors might choose bonds to chase promising gains. Either way, corporate bonds can add diversity to your portfolio or play nicely with other fixed-income securities. They typically yield higher returns than government bonds of similar maturity and can be sold before maturity in a large secondary market, offering liquidity if needed.

Once a company figures out how much it would like to borrow, it issues a "bond offering" in that amount. Unlike stocks, ownership of corporate bonds doesn't mean you own any stake in the company that has issued the bond. If, hypothetically speaking, some well-funded internet troll decides to take over his favorite social media site, he will be forced to pay all stockholders $54.20 for each share they own (Hi, Elon!). In contrast, bonds stay with the investor no matter who owns the company. You're just effectively lending them money, and the company pays you a rate of interest over a period of time and repays the principal at the maturity date. Most are generally categorized into the following maturity ranges:

- *Short-term notes* (with maturities of up to three years)

- *Medium-term notes* (with maturities ranging between four and ten years)

- *Long-term bonds* (with maturities greater than ten years)

It's not just age that matters; corporate bonds are also ranked by credit quality. Moody's and Standard & Poor's are like the Siskel and Ebert of bonds: they check out each corporate bond issuer, too, and give them a thumbs-up or a thumbs-down. They don't actually use thumbs. They give you letter grades, but when they get below about a B it's thumbs-down for most investors. These grades make up a bond issuer's report card, and issuers with low scores earn a pass to the high-interest rate club. That can mean a big payout for investors but also signals a big risk. It's important to note: *not all corporate bonds are junk bonds.*

MONEY TIP

TAKING THE TOP OFF

Occasionally companies will offer a "convertible bond," which is a special kind of bond that can be converted from debt security (bond) to an equity security (share). The downside? These bonds pay less interest than traditional bonds in exchange for doing this magic transformation trick.

IS THERE JUNK IN YOUR TRUNK?

Corporate bonds are basically split into two credit categories: you've got your classy investment-grade ones, and the more adventurous speculative-grade (or high-yield or junk—tomato, tomahto) ones. Speculative-grade bonds are like the bad boys of the bond world. Accountants over at the credit agencies looked them over and thought they were a bit shaky compared with the more respectable investment-grade crew. The investment-grade category has four rating grades while the speculative-grade category has six. The report cards are different for each category.

	MOODY'S	STANDARD & POORS
Highest quality (Best quality, smallest degree of investment risk)	Aaa	AAA
High quality (Often called high-grade bonds)	Aa	AA
Upper medium grade (Many favorite investment attributes)	A	A
Medium grade (Neither highly protected nor poorly secured)	Baa	BBB
SPECULATIVE GRADE		
Somewhat speculative (Have speculative elements)	Ba	BB
Speculative (Generally lack characteristics of a desirable investment)	B	B
Highly speculative (Bonds of poor standing)	Caa	CC
Most speculative (Poor prospects)	Ca	CC
Imminent default (Extremely poor prospects)	C	C
Default	C	D

When you see that junk rating or low score, it means these bad boys have a higher chance of ghosting you or defaulting. Nobody wants to get ghosted, so they have to make their profile look extra sexy. They do that by offering higher interest rates to brave (or foolish) investors. As a financial linguist, I particularly like some of these corporate bond terms:

- "Fallen angel"—this is when an A-lister takes a nosedive from the top-shelf all the way down to the junk drawer because life got tough or due to some real poor decision-making.

- "Rising star"—the opposite of a fallen angel. Here a company is leveling up after getting an upgrade from a credit agency because it's finally gotten it together.

- "Split ratings"—occurs when the different credit rating agencies don't agree on a rating.

HOW GOOD IS THE GETTING?

Generally speaking, investment-grade corporate bonds offer interest rates ranging from 2 percent to 5 percent, while speculative corporate bonds could offer rates upward of 5 percent to 10 percent or more, depending on the level of risk. The pricing is influenced by maturity, the credit rating of the company issuing the bond, and the general level of interest rates.

Here's how the whole interest rate to corporate bond rates situation plays out: If the interest rate is high, bond rates will be higher to remain competitive. If you can make 5 percent by buying US bonds or CDs, which are super safe, why would you lend money to anyone less reliable than that? Because they would pay you more than 5 percent. Conversely, in a low-interest-rate environment, bond rates will be lower. If that nice insured CD is paying 1.75 percent, why would a corporation offer you too much more than that? They're going to start their negotiation at 1.75 percent instead of the 5 percent in the last example. Economic factors such as inflation, economic growth, and central bank policies can affect corporate bond interest rates. For example, in times of high inflation, higher interest rates may be offered to attract investors.

The two flavors of bonds come with their own risks and yields. Corporate bonds are usually a sweeter but riskier deal than the safer (if less rewarding) bonds offered by the government. This split is what creates the "credit spread" between corporate and government bonds. This spread can be tracked using a line graph that compares just how big a difference the spread is.

Credit Spreads

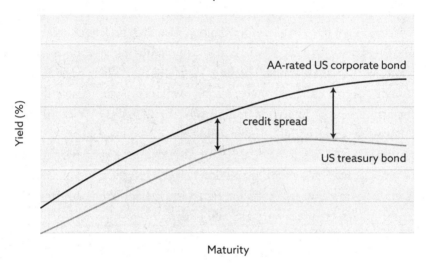

Here are a few examples of recent high-quality corporate bond issuances where the interest rates were reported:

Apple. In 2019, Apple issued bonds with various maturities. They had a number of offerings from short-term notes with a 1.7 percent interest rate to a 30-year bond with an interest rate of 2.95 percent. This bond issuance was part of a larger strategy to raise capital for corporate activities like share buybacks and dividend payments.

Amazon. In 2020, Amazon issued bonds worth $18 billion across different maturities. One tranche included 3-year bonds with an interest rate of 0.25 percent, reflecting the company's strong credit rating and the low-interest-rate environment at the time. Then, the speculation was that Amazon didn't even need the money. They were just taking advantage of the low rates.

AT&T. In March 2021, AT&T sold bonds worth $14.7 billion, in various tranches. One of the tranches was a 10.5-year bond with an interest rate of 3.25 percent. This issuance was part of AT&T's efforts to refinance its existing debt.

These bonds are typically available to both institutional and individual investors. They trade in a number of places including brokerage accounts. To find them, look for a section dedicated to bond trading on your brokerage's platform. It may take a bit of digging, but it will be labeled "Fixed Income," "Bonds," "Bond Market," or something similar. You can usually find it in the main menu or under the trading/investment options. Once there, you can use the search and filter tools to find specific bonds. You can search for corporate bonds by name or CUSIP number (a unique identifier for securities; stocks have these too). If you don't have a specific bond in mind, use filters to narrow down your options. Filters can include bond type (corporate), maturity date, credit rating, yield, and issuer.

A JUNK BOND BY ANY OTHER NAME

To sum it all up, issuers of high-yield/speculative/junk bonds are often companies with unstable financial histories, operating in volatile industries, or in a phase of aggressive growth or restructuring. At The Money School we're here to learn about different assets. Sometimes understanding them helps you know what you want to invest in or, rather, what you don't; other times it helps you make sense of the broader markets. Unless you're the Junk Bond King, you don't want to make them your whole deal. Be aware that their values can fluctuate considerably based on the economic environment, performing well during times of economic growth and potentially suffering during downturns. But yes, even junk bonds can have a place in a balanced portfolio.

> **CONFESSIONS OF A PROFESSOR** | **TESLA'S JUNK DEBUT**
>
> "That's right, Bob. Tesla's $2.6 billion acquisition of SolarCity in 2016 was a sign that Elon wanted to expand his clean energy footprint," I said during an interview on a business show.
>
> "And to finance the acquisition, Tesla issued bonds, right?" Bob asked in an anchorman kinda way.
>
> "Yep. It was $1.8 billion in bonds in August 2017 at a 5.3 percent interest rate. This move was controversial, as SolarCity was facing financial difficulties at the time, and both companies were founded by Elon Musk, raising conflict of interest concerns. But, despite skepticism from some investors and analysts, Tesla's bond issuance was oversubscribed, indicating strong investor demand," I replied, dialing up my former anchor-lady ways.
>
> "Ya, there's always demand for Elon's junk," Bob said.
>
> Silence. *What the actual . . . Is that joke?!* I thought.
>
> "I mean junk bonds," he said in a half-creepy, half-embarrassed tone.
>
> "Well, Bob, I am not really sure but I'll take your word for it."

Junk bonds are sometimes born but also sometimes made through unexpected downgrades and defaults. Case in point: Lehman Brothers' corporate bond fallout. The downfall of Lehman Brothers in the fall of 2008 is a major plot point in the Great Recession. Lehman, a global financial services firm, was heavily invested in the subprime mortgage market. As the housing bubble burst and mortgage defaults soared, Lehman's extensive exposure to mortgage-backed securities led to massive losses. Unable to secure additional funding or a buyer, Lehman filed for bankruptcy, which was the largest in US history at the time. Investors holding Lehman's corporate bonds faced

---

* Not his real name and you'll see why.

enormous losses. In a bankruptcy, secured creditors get paid out first, then unsecured creditors (like bondholders). Stockholders get a cool story to tell and exactly zero dollars. In the case of Lehman Brothers, unsecured creditors recovered less than half their initial investment or about forty-one cents for every dollar invested. This event exposed the risks of highly leveraged and risky investments in the banking sector and led to increased regulatory scrutiny and reform in the financial industry.

Another example and a good segue into the next section is the Asian Financial Crisis of 1997–98. The crisis began in Thailand with the collapse of the Thai baht (its currency) and spread across East Asia, affecting currencies, stock markets, and other asset prices. Many corporations in these countries had issued bonds in US dollars to take advantage of lower interest rates compared to local currencies. But as local currencies devalued dramatically against the dollar, the cost of servicing this dollar-denominated debt skyrocketed, leading to widespread defaults and financial distress. This crisis showed how risky it can be when companies borrow in one currency but make profits in another, especially when the currencies are unequal. The Lehman and Asian crises both show how corporate bonds can affect the economy and financial system, as well as illustrate the complications that can happen with this type of investment.

INTERNATIONAL BONDS

Now that I've told you a horror story about foreign bonds, let's double-click on the idea of them. Honestly, I really don't recommend dabbling in international bonds for a newbie American investor.* The biggest reason is because they are traded in a foreign currency, and the currency risk against the American dollar is tricky to track. For example, the interest rate could look like it's rocking, but if the currency denomination the bond is in is faltering against

---

* You may already be an investor in foreign bonds. If you're Jewish, you may have gotten Israel bonds as a bar or bat mitzvah gift. Mazel tov! These bonds have comparable rates to those of US Treasuries, and the Israeli government has never defaulted on its debt. The Indian community also has a tradition of diaspora bonds, and some countries in Africa are experimenting with them as well. If you may have gotten one as a gift, this is your sign to go check and potentially cash them out.

the dollar, then it's not rocking; it's rolling away from you—along with your profits.

If the US or Germany issues bonds, you can be pretty sure that you'll get your initial investment back. After all, those countries are economic powerhouses and unlikely to go under. Therefore, they don't have to pay as much interest (that becomes your profit) because there are a lot of investors like you who would take that bet. But if Portugal, Italy, Ireland, Greece, or Spain (known by the offensive acronym PIIGS, these are the EU countries whose economies are struggling) asks you to give them money, there's a chance you'll never see that cash again, so you'll want more of a return to take on the risk.

If you want some exposure to other parts of the world, then here are some dos and don'ts:

- *Do* try to find international bonds in bond funds to start. There are "dollar-hedged" funds that use tools to safeguard against currency fluctuations of the foreign bonds in the fund.

- *Don't* go for emerging markets like Indonesia, Malaysia, and Kenya unless you happen to be an expert on those places—like you speak the language and you majored in studying that country in college.

- *Do* stick to developed countries like the United Kingdom, France, and Germany.

- *Don't* forget our Canadian friends, whose banks rode the Great Recession hurricane out like a boss. They are technically international but just as safe, if not safer, than buying homegrown Treasuries.

GRADING THE STATE

When it comes to the world of finance, everyone gets a score. Even countries' creditworthiness can be quantified. This score is known as a sovereign credit rating. Their primary purpose is to evaluate the likelihood of a country fulfilling its financial obligations, namely repaying debt. This score is used by investors and financial institutions to gauge a country's risk level. The ratings are provided by the usual friends—Moody's, Standard & Poor's, and Fitch Ratings, each employing its own methodology and rating scale.

When reducing a country's entire economy to a letter grade, the credit bureaus zoom all the way out and look at the full picture. They start with economic aspects like GDP growth, economic stability, and wealth level. From there they look at other hard stats like inflation rates and currency stability. But then they account for political factors such as government stability and policy continuity. They get all up in the national budget. How much debt does the government have? Are there budget deficits? They also check external factors like balance of payments and foreign exchange reserves. It's a very involved process.

We've covered this before but as a refresher, ratings are typically expressed in letter grades, where AAA represents the highest rating, indicating an extremely strong capacity to meet financial commitments, and D signifies default. Ratings from AAA to BBB– are categorized as "investment grade" (lower risk), while those from BB+ to D are considered "noninvestment grade" or "speculative" (higher risk). If these seem repetitive, that means you're learning. If it doesn't, don't worry. We'll get it to stick in your brain by the end of the book. Just like learning to read starts with the ABCs and goes all the way to the mysteries of the semicolon, financial literacy starts with its own building blocks and gets more complex as it goes.

These ratings are a big deal when it comes to a country's ability to borrow money and attract investors. Conversely, a downgrade can increase a country's borrowing costs, reflecting higher perceived risk. These ratings not only reflect but also influence a country's economic outlook, affecting its financial markets and economic policies. They are constantly being updated and changed regularly based on economic and political shifts. Some of the mainstays in the AAA club are Canada and Australia, while on the other end we have Sri Lanka and Lebanon.

FYI: CRY FOR ME, ARGENTINA

In a surprising move in 2017, Argentina issued a 100-year bond, known as a "century bond," which was notable given the country's history of economic volatility and defaults. The bond was issued with a yield of 7.9 percent, attracting investors with its high return despite the long-term risk. This issuance was remarkable because it was a surprising indication of investor confidence in a country that had defaulted on its debt as recently as 2001. Unsurprisingly, Argentina defaulted on the bond. After the default, restructuring investors managed to recover about fifty-five cents on the dollar.

I've talked a lot about how bonds can be used to add a little diversity to your portfolio. Just remember to peep that credit rating to make sure you're comfy with the return and the risk. Now if only we had a credit rating agency to assess the trustworthiness subjectively of the people in our lives. If you want to start a company that does that, *that's* a bond I would definitely buy.

ADVANCED MARKETS 101
Commodities

I shed my financial world training wheels in the pit at the Chicago Merc, which is an exchange where commodities are traded. I hadn't seen the movie *Trading Places* yet, so I had no idea that commodity trading meant the exchange of physical items like coffee, oil, gold, silver, and even frozen concentrated orange juice. (I thought I was getting punked when I was told I was going to work at a stock exchange that sold orange juice.)

While I was thrown into the deep end of financial markets (as was Billy Ray Valentine, Eddie Murphy's character in *Trading Places*), commodities trading is not the place to start off as an investor. Unlike stocks and bonds, commodities and the investment vehicles we explore in this course are more advanced. They are volatile and complex. But stick with me here. In a few lessons we will put it all together and talk about how to structure your portfolio. Some of the best portfolio setups include a little exposure to commodities.

You'll likely only have a baby bit—if anything—invested in advanced markets, and even that little exposure will be via funds. You don't need to shop in anything but beginners' markets to have a portfolio of your dreams. But just in case your dreams get bigger and/or your OJ craving gets stronger, this course will always be there for you.

WHO YOU CALLIN' "A COMMODITY"?!

Technically, *commodity* means a basic good that's not special, as in it can be swapped for the exact same thing and no one would really notice. I remember for a while when I was on the news, I felt "commoditized" because I could have been replaced by some other young lady telling old rich white men what the Dow was doing. In other words, it's "fungible" (RIP NFTs) in the same way as if I gave you a twenty-dollar bill and you gave me another one back, we would have the same value. But the colloquial use of the term *hot commodity* means that something is highly valued, as in "that actress is such a 'hot commodity' in Hollywood right now."

In the investing world, both are somewhat true. Investing in commodities is both common and extraordinary. Honestly, most of investing is this way, as in, it feels so special until . . . it doesn't.

Just like eggs, commodities come in two types: hard or soft. Anything that has to be grown or harvested like soybeans, cotton, cattle—or yes, eggs—is classified as a soft commodity. Hard commodities are resources that are mined or drilled from the earth, such as palladium, silver, platinum, gold, crude oil, and natural gas.

HARD COMMODITIES

The gold standard of commodities for your average investor is, obviously, gold. The US has a long and storied history with gold. It has been the universal symbol of wealth since ancient times and had backed the US dollar all the way up until 1971. Gold is considered to be a safe haven by many investors. While some opt for gold as a bulwark against the zombie apocalypse / an alien invasion, it's also a popular choice because it's a hedge against inflation. Remember, in the words of John Pierpont Morgan Sr. (as in J. P. Morgan), "Gold is money. And nothing else."

Of course, gold isn't the only hard commodity. There's also oil, which is sometimes considered liquid gold. But let's start with gold.

Gold

J. P.'s view is shared by many investors to this day. Many investors turn to gold in times of economic uncertainty or when inflation is high, as it has proven to maintain or increase its value while other assets may lose theirs. Gold tends to have a negative "beta" value, meaning its price often moves inversely to the stock market.

Gold has long been considered a "hedge," which is an investment that has a negative relationship to the price of the asset you are hedging against. Hedging in the financial world means pretty much the same thing as it does in life. If you're hosting a party and you know all your friends drink beer and beer is always a big party hit, you still buy water, just in case. Maybe it's hot outside, maybe someone is pregnant, maybe someone just doesn't want a beer. Whatever the reason, if someone says no to a beer, they now have something else to drink. You've hedged against people turning down a beer.

In the financial world, hedges are also about investing in future protection, but we do this in other ways too. You pay for car insurance as a hedge against getting into an accident. It costs you a little bit of money each month, but if something goes catastrophically wrong, insurance will kick in and cover the cost of repairs. You get a prenup to hedge against a divorce. That will also cost you some money up front, but helps you in case marriage disaster strikes. You hope you don't need to rely on car insurance or a prenup because you're not planning (hopefully) on getting into an accident or divorced, but it's there just in case. In the business world, large companies do this all the time. If a company sells chicken sandwiches, they will buy futures contracts that let them buy chicken in the future at a set price. That way, no matter what happens during that time, they are able to buy chicken at the agreed-upon price. It gets more complicated than this, but that's the basic theory.

If the stock market is like a roller coaster, then gold is like a train ride in the kiddie section of the park. In the long run, stocks tend to outperform gold as an investment, but in the short term, gold can steal the show, especially in times when everyone is feeling nervous. If you have an upset stomach from stress, which would you rather ride: the roller coaster or the kiddie train? Just like a coaster and a train are on two different tracks, gold performance is unrelated to stock market performance. This makes it a reliable ride in times when the stock market roller coaster goes upside down, like during the 2008 financial crises or the 2016 Brexit drama.

There's no actual causational relationship between the price of gold and stock market returns. Think of it this way—in the summer, ice cream sales and shark bites increase. So you could look at those facts and think eating ice cream causes sharks to bite people. But that's not the connection. When it's hot, people eat more ice cream and go in the water, where the sharks live, to cool off. The environment connects the two events. It's the same with gold prices. When people are anxious about the future, they are more likely to invest in gold. Whatever makes them anxious, say a global pandemic or a recession, can also cause the stock market to go down.

Investor anxiety can be one part of what drives gold prices up during a stock market downturn or any crisis, but gold is also an important investment as a hedge against inflation. Gold is priced in dollars. So, when the dollar weakens, it takes more dollars to buy the same amount of gold, which increases the price of gold in dollar terms. Over an extremely long timeline—decades or more—gold can be an excellent hedge against inflation. However, in the shorter term, the fluctuation in gold prices can make it less effective.

If you've been having an anxious few years, the gold market would suggest you're not alone. Amid a tough year for commodity returns in 2023, gold shined by reaching an all-time high. This surge was largely driven by the growing likelihood of rate cuts in 2024 and a weakening dollar. And when something—anything—is high-flying like that, there are always predators looking to take advantage of the situation.

MONEY TIP

INVESTOR BEWARE: GOLD SCAMS

1. **Gold IRA Scams:** These include high-pressure sales tactics, exorbitant fees, fraudulent companies, unlicensed IRA "experts," high markups, leveraged accounts, shady custodians, and unapproved "collectible" coins. Scammers often take advantage of those looking to invest in gold as part of their retirement savings.

2. **False Promises of High Returns:** Scammers often lure investors with the promise of lucrative profits from rising precious metals prices. They create a sense of urgency and use bait-and-switch tactics, impersonating reputable companies or individuals and creating fake websites or apps to scam people out of money and personal information.

3. **The Vanishing Company Scam:** This involves convincing buyers to send money for gold at a lower price, but the company disappears after receiving the money. The victim ends up with no gold and no way to recover their money.

4. **The Inheritance Scam:** Scammers pretend to have inherited gold and need help moving it out of their country. They often ask for a partner, a bank account, and some bribe money, only to disappear once they receive the cash.

5. **Coins That Don't Exist:** Scammers convince buyers to purchase gold coins and offer to store them in escrow due to risks of theft or disasters. But these coins don't exist, and the buyer is charged storage fees and insurance for a nonexistent gold coin collection.

Also, there are gold scams that specifically target the elderly, and there is a special place in hell reserved for those people.

You can legitimately invest in gold in a few ways. First, you can buy actual gold "bullion," although that's not my favorite way because it becomes tricky to buy, sell, and store actual gold bars. You can buy gold mining stocks. Or you can buy into gold ETFs, the most popular being ticker symbol GLD.

Oil

It's important to note that the nongold commodities are a trickier investment because the prices are based on physical supply and demand. Of course, the physical supply and demand can be impacted by things—black swans—out of our control like pandemics (hello, 2020) and extreme weather events (hello again, 2020). There are a whole lot of white papers being written on climate change's impact on the commodity market. Even nonextreme variations move markets. On a non-catastrophic scale, just imagine how much less demand there is for natural gas and oil in a mild winter.

Oil is globally traded in US dollars, so fluctuations in the value of the dollar can directly affect oil prices. It's a little wonky, but imagine the global oil market as an international carnival where all the rides and games (oil) are priced in tickets (US dollars). Now imagine that people from different countries come to this carnival with their own currencies and need to exchange them for tickets (dollars) at the entrance.

When the US dollar is strong, it's like the ticket booth raising its prices. People from other countries find that their currency buys fewer tickets (dollars), making the rides and games (oil) more expensive for them. As a result, they might decide to spend less and go on fewer rides. Conversely, when the US dollar is weak, it's like the ticket booth offering a discount. Now people from other countries get more tickets (dollars) for their currency, making the rides and games (oil) cheaper. They might decide to enjoy more rides since they can afford more.

The strength of the US economy affects the dollar like the reputation of the carnival affects ticket sales. If the carnival (US economy) is seen as exciting and well managed, more people want to come, and the demand for tickets (dollars) increases, making them more valuable. But if the carnival seems poorly managed or uninteresting, fewer people come, and the value of tickets (dollars) may decrease.

If you hate the carnival analogy, basically, the dollar and oil have an inverse relationship. When the dollar decreases, the price of crude oil increases, and vice versa. When the dollar is weaker, it takes more dollars to buy the same amount of oil.

FYI

OH, OPEC!

Even if you don't end up investing in oil or commodities, following geopolitical happenings never hurts. And one of the big players to keep your eye on is OPEC, or the Organization of Petroleum Exporting Countries (pronounced oh-peck, not spelled out O-P-E-C), which is made up of oil-producing countries like Saudi Arabia, Iran, Iraq, Kuwait, and Venezuela. Since they control basically all the world's oil supply, their moves can lead to a decrease in the global oil supply, potentially driving up oil prices. Higher oil prices can lead to increased costs for transportation and manufacturing, often affecting consumer prices as a result. Conversely, lower oil prices can reduce costs for businesses and consumers. Predictable and stable policies from OPEC can contribute to market stability, while unexpected changes or conflicts within OPEC can cause the market to go cuckoo bananas (not a financial linguist term).

Unlike gold, please don't go out and buy a barrel of oil or a well. Like gold, there are individual oil companies (some listed at the end of this lesson) that are known for doing big dividends and share buybacks. Or you can invest in an ETF, with one of the most popular being ticker symbol USO, which is up about 25 percent for the year at the time I'm writing this. While that might sound enticing, you may not feel good about investing in oil, and I feel that. If you want more sustainable options, take a look at how companies are graded using ESG (environmental, social, and governance) factors. There are rankings for oil companies* as well as funds with exposure to commodities that exclude fossil fuels altogether.

---

* Interestingly, Tesla ranked lower than some of the oil/gas companies recently. Yes, Elon posted about it. Keep in mind that the rankings take a lot of different factors into consideration and are said to be influenced by opinions of the companies and their players rather than the straight data.

SOFT COMMODITIES

Commodities that are "soft" are grown and harvested, as opposed to "hard" commodities like metals and oil that are mined or drilled. Soft commodities refer to agricultural products and livestock, like most of what we eat and drink. Yeah, now I'm hungry too. But seriously, they can be classified in five categories:

1. Grains and cereals like wheat, corn, rice, oats, and barley. Think staple foods for humans and animals alike.

2. Oilseeds like soybeans, canola, and sunflower seeds. These are crucial for producing vegetable oils and also important for making biodiesel (renewable fuel similar to diesel but sans the fossil).

3. Tropical products like coffee, cocoa, and sugar. Their production is often concentrated in specific tropical regions, making them sensitive to weather conditions and political stability in these areas.

4. Fibers like cotton and wool, used in the textile industry.

5. Livestock like live cattle, hogs, and poultry.

The volatility of soft commodities is real. These are plants and animals, y'all. As anyone who has tried to grow a tomato can tell you, too much water, too little water, or a random bug infestation and the whole thing just flops over and dies. Soft commodities are supersensitive to seasonal factors and weather conditions. If there's more rain one year and the crop thrives under those conditions, prices will go down if all the farms are producing more. But if there's too much rain and the field floods, it could kill the crop, driving up the price by reducing the available amount. When it comes to market fluctuations with this asset, an awful lot is determined by factors way beyond anyone's control. As if acts of God weren't enough, changes in dietary habits, population growth, and economic development can influence the demand for various soft commodities. Since many soft commodities are grown in specific regions, they can also be affected by political instability, trade policies, and economic conditions in those areas. Agricultural markets can be significantly affected by government policies and regulations, such as subsidies, tariffs, and trade agreements.

CONFESSIONS OF A PROFESSOR

HAMMER TIME

"What the heck is that guy carrying?" I heard one guy in the middle of the pit shout.

"A hammer?! Is that skinny guy coming for us? Bring it, buddy!" I heard another shout to laughs on top of the baseline roars and rumbles during trading hours.

There was a short slender guy who walked onto the floor of the exchange when I was working there. He carried a hammer, a nail, and a plant.

"What the heck, dude?" someone else yelled.

"Is that weed?? I'll take some over here!"

More laughs and roars from a crowd full of guys who were only slightly distracted by this weird occurrence while still making trades for their firms.

"What is he doing? Don't you see we are working here?" a sweaty big guy screamed.

The mystery man hammered the plant to the wall and just walked away.

"What is that??" a few different guys howled.

It was a soybean plant. They had been trading soybeans for years, decades in some cases. And they never knew what one looked like. They never really had to until now.

HOW TO COMMODITIZE

If you opt to invest in commodities, there are four ways to go about this. You can choose the ETF route as I suggested with gold and oil because there are ETFs for everything, both in the US and abroad (much more on ETFs in the next course—I promise!). If you're a glutton for more complexity, you can also invest through options, futures contracts, or by heading to the commodity store and buying a physical commodity. While it's not my favorite, I will say purchasing a gold bar is likely easier to store than, say, fifteen hundred pork bellies, but you can buy both at Costco if you really want to. If you're in a city apartment and are already keeping your sweaters in the oven because space is at such a premium, you can invest in a commodity-producing public company, such as Archer-Daniels-Midland, which covers the gamut from wheat to corn to cocoa and beyond and takes up zero space.

Futures Contracts

The most difficult/advanced type of commodity investment is via a futures contract. Futures are important to the commodity producers because those futures contracts enable them to lock in future prices, which helps protect the producers from the aforementioned extreme bouts of weather. Let's say Farmer Sue wants the peace of mind knowing that she's going to get market price for her corn crop, no matter what. Basically, with a commodities futures contract, she'd be locking in a price to hedge against uncertainty.

Now, there's a good reason why this kind of trading was relegated to professionals only for many years. In the commodities biz, even a little bitty movement can make the market swing wildly. Great when it's a return, but devastating when it's a loss.

A futures contract is an agreement to buy or sell a specific quantity of a commodity at a set price on a future date. This sounds confusing. It's not. That's a fancy way of saying that an apple cider maker signs a contract with an apple farmer agreeing to pay three dollars a bushel when the apples are ready in the fall. These contracts are standardized in terms of quality, quantity, and delivery time, traded on specific commodities exchanges like the Chicago Mercantile Exchange (CME) or the New York Mercantile Exchange

(NYMEX). PS. This is your first exposure to derivatives, which we will dig more into in the next lesson.

One of the earliest examples of futures trading comes to us from ancient Greece (I guess I wasn't done with the Greeks!). In ancient Greece, there was a philosopher and expert astronomer named Thales of Miletus. Through observing certain patterns in the stars, Thales anticipated that there would be an excellent, off-the-charts olive crop that season. Thales wanted to figure out how to monetize his research. He thought that if there were to be an awesome olive crop that he should purchase olive oil presses now, before they got scooped up closer to the harvest. Although Thales had a good feeling this prediction would pay off, he wasn't entirely sure. He was pretty confident in his astronomical readings, but it wasn't an exact science. So, he negotiated a deal with local olive oil makers: he would pay them a fee in order to get the right to all of their presses at the beginning of the harvest season. That way, at the beginning of the harvest, Thales could decide once and for all whether to buy the olive presses or not. Then the time to farm olives rolled around and Thales's readings were correct! There was an amazing crop, and when it came time to decide on whether to take the option and buy the olive presses, it was an easy yes.

Fast-forward a couple thousand years, and this is essentially how futures are negotiated today. As you may be able to see from this very early example, this is a type of security that is helpful for farmers and other people working in agricultural or other commodities-based industries. You can certainly get involved but it doesn't make as much sense for regular investors to go deep into this world because we don't have the same skin in the game.

Because derivatives involve a lot of guesswork on how the underlying asset's value is going to change over time, derivatives are dripping with speculation. In everyday life, speculation may be used synonymously with gossip and rumor. Like, "there's speculation she has a thing for the pool boy." In the financial world, the use isn't so different. Speculation is finance speak for a guess. This guesswork doesn't always pan out, and so derivatives can turn sour very quickly. Speculation is a loaded word on Wall Street because speculative investments have led to huge economic crashes, including the subprime mortgage crisis and the dot-com bubble. That's why derivatives are often an investment category that ends up being counted as a "liability" rather than an "asset."

Futures contracts attempt to have investors benefit from what happens to an investment in the future. If the contract goes up, a buyer gets more value while the seller takes a loss. That of course means the opposite is true: if the price goes down, the buyer suffers a loss, and the seller gets more value. When we talk about the futures market, we're often referring to the price of commodities like orange juice, metals, oil, and livestock. But people can also buy futures contracts for Treasury bonds, stocks, index funds, and cryptocurrencies. While futures contracts are now associated with Wall Street and all the hullabaloo therein, they did just initially become popular because it was such a useful tool for sweet farmers.

You know the expression "Youth is wasted on the young"? It's a phrase typically used by older folks to articulate that the Benjamin Button aging backward thing sounds pretty dang nice. That way, you get all of the wisdom of old age, with all the energy and physical ability of youth. With "youth is wasted on the young," our elders are complaining that the youthful glow and bouncy step comes at the wrong time. I think entrepreneurs feel something similar when it comes to money: when you're a business owner, the money comes at the wrong time. Say you are an aspiring farm mogul and want to have the biggest apple orchard and make the best apple cider in all the land. When the apple cider has been made and is ready to drink, that's when you'll get your money. But that's not when you'll need the money most, right? It's everything that comes before it: it's buying the orchard, the costs involved with taking care of the land, and it's getting the equipment for making apple cider (whatever that equipment is). When it all comes down to it, the farmer boss needs the money that she will earn from the apple cider before the apple cider can be made. That's where futures contracts become super helpful.

Let's say you were that pre-mogul farmer and you needed some cash for start-up costs. You could come to me and say, "Hey, Prof, are you interested in paying me $5,000 now, and in exchange, you can get all of my apple cider as soon as it's done?" Maybe I have an idea for distributing the apple cider to a local grocery store, or maybe I just love apple cider, but either way, I say yes, and we have ourselves a little futures contract. The lingo here is that the person who is paying the forward price (me, in this example) is the person who "goes long." The person who "shorts" the contract is the one who is selling the asset (you, the farmer, in this example).

Futures help suppliers and manufacturers lock in prices so that random changes in circumstances don't totally screw them. So, a farmer might want a futures contract for next year to ensure that, no matter what happens, they can get the market price for their crop. In essence, they are locking in a price to hedge against whatever the heck might happen. On the flip side, let's say a manufacturer makes canned soybeans and they want to make sure that they can count on a certain price for soybeans next year so that if the price goes higher, it doesn't screw up their business. Then the manufacturer is *going long*, and the farmer is *shorting* their soybeans. The same thing goes for an airline company that needs to lock in the price of fuel for their operations.

Not all brokerages trade futures contracts. The ones that do want to make sure an investor knows the risk of futures trading. They also may set a minimum net worth, or a minimum deposit requirement, just to get in the game. If the value of the contract goes down, you may get a margin call, which means you have to deposit more money in the account to keep it open. Remember: for a long time, this kind of trading was relegated to professionals with deep knowledge of the history and how these types of goods tend to move.

My advice is, unless you live, work, and breathe smack in the middle of corn or coal country, know how futures contracts work but leave them to the pros.

Commodity Stocks

Commodity stocks are just shares of companies involved in the production, exploration, or processing of commodities. These stocks are directly affected by the prices and demand for the specific commodities they deal with. Here are some examples of commodity stocks, categorized by the type of commodity:

Energy
- Exxon Mobil Corporation (XOM): A leading company in the oil and gas industry, involved in exploration, production, and refining.

- Chevron Corporation (CVX): Another major player in the oil and gas sector, with operations worldwide.

- Schlumberger Limited (SLB): A company that provides technology, project management, and information solutions to the oil and gas industry.

Metals and Mining

- Barrick Gold Corporation (GOLD): One of the world's largest gold mining companies.

- BHP Group (BHP): A leading global resources company that produces various commodities, including iron ore, copper, and coal.

- Rio Tinto (RIO): An international mining group that focuses on finding, mining, and processing mineral resources, including aluminum, copper, and iron ore.

Precious Metals

- Newmont Corporation (NEM): The world's largest gold mining company.

- Wheaton Precious Metals Corp. (WPM): A company focused on silver and gold streaming.

Agriculture

- Archer-Daniels-Midland Company (ADM): Processes ingredients for food and feed, including corn, oilseeds, and wheat.

- Deere & Company (DE): DBA (doing business as) John Deere, primarily known for its agricultural machinery.

- Mosaic Company (MOS): A producer of phosphate and potash, two essential nutrients for crop fertilizers.

Soft Commodities

- Bunge Limited (BG): Operates in the agribusiness and food sector, particularly in the processing and distribution of agricultural goods.

- Tyson Foods, Inc. (TSN): One of the world's largest processors and marketers of chicken, beef, and pork.

Specialty Chemicals and Materials

- Dow Inc. (DOW): Specializes in the production of chemicals, plastic materials, and other specialized products.

- Ecolab Inc. (ECL): Provides water, hygiene, and energy technologies, which are essential in processing various commodities.

Diversified Commodities

- Glencore PLC (GLEN.L): Engages in the production, refinement, processing, storage, transport, and marketing of metals and minerals, energy products, and agricultural products [Trades on the London stock exchange].

Utilities (Water)

- American Water Works Company, Inc. (AWK): The top dog when it comes to water and wastewater utility companies that are publicly traded in the US.

Now to be 100 percent clear, this is not me suggesting you run out and buy these stocks. It's just me giving you other options to start looking for exposure (in finance speak, "exposure" just means to invest in) to commodities. It's also a good exercise in starting to see the world as an investor. It's like if you've ever gone to see a movie with a sound editor, you know they cannot watch the movie like a normal person. They are constantly picking up on little glitches and pops. That's because they can't help themselves from using their expertise everywhere they go. They can't turn it off.

Being a "professional" investor is basically starting to invest your money, no special certificates or certifications required (well, except The Money School cert, but you're more than halfway there, so congrats, almost grad!). The more you get into it, the more you see the world in terms of investments. A great experience with the customer service people at your water company gets you wondering if it's a public company because they are doing something right. A cool scene about a coffee brand in a movie gets you looking up the ownership of that company. It opens you up to a new way of viewing the world through the lens of an investor. Green-colored glasses, anyone?

The Advanced Markets

ADVANCED MARKETS 201
Currencies

Who's ready to make money investing in money? Apparently everyone, because currency trading is the largest by volume of all investments out there. Six trillion dollars (say it Dr. Evil style) is traded every day. For comparison, only about $250 billion is traded daily on the NASDAQ in early 2024.

Some of the volume of currency trades comes from it being traded twenty-four hours a day, all over the world, versus the traditional stock market, which keeps the 9:00 a.m. to 4:30 p.m. ET hours of a recalcitrant employee who's basically daring the boss to fire him.

You may have also heard of currency trading referred to as "forex" trading, meaning "foreign exchange trading," and it's literally just that—trading currencies. It's based on the speculation of what these currencies will be worth, and it's not for the faint of heart . . . or for those who aren't up to date on geopolitics.

Only recently has currency trading opened up to the masses (read: us), much like commodity trading. What some call democratization, others may label "beware!" The only real statistic you need to know is that 75 percent of beginner investors walk away from forex trading empty-handed, because it's a market ruled by insiders. I'm not saying you can't become a kick-ass forex trader; I'm just saying don't join a David and Goliath fight without knowing which one you are. By the end of this lesson, you'll know which one you're destined to be.

FIAT WHAT?

Fiat currencies are ones that are backed by a government (as opposed to those that are decentralized, which we will talk about soon enough). They can be traded against each other, meaning a currency like the Japanese yen (JPY) may trade against the US dollar (USD). There are eight currencies traded most often, and seven pairs of these make up more than 80 percent of all trades. One half of each pair is always USD because the US is currently the largest economy in the world. The pairs are:

- Euro (EUR) / USD

- Great British Pound (GBP, nicknamed Sterling) / USD

- USD / Yen (JPY)

- USD / Swiss Franc (CHF, nicknamed Swissy, which sounds delicious)

- USD / Canadian Dollar (CAD, nicknamed the Loonie, which sounds adorable)

- Australian Dollar (AUD, nicknamed Aussie) / USD

- New Zealand Dollar (NZD, nicknamed Kiwi) / USD

The most traded pairing by far is EUR/USD, making it most popular for speculators because of its high volume.

FYI · IF COMMODITIES AND CURRENCIES HAD A BABY

There are some "commodity currency pairs" in forex. Investing in forex can be a way of indirectly getting exposure to commodities markets.

For example, Norway regularly makes the list of the top 20 oil-producing nations and the price of oil tracks with the value of the Norwegian krone. Some investors will choose to trade the krone instead of or in addition to oil futures.

As well as Norway, Australia, Canada, and New Zealand all have currencies that are influenced by the price of their chief commodities.

There are also minor currency pairings, known as Cross Currency Pairing, such as EUR/GBP, EUR/CHF, and GBP/JPY (note: those don't include USD). Like most things in the financial world, the currency's value is based on supply and demand.

For example, the price of USD goes up when other countries are importing more of our goods and goes down when there are too many US dollars in the world.

THE ROOM WHERE FOREX HAPPENS

Regular brokerages don't play in the forex party. To get into the rager, you need to use a forex-specific brokerage like MetaTrader that specializes in the foreign exchange market, offering the ability to trade currency pairs (for example, EUR/USD, GBP/JPY).

These platforms are tailored for forex trading and often include sophisticated tools for technical analysis, such as real-time currency price charts, technical indicators, and news feeds related to currency markets.

Forex brokers primarily make money through spreads (the difference between the bid and ask price of a currency pair). Some may also charge commissions per trade. They often offer high leverage, which allows traders to control large positions with a small amount of capital, but this also increases risk. They are regulated by different organizations than traditional brokerages, the Commodity Futures Trading Commission (CFTC) and National Futures Association (NFA) in the US compared to the SEC and FINRA. To be clear, forex brokerages primarily cater to active traders speculating on currency price movements, not long-term investors.

CONFESSIONS OF A PROFESSOR

BUTCHERING THE PIG

"So how is the new guy you're chatting with online going?" I asked my girlfriend Lena.

"I'm so done with dating. Done. Forever. All the apps are deleted," she said in a defeated huff.

"What?! What happened?"

"So all was going well with the guy. We talked for months at this point. Like every day. About everything. We developed this really deep connection, I thought. He invited me to Geneva with him where he was on 'holiday.' I was so excited," she said with a big breath signaling the story was about to turn.

"All that sounds great . . ." I said reaching for her arm in anticipation of whatever else was coming next.

"Well, see, he's older and richer and more well-traveled. He started taking an interest in my career and future. He said he wanted to help me build wealth on my own to make me feel more secure and confident even if he ended up treating me and paying for everything in our relationship," Lena said, her voice starting to quiver.

"Okay . . . well . . ."

"Oh my God! You specifically are going to think I'm a stupid idiot. Urgh, I can believe it . . ."

"Lena, I promise I'm not going to think that. You are one of the smartest, most accomplished women I know," I said reaching for a tissue I assumed she would need.

"He started showing me account statements of like a lot of money he was making, $50,000, $75,000 . . . it was all real. I thought. And then he said he could help me do the same thing and he would be there to be my backstop as I learned the ropes of investing in . . . oh, you know this stuff already but I didn't," Lena said, starting to cry but also talking quickly to explain herself to me.

"Investing in what, babe?"

"Well, he introduced me on WhatsApp to his broker. It was a Brazil number, but I don't know, they are all international. He had me download this thing called MT5 . . ."

"MetaTrader5? For forex?" I said, now knowing exactly where this was going.

"Yes, I think so . . . Damn, I should have called you earlier but it looked so legit. He showed me a demo account and made it seem so easy. My guy even put the initial amount of money in my account to get me going on a real one," she said.

"Oh, Lena . . . and let me guess. You started putting in your own money after that and then they showed you some increases in your account to get you to put more in and then when you tried to take some out they either told you there were high fees to do that or then started showing you that the account was way down and you lost your money or they disappeared?" I said so sad that she had fallen for a type of scam known as a pig-butchering scam where victims put real money in fake accounts.

"Basically yes. I put in $500, which is a lot of money for me. Then another $500 and they said my money grew to $5,000 at that point and if I had another $1,000, I could likely clear $10,000 in a couple weeks," Lena said, starting to tear. "But then my car broke down again and I thought it might be time to get a new one so I asked for even just half of my profits back. As soon as I said that, they showed me my account was down to $500. They said it was a fluke but maybe they could get it back if I gave them another $500."

"Ah, baby girl, I think you know that $2K is gone, right?"

"Well, then I got this message from him," she said grabbing her phone to read it directly. "'My dear Lena, ever since I helped you open up your real account, your interest and enthusiasm towards me has waned. I don't think Geneva is a good idea anymore as I don't feel the same connection with you.'"

"Can I see that? Can I write down all these numbers? And also I'm going to write back, okay?" I said, not really asking but taking charge of this.

"I mean, I guess what's the—"

"'I totally agree, my dear,'" I said as I started typing. "'I should have voiced my discomfort with a new and unregulated broker much earlier. Since I didn't get the chance to do that with you, I think it's best I send all of these messages, images, and numbers to the CFTC. Bisous, Lena.'"

And that, we did. Sweet Lena never saw that $2K, but she did get some sweet revenge. And she's back on the apps, in case you were wondering.

Be careful of the TikTokers, people on dating apps (this is a big problem, and many of the scammers play the long game), and even random WhatsApp messages from strangers who peddle forex as a get-rich-quick hack. It's just not. Well, actually it is . . . for them to get rich quick off you. Please don't fall for it.

CRYPTOCURRENCY

Cryptocurrency is digital money, meaning you can't see it, hold it, or stuff it under a sink for safekeeping, and it's traded on what's called the block-chain. The blockchain is a decentralized monetary system, free (for now) of any government control, that tracks all the trades made in the crypto world. During crypto's rise, stans believed that it would be a new hedge against inflation and economic instability, just like gold. But during times of market woes, crypto didn't act as the safe haven it was intended to be. At all. In fact, it moved in lockstep with the stock market, which is the exact opposite of a hedge for it.

There are a lot of cryptocurrencies other than the well-known Bitcoin, but I think that's really the only one worth double-clicking on. As famed economist Nouriel Roubini (the one who predicted the financial crisis) said on *Money Rehab*, the rest are "shit coins" hocked by "carnival barkers" who steal people's money to drive Lamborghinis and go to strip clubs in Miami. Yes, he said all that. He even came back on the show a year later and clarified that calling them "shit coins" was offensive to manure because manure is actually useful.

Digital currency's objective is to enable peer-to-peer transactions, decentralizing the need for overseeing bodies like banks or governments. While I don't think crypto is unseating the dollar anytime soon, crypto does have some elements that the good old dollar does not. For example, if you want financial privacy? You've got it with crypto. As I mentioned, cryptocurrency is decentralized, and instead of a central banking institution, it depends on a network of users that oversee the system. Cryptocurrency buffs would hate that I'm saying this, but the work that this network does is pretty comparable to what banks do—the network verifies that people spending the cryptocurrency actually have the coin to spend, and the network keeps track of these transactions and adds them into a big record known as the "ledger." Whenever you get lost thinking about it, just remember the ledger is basically a blanket term for a list of transactions. I remember this by repeating to myself: "l" for list and "l" for ledger.

To understand how the ledger works, you need to understand how crypto is created. I'll use Bitcoin as an example—because, again, practically everything else is you-know-what. Bitcoin is created in a process called Bitcoin mining. But I promise you, Bitcoin mining is not what you think of when you picture traditional mining. When you think of mining, you probably think of, well, a mine—with hard hats and caves and canaries. But Bitcoin mining doesn't happen in a mine; it happens on a computer.

This is the interesting part about Bitcoin. Anyone can mine Bitcoin; and you can do it anywhere in the world, so long as you have access to a computer. That makes Bitcoin completely different from government-backed currencies, like the US dollar. Can you imagine if anyone could print dollar bills? Not only that, but imagine that you could print dollar bills and do it at home, without even getting out of your pj's! If this was a thing, I would do it, wouldn't you? So why isn't everyone making Bitcoin?

Well, here's the catch. While you can mine Bitcoin through a computer—it's a pretty complicated process. In order to create one Bitcoin, you need to program your computer to solve billions of calculations per second. So, to quote the great poet Hilary Duff: "If you can't do the math, then get out of the equation." But if you can do the math, you can mine Bitcoin. As you can imagine, it takes a lot of heavy-duty computing equipment and energy to solve so many calculations (I personally am exhausted just thinking about it).

Calling the process "Bitcoin mining" is a bit misleading. To me, mining implies that you're doing some work to find something valuable, and then you get to keep it. In actuality, Bitcoin miners are doing work to upkeep the entire Bitcoin network, and in exchange for their work, they (sometimes) get rewarded with Bitcoin. It's a really brilliant system when you think about it. Cryptocurrency creators really wanted their currency to be defined by this decentralized network that keeps the system running; but how could they get people to join this network? How many people are so passionate about decentralized currency that they'd spend their time verifying crypto transactions? Not many, the crypto founders thought. So they created a system, where the incentive to upkeep the Bitcoin network is the promise of earning Bitcoin. Bitcoin mining happens in two steps.

Step 1: Confirming Transactions

Bitcoin mining starts by confirming transactions that folks have recently made with Bitcoin. As you recall, Bitcoin creators really want a decentralized currency, but this desire presented an issue: because while the creators did want decentralized currency, they didn't necessarily want unchecked currency. While Bitcoin fans eschew banks, banks do perform essential functions that prevent fraud. For example, if I went to Bill Gates and said I will take your $127 million home and pay for it in cash, Bill Gates would be able to go to my bank and say: "Hey, guys! Does Prof Lapin have this cash ready to roll?" At which point my bank would call me and say, "Prof Lapin! While you may be the illustrious professor of The Money School, you don't have $127 mil sitting in your checking account."

So, without that central figure guaranteeing whether someone is good for their money, how would Bitcoin prevent fraud? Bitcoin creators solved this problem with the network. Each time a buyer pays someone in Bitcoin, the transaction gets funneled into transaction limbo, known as transaction pools or memory pools (mempools as the kids say). It's the miner's job to then confirm whether the transactions in the mempools are legit. They check things like whether the person paying with Bitcoin actually has Bitcoin and that they haven't already spent their Bitcoin on something else.

Miners aren't just confirming Bitcoin transactions because they want to prevent fraud; they are confirming transactions because it's the first step on the road to earning Bitcoin. That brings miners to their next step . . .

Step 2: Creating a Block

At a top level, the next step is to take some confirmed transactions that are chilling in the mempool and group these transactions together in a unique combination. The unique combination of transactions acts as a key that opens a spot on the ledger. The Bitcoin ledger is built with blockchain technology, which is essentially a database that uses cryptography (aka codes) to make the information stored in the database ultra-secure.

In the crypto world, blockchain is where the network stores the records of transactions. Here's where we zoom in and things get a little clearer: blockchains were actually named somewhat intuitively. Information on verified transactions is stored in virtual compartments (or blocks) and those blocks are strung together in, yep, chains. Think of it like a bookcase, and each block is like a shelf. Once one shelf is filled up, you go on and start filling the next one. Only instead of books on a shelf, these blocks are storing the records of Bitcoin transactions. Once miners confirm transactions, their next goal is to add these transactions into the next block on the Bitcoin blockchain; thereby creating a record of the transaction on the Bitcoin ledger.

Here's where mining gets extremely competitive: Remember when I said that miners group transactions together that form a key to unlock the next block on the blockchain? Not every group of transactions will make a key. So miners need that supercomputing power to generate a ton of different combinations of transactions. The goal is to beat all other miners in making a combination of transactions that successfully unlocks the next block on the blockchain. When a block is added to the chain, it gets a digital time stamp. This helps miners verify and track transactions, by allowing them to see the timing and reference previous transactions. If you can do this, you will earn your payment: Bitcoin, plus any fees that were associated with the confirmed transaction you grouped together (more on Bitcoin transaction fees in a sec).

FYI

BITCOIN BOUNTY

A miner currently earns 3.125 Bitcoin for successfully validating a new block on the Bitcoin blockchain. That's about $200K at the time of writing this.

ONE IN 21 MILLION

Unlike how the Fed can influence the amount of money in circulation, Bitcoin has strict limitations on how many coins can be mined. There is a finite number of Bitcoins (twenty-one million). Once the twenty-one-millionth coin has been mined, that's it! No more new coins. At the time I'm writing this, nineteen million Bitcoins have been mined, but by the time you read this, that number will be higher. Under the current system, a new Bitcoin is mined approximately every ten minutes. It's estimated that all twenty-one million Bitcoins will be mined by 2140.

Here's the deviously smart thing: not only is mining hard, but it actually gets harder depending on how many people are on the network trying to mine. Cryptocurrency founders built the mining system this way to prevent against the value of the currency swinging haphazardly. Their thinking was: if, for example, it took one minute to solve the math required to get a block added on the Bitcoin blockchain, and one million people were mining all at once, then all twenty-one million Bitcoins would be mined in twenty-one minutes. That would mean that the entire finite supply of Bitcoin would flood the market all at once, which would drive the value of the currency down (remember: excess supply means lower value). Because Bitcoin creators are purists when it comes to value, they wanted a way to keep the pace of mining in check. Therefore, they programmed Bitcoin mining difficulty to be dynamic: the more people that are mining, the harder it is to get a block added on the blockchain.

Another way Bitcoin founders built for steady pacing of the new currency is to ensure that, over time, fewer coins would be awarded for each block added to the chain. In the earliest dates of Bitcoin mining, there were 50 Bitcoins awarded per block added to the blockchain. Bitcoin blockchain is programmed so that the number of Bitcoins awarded per block is cut in half every time 210,000 blocks are added to the blockchain. This happened in the spring of 2024. It takes around four years to add that many blocks to the blockchain. The next time the reward will be halved is 2028, when miners will be able to receive only 1.562 Bitcoins awarded per block.

I HAVE CRYPTOCURRENCY . . . NOW WHAT?

When I was at CNBC I befriended the assistant to one of the execs. We would normally be the first two people to get to the office every morning. Every day she would bounce into work with her boss's breakfast order: a carrot muffin and a green juice. Breakfast of champions. One day, she came in looking a little pale. That struck me as unusual because she normally took the stairs at least part of the way up to the office, which gave her this great, albeit slightly sweaty, glow. "Is everything okay?" I asked her. She started saying slowly: "Well, the big boss and I have the same colored credit card—if you look too quickly, they look exactly the same." She paused, looking down at the muffin in her hands. Then, she blurted out: "And I accidentally used his card for a bikini wax at the European Wax Center."

She was horrified, and I felt her pain, but it was hard to stifle the laugh. Her boss was easygoing; it was definitely not a fireable offense, and she knew it, but she was cringing at the thought of him going through his credit card statements and seeing a charge from the European Wax Center. She did the right thing and owned up to it and reimbursed her boss for the charge. I'm sure a lot of people have purchases like these—things that would be blush-worthy if anyone got a hold of your credit card statements.

It was 2010, the year after Bitcoin launched, so there were a few stories and rumblings about it. I'll never forget that she said, "I mean if I had that Bitcoin thing, I guess I could have gotten my wax in peace."

Well, she was right. The Bitcoin user interface is designed to ensure everything is anonymous. The issue, however, is that it's very difficult to spend your Bitcoin while staying completely undercover. To do that, a name has be linked to the account, and the blockchain usefully records every trans-action made by the account. Plus, if you used cash (rather than mining for them) to buy those coins in the first place, without some extra steps, your real identity is already linked to those coins. If you have a mix of coins that you got anonymously and coins you bought at an exchange and you keep them in the same wallet? Now both of those coins can be traced back to you too. So, how private is crypto really? That's TBD—but it's undeniable that it is *more* private, and further from the reach of oversight, than traditional currency but it's not completely anonymous. So my assistant friend's boss wouldn't find her wax transaction. But if she used Bitcoin to buy a bomb to blow up the building, he (via the authorities) would likely be able to figure it out. There are a couple of criminal cases suggesting that it's not nearly as foolproof a way to pay a hit man as many people think.

The Bitcoin Blue Check

If you're getting paid in Bitcoin, or buying something using Bitcoin, your transaction will need to be verified by the network. By now, we know this. But this process doesn't happen completely automatically. It's actually more like posting a job on TaskRabbit or Upwork; you let the network know you have a transaction that needs to be confirmed, and you detail how much money you'll give to the miner who gets it added to the blockchain.

Yep. Time to circle back to the fees. Remember I mentioned when a miner gets a block added to the blockchain they receive all of the fees associ-ated with the transactions in the block? This is where the transaction fees come in. If you're paying someone in Bitcoin, you'll essentially go to the network and say: "Hey, fam, I'm looking for a miner to verify a transaction of one Bitcoin that I'm sending. My rate for validating this transaction is

0.000001 Bitcoin." Bitcoin miners on the network see all of the transactions in the memory pool that have yet to be validated and can choose which ones to prioritize. Obviously, they'll try to scoop up the transactions that are offering the biggest fees. This can affect the amount of time it takes for a Bitcoin user's transactions to be verified.

Once a block holding your transaction is added to the blockchain, your transaction counts as being verified one time. Each block that's added to the blockchain after yours is another verification. Some people who accept Bitcoin as payment will consider themselves paid as soon as a transaction is verified once. But, more commonly, vendors will require three to six verifications before they consider your payment as legit. For example, if your transaction was grouped into Block #100, some vendors would not consider themselves "paid" until the greater blockchain had reached Block #105. The rationale behind waiting for up to six verifications is that there is a circumstance in which a cryptocurrency transaction gets reversed. It's unusual, but here's how that would happen:

1. *There's a battle.* Let's keep with our example and say that we just made a transaction that is now in the mempool. The most recent block added to the blockchain is #99, and miners are hard at work competing for the block #100 slot. Two separate miners, let's call them Thelma and Louise, solve the puzzle at the same exact time, and both get to add #100 to the blockchain. Your transaction is in the block Louise added to the chain.

2. *Confusion ensues.* This creates what's called a "fork" in the blockchain, where the chain splits in two directions. Consequently, miners can add block #101 to Louise's #100 block or to Thelma's #100 block. Pretty quickly, the network catches these types of forks.

3. *There's a tiebreaker.* The rule in the network is that there can't be repeat blocks, so either Thelma's or Louise's branch of the blockchain needs to be deconstructed. The rule is that the shorter chain loses; so if Thelma's branch has reached #104 block, but Louise's branch has only reached #102 block, Thelma's branch is the one

that gets to remain. Therefore, Louise's block #100, 101, and 102 all get unverified, and those transactions (including yours!) go back in the mempool.

On average, it takes around ten minutes for a transaction to be confirmed by the network. But because miners will prioritize validating the transactions that have the biggest fees, people who want their Bitcoin transactions verified have to choose: Do they want to offer a higher fee to get their transaction validated? Or are they okay waiting a while for a transaction to go through? As more transactions get added to the memory pool, the demand for miners to confirm transactions goes up. As a result, transaction fees creep up. The transaction fees can be as high as fifty-nine dollars, which could feel ridiculous if you used Bitcoin to buy something worth twenty dollars.

SO, TO BITCOIN OR NOT TO BITCOIN?

Despite recent bobbles in the digital currency market, crypto investing might just be here to stay, and we're starting to see the advent of crypto index funds. The thing about crypto is that a lot of people have gotten insanely wealthy trading crypto . . . *but many more people haven't.*

If after knowing all this and understanding that there's no intrinsic value, like it's not tied to gold or salt or any other asset for that matter, you're still looking to get some exposure to Bitcoin, know that buying Bitcoin directly isn't the only way to do that. Now this is *not* me telling you to get exposure to Bitcoin or to buy any of these. The SEC approved Bitcoin ETFs in 2024, which invest in coins and sell shares, which means that now there are lots of funds that allow you to invest in Bitcoin without buying coins yourself.

You might be wondering, "Um, don't we need bank or government oversight for this to work for the long run?" Now that is a great question, and currently legislative control is being fought for by entities like the International Monetary Fund (IMF) and the SEC. Also, our friends at the Federal Reserve's Oversight Program have started to oversee banks' cryptocurrency activities. This move is part of the effort to ensure proper regulatory compliance and risk management at least as it relates to banks' involvement with crypto.

> **MONEY TIP**
>
> ## GET A WALLET
>
> Buying and selling crypto is similar in practice to trading stocks, and you do so on exchanges like Coinbase, although you can also trade on Robinhood and Public, now, and on some traditional brokerages. Because crypto isn't regulated, you don't have the protections of traditional investment trading, meaning you can be hacked and lose your entire net worth in a keystroke, so it's important to protect your assets by using a digital wallet. Coinbase has one but there are tons of others depending on what you're storing and what you're optimizing for.

In the last two lessons we've gone from some of the oldest investments in history—gold and food—to cryptocurrency. For some investors, these may be a dynamic part of their portfolio. But for most of us, it will probably be secondary via an investment in companies in that sector or in ETFs that offer exposure without requiring as much in-depth knowledge. My advice is that you should invest no more than 1 percent of your assets in cryptocurrencies or anything risky like storing OJ in your swimming pool. And if you're storing sweaters in your oven, please stop. It's a fire hazard.

The Advanced Markets

ADVANCED MARKETS 301
Derivatives

While stocks and bonds are different assets, they have some general overlap. With both, investors purchase the security, and then they own it. The end. Derivatives play a whole different game because, as the name suggests, they are not necessarily outright assets. They are investment opportunities that *derive their value from another asset.*

Derivatives are different from buying stocks and bonds where investors are buying a financial asset (shares) and what they're paying is directly linked to what they're buying; the price is not derived from anything other than the exact asset the investor is buying. And to complicate matters further, derivatives are often valued based on projections of future market trends, which makes these securities highly speculative (read: the riskiest).

The derivatives market has gotten a bad rap, understandably so, from the 2008 financial crisis during which banks were selling such complicated versions of investments that they ultimately sank themselves, bringing the whole global financial world with them. But not all derivatives are bad or BS. Derivatives, if used correctly and responsibly, can help you derive some serious gains. Now, whether or not you should be taking big risks with your portfolio comes down to how much risk you feel comfortable with and how much risk makes sense given your overall financial picture.

POP QUIZ

ARE DERIVATIVES RIGHT FOR YOU?

1. How old are you?

   a. 45+

   b. 35–44

   c. 18–34

2. Your interest in the financial world looks like . . .

   a. Dipping my toes in.

   b. Wading knee deep.

   c. Diving right in.

3. What is the next big purchase you are focused on?

   a. Living a sweet retirement.

   b. My kids' college education.

   c. Nothing on the horizon, but a second house or car would be nice!

4. When will you be making your next big purchase?

   a. 5 or so years

   b. 10–15 years

   c. 15+ years

5. I expect my income to:

   a. Decline in the next few years; unfortunately, my job is on shaky ground.

   b. Stay the same. I'm tenured and have no worries that my salary will change significantly in the next few years.

   c. Increase! I am getting a raise or jumping to another job with a higher salary.

6. The amount of time you can dedicate to your investments is . . .

    a. Zero time.

    b. Five hours a month.

    c. I will be spending several hours a day. This is my full-time job!

7. You have experience in the investment world . . .

    a. Zero.

    b. I've been teaching myself (hello, I'm here after all).

    c. I have a background in financial services but am still in The Money School because I was embarrassed to admit that I didn't know terms everyone else *seemed* to know.

8. Your budget is . . .

    a. Airtight. I have everything budgeted to the penny.

    b. Comfortable. I have some wiggle room in my budget, and for the right opportunity, I would put some more money into investments.

    c. Flex! I have the cash to take on some big risk for a big potential reward.

9. Is your emergency fund in check and your debt paid down?

    a. Not quite. I have a plan to finish paying off my debt, but I'm not there quite yet; and I'm prioritizing paying off debt before really getting serious about my emergency fund.

    b. I've paid off my debt, and I'm almost done getting an emergency fund together.

    c. Yep! Debt is gonzo and emergency fund is on point!

If you answered all or mostly As, you're probably not in a position to take on a lot of risk. Either the idea of losing money makes you queasy, or you're in a position where you can't shoulder the risk of losing a lot of money. And by no means is that a bad thing! We all go through times in life when it makes the most sense to cling to our assets a bit tighter. You happen to be in that phase right now. That means that derivatives are probably not the best money move for you. Instead, your portfolio should focus on stocks and bonds—perhaps with a bit of a greater emphasis on the safer stuff.

If you answered all or mostly Cs, you might be in a position where you can risk-it-for-the-biscuit, and derivatives might be a good *option* for you (pun intended). But again, I'm waving the red flag your way: derivatives are complicated and have a history of screwing people over. If you want to get serious about derivatives, you shouldn't try to DIY your first move. Talk to a financial advisor and really hammer out the best derivative strategy for you.

If you answered all or mostly Bs, or a mix of As and Cs, you're likely best suited for a middle-of-the-road portfolio. You're in a good position to be investing, but it doesn't make sense for you to opt in to a really risky investment like derivatives. Instead, your portfolio should focus on stocks and bonds—likely with a greater proportion of stocks than bonds. Nonetheless, I do believe it's important to understand how all parts of our crazy financial system work to be the best investor in whatever you end up investing in that you can be.

YOU'VE GOT OPTIONS

As we're about to roll into derivatives, I want you to remember that you have the ability to purchase shares of stock. Such purchases fall into the "equity security" category. But there's also the option to buy a derivative security involving that same stock. You guessed it: with options.

Options are just what they sound like: purchasing one gives you the *option* to buy a stock or commodity at a set price in the future. There are two kinds of options: call options and put options. Call options give you the option to buy. Put options give you the option to sell.

Options are lower risk than futures contracts themselves since they come with an out. You are basically paying a small, token amount for the option to buy it at a certain date. Of course, you can choose not to pay when the time comes, but you will lose your deposit. The investor doesn't have to "exercise" or use their options. If the spot or current price of the asset is more favorable to the investor than their option price, they can say, "Psych, just kidding!" and go on their merry way. Essentially, investors will exercise the option only if their hunches were correct; if they weren't, they don't need to take the option. This way, options almost act like an insurance policy for investing decisions.

CALL OPTIONS

When you're looking at call options, you are looking at the option to *buy* a stock at a certain price. I remember the terminology by thinking of one of those old-fashioned telethons, where people call in to donate or to buy something. Or, if that doesn't jibe with you, try thinking of it like you're calling dibs on buying a stock at a certain price. Whatever trick helps the definition stick: call = buy.

As we go through some examples, there will be moments where it feels like a lot of information is being thrown at you. When that happens, don't panic! There's a foundational golden rule that you can always return to when things get a little fuzzy: the motivation for a call option is that you have a hunch that the price of a stock may go up, and so you want to be able to buy it now at a lower price. You may be thinking: *If you have a hunch that the value of a stock is going to go up, why wouldn't you just buy the stock now?* Well, with a stock option, you have the option to buy the stock at a certain price later on. So if your hunch is incorrect (happens to the best of us!) and the stock price actually drops, you can decide not to buy the stock at the price you reserved. When you decide to buy the stock, it's called "exercising" the option.

Let's dig into this concept with an example. Meet Lily Long. She likes piña coladas, getting caught in the rain, and stock options. It's New Year's Day, January 1, 2033, and part of her New Year's resolution is to make her money work for her. She's interested in buying stock in a company called The Money School Company. Right now, the stock price of MSKL is $15 per share. She thinks that this company is incredible (Lily is so smart) and that the stock price is going to climb in the next few months. She goes online to her brokerage company, and she looks at the list of people selling MSKL call options. That list is called an "options chain." Each entry is a different investor selling a call option for a different price. Typically, an entry in an options chain will look something like this:

EXPIRATION DATE: MARCH 18, 2033

ASK	STRIKE PRICE
$0.05	$20

The *expiration date* is important. It's the big day; it's D day where the "D" stands for decision. If Lily is to buy an option, she will need to decide on whether or not she's going to exercise the option by the expiration date. In this example, the expiration date is March 18, 2033. Now some fun facts:

Fun fact one: The third Friday of every month is when monthly stock options typically expire.

Fun fact two: Typically, with US options, you can exercise the option anytime up until the expiration date. In some other countries, you can only decide to exercise an option on the expiration date.

Fun fact three: The option price typically goes up the further you go out, because you're essentially paying for more time to decide whether or not to exercise the option. In your life, have there been times when you would have paid money in exchange for a little extra time to make a decision? I certainly know I've had a moment or two like that, where I wish I could have bought some more time.

The strike price is the term for the price that you will have the option to pay if you buy the option. But Lily can't just take this option for free. That would be too good to be true. Lily has to pay for the option, and that's where the *ask* comes in. The "ask" price is the price per share that you need to pay in order to get the option to buy the shares at the strike price on the expiration date. In other words, if Lily buys this option for the $0.05/share ask price, she will have the option to buy the stock at $20/share by March 18.

Stock options are typically sold as a bundle of a hundred shares; and yet, when you look at your pricing options online, you're going to see prices per share. That's an important thing to remember: even though it looks like Lily is buying the option to buy one $20 share at $0.05, she's not. We're talking about multiples of a hundred here. Don't get that twisted.

So, the *full story* is that Lily would need to pay for a hundred shares at the ask price of $0.05/share in order to have the option to buy a hundred shares of MSKL at $20/share. So what will Lily actually pay for the option? It will be the ask price multiplied by a hundred shares, or:

$$\$0.05 \quad \times \quad 100 \text{ shares} \quad = \quad \$5$$

This five dollars is neither a down payment nor a deposit. It is the amount that Lily pays to purchase the option. If she exercises the option, this does not count toward the amount she needs to pay to buy the stocks at the strike price. And if Lily does not exercise this option, she does not get her five dollars back.

If Lily buys the option, a few different scenarios could play out. Let's look at a situation where she does want to exercise the option and a second scenario where she lets the option expire.

Scenario A
(spoiler alert: this scenario means more returns for Lily)
On March 18, 2033, MSKL stock is trading at $25/share.

Investors typically exercise call options if their strike price is lower than the market price of the stock; because essentially what that means is that they get to pay less than what the suckers on the open market are paying for the same stock. In other words, they get to buy a stock for a discount! And who doesn't like a discount? When the market price is bigger than the strike price for a call option, it's called being "in the money." That one is easy to remember because it doesn't take a lot of brainpower to wonder whether being "in the money" is a good or bad thing. We want to be *in* the money. Duh.

In this scenario, MSKL stock is trading at $25/share. So, Lily will say, "Hell yes! You bet your bottom dollar I'll be exercising my option to buy this stock at $20."

Of course, exercising the option to buy the stock does mean that you have to buy the stock, which is going to cost you a hundred shares of the stock at the strike price, or:

$$100 \text{ shares} \quad \times \quad \$20/\text{share} \quad = \quad \$2,000$$

If Lily had not bought the option all those months ago and wanted to buy a hundred shares of MSKL on the market, that would have cost her a hundred shares of the stock at the market price, or:

$$100 \text{ shares} \quad \times \quad \$25/\text{share} \quad = \quad \$2,500$$

Lily knows that she made a good deal. But how good of a deal was it? The way to answer this question is to determine your net change, which will tell you how much you've benefited, or lost, from the investment decision you made. An important note here: we're calculating change, not profit. Lily will profit from these MSKL stocks only once she sells them. In this case, the general calculation for net change is:

$$\text{MARKET PRICE OF 100 SHARES} \quad - \quad \text{PREMIUM} \quad - \quad \text{STRIKE PRICE FOR 100 SHARES} \quad = \quad \text{NET CHANGE}$$

Using this formula to calculate Lily's numbers, we get:

$$
\underset{\substack{\text{(current price} \\ \text{of 100 shares)}}}{\$2{,}500} \;-\; \underset{\text{(premium)}}{\$5} \;-\; \underset{\substack{\text{(the strike price} \\ \text{for 100 shares)}}}{\$2{,}000} \;=\; \$495
$$

A $495 gain. Nice! Piña coladas are on Lily tonight.

Now let's look at a scenario where Lily would not want to exercise the option.

Scenario B
(spoiler alert: this scenario means less returns for Lily)

On March 18, 2033, MSKL stock is trading at $16/share.

Yes, the value of the MSKL stock is up from the price when Lily bought the option ($15), but that doesn't matter to her. The only thing that matters to Lily is whether the market price on the expiration date ($16) is higher than the strike price ($20). In this case, no.

Thankfully, Lily only paid for the *option* to buy a hundred shares at $20/share. She does not *have* to buy them. As we now know, with call options, when the stock price has exceeded the strike price, it's said to be "in the money." In a situation like Scenario B, where the strike price is higher than the market price, the option holder is considered to be "out of the money." Boo. Bummer. Sure, it sucks, but the condition where an investor is "out of the money" by the expiration date happens all the time. In these situations, investors simply choose not to exercise the option. But let's do the math to get a sense of what the loss would be if Lily were to exercise the option: she would need to pay $20 to buy shares that are valued at $16, and she'd need to pay for a hundred of them:

$$
\underset{\substack{\text{(current price} \\ \text{of 100 shares)}}}{\$1{,}600} \;-\; \underset{\text{(premium)}}{\$5} \;-\; \underset{\substack{\text{(the strike price} \\ \text{for 100 shares)}}}{\$2{,}000} \;=\; -\$405
$$

And . . . uh-oh. That's a $405 *loss*. We do not want that. So, it's an easy decision. Lily does not take the option to buy the shares at the strike price. If she really wants to buy the shares still, she's better off buying them at the $16/share current price. But she does not get back the five-dollar premium she paid for the option, and she's not paying your bar tab this evening.

Scenario C:
You Might Not Want to Try This at Home

There's another way this could play out. It's not something I recommend newbie investors integrate into their financial habits, but it is something that happens every day on the financial markets. And the more you understand how the markets work, the more you can see various factors that affect your own portfolio and profits. Okay, so let's say it's the beginning of March 2033 and MSKL stock is trading at $24, $4 over Lily's strike price. So she's in the money. Yay! But wait, what if Lily doesn't have $2,000 on hand to buy the stock? Or she doesn't want to deal with the hassle of buying the stock and then trading it to get her money back? Or she's just somewhat of a gambler?

Well, in this situation, Lily can sell her option. That is, she can sell the contract she bought for five dollars to another trader for more than she paid for it. Since the option is in the money, and there's time left on the contract, she will be able to make a profit. But she has to act fast before theta decay sets in. ("Theta decay" is a sinister way of saying that options become less profitable the closer they are to the expiration date.) This is a way that some investors make money when they don't have enough cash on hand to buy a hundred shares of anything. I don't recommend it for anyone but the most advanced traders because it can get complicated fast, but I do want you to know that it happens and generally how it works.

Here's the golden rule that we can draw from these examples: with call options, the hope is that you reserve a low price for an awesome stock that ends up skyrocketing in price per share. The best-case scenario is: that happens, you exercise the option, and you get a discount on a great stock. The worst-case scenario is that the market price is lower than the strike price you bought with your option. In other words, you can buy shares cheaper on the market than it would cost you to exercise the option. In that case, you do not exercise the option, and you lose whatever premium you spent to buy the option. But on the bright side, you didn't lose a ton by sinking all of your money into a bad stock.

I know this concept is a bit dizzying. For me, I didn't really internalize these scenarios until I started doodling notes to myself. Here's roughly what my doodles looked like at the time. But feel free to make whatever graphs, shapes, charts, or arrows you need to bring this concept home to you.

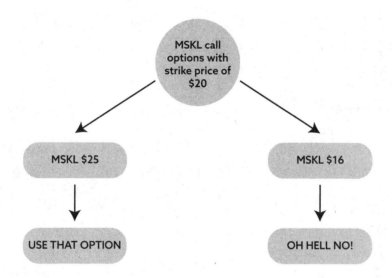

PUT OPTIONS

In contrast, put options are the options to *sell* a share at a certain price. For example, say Lily owns shares of a company called ICK. Currently, the market price is $25/share. But say that Lily has concerns that ICK's price may tank. Maybe she knows that the company is undergoing an investigation and the report will be published on March 15. She's worried that the results of that report may be negative and that the stock price will plummet. For whatever reason, Lily not only has a sneaking suspicion that the stock price will fall, but she also believes that today's price of $25/share is the highest ICK's price will ever reach. She may want to purchase the option to sell her shares at the current market value. If this isn't quite clicking yet, stay with me; it will soon.

So, Lily pulls up a list on her brokerage account of the put options for ICK. She sees the intel below:

EXPIRATION DATE: MARCH 18, 2033

ASK	STRIKE
$0.05	$25

Again, if Lily buys the option, a few different scenarios could play out. Let's look at a situation where she does want to exercise the option and a second scenario where she lets the option expire (no spoiler alerts this time).

Scenario A

On March 18, 2033, ICK stock is trading at $20/share.

In this scenario, Lily has the option to sell her shares at $25/share, when the market price of the stock is $20/share. In other words, she has the opportunity to sell her shares for greater than market value. Will she do it? Hell yes, she will! Let's look at how much this move saved her. If she had not purchased the put option, she would have sold her hundred ICK shares at $20/pop: 100 shares × $20/share = $2,000.

But Lily will exercise her option to sell her hundred shares at $25/share:

$$\underset{\substack{\text{(current price} \\ \text{of 100 shares)}}}{\$2{,}500} - \underset{\text{(premium)}}{\$5} - \underset{\substack{\text{(the strike price} \\ \text{for 100 shares)}}}{\$2{,}000} = \$495$$

By exercising the put option, Lily was able to make $495 more than she would have by selling her shares on the open market. Woohoo!

Scenario B

On March 18, 2033, ICK stock is trading at $30/share.

In this scenario, Lily has the option to sell her shares at $25/share, when the market price of the stock is $30/share. The choice here boils down to whether or not she wants to sell her shares for less than what she can get on the market. Her answer: hell-to-the-no! Why would she give the market a discount on the shares that she bought with her hard-earned money? She wouldn't!

As you can see, with put options, the conditions under which you'll exercise an option are flipped from call options; you will exercise a put option when the strike price is higher than the market price. This should really drive home how investors use options like an insurance policy. We gave an example of Lily wanting to pursue a put option because she had reason to believe that the price of ICK shares would go down. By buying a put option, Lily created a little safety net for herself so that she didn't lose too much.

CHEAT SHEET

When the strike price is less than the market price:

- you will choose to exercise the call option.
- you will let the put option expire.

When the strike price is greater than the market price:

- you will let the call option expire.
- you will exercise the put option.

THE LONG AND SHORT OF IT

In long positions, you're the one buying the option. You could be buying the option to buy a stock at a price (call option) or sell a stock at a price (put option), but the option is yours. You are in control! You can also *sell* options, and take the "short position."

Taking a short position with options is very risky, and I don't recommend The Money School students try this at home. That said, I do think that you should understand how this money move works. Remember: "short" is not the opposite of "tall" in the financial world and it just means you think something is going in the pooper.

A short position is basically the opposite of Lily's transaction. Lily bought options with her long position; in a short position, you are the one selling the options. Let's say that the person on the other end of Lily's transaction is named Sammy Short. When Sammy takes a short position on a call option, he is selling the option for an investor to buy his shares at a certain price. When he is taking a short position on a put option, he is selling the option for an investor to sell him the shares for a certain price. The tricky thing about selling options is exactly that: you are selling the option—the decision-making power, the control—to another investor.

Let's revisit the last example. Say Lily had purchased the put option from Sammy. In nonfinance speak, this means that Sammy sold Lily the options to sell her ICK shares to him at $25/share. That would mean that if Scenario A played out—and on the expiration date ICK shares were trading at $20/share, and Lily decided to exercise the option—Sammy would *have* to buy Lily's shares at $25/share. Meaning, he would *need* to spend $2,500 to buy shares that are actually worth less than what he's paying. In short (pun intended), with short options, you might need to fulfill an obligation that ends up with you losing money.

CHEAT SHEET

1. With a long position, you're buying the *call option* because you think the price will go up.

2. With a long position, you're buying the put option because you think the price will go down.

3. With a short position, you're selling the call option because you think the price will go down.

4. With a short position, you're selling the *put option* because you think the price will go up.

Here's something that adds an extra element of risk with options: you can sell the option for an investor to buy shares from you, even if you don't own the shares. In other words, Sammy Short could sell the option for Lily Long to buy a hundred shares of MSKL stock from him even if he doesn't have a hundred shares of MSKL stock. Why would Sammy do this? The biggest reason would be that he is confident that Lily will not exercise the option. Therefore, Sammy has no need to own any shares. But if Lily does exercise the option, Sammy, to put it simply, is screwed. If you sell the option to buy shares that you don't own, it's called an "uncovered option," or a "naked option." Do you want to be naked in the middle of Wall Street? No? Let's keep our clothes on, please and thank you. So stay away from naked options. (Or naked anything with your money, really.)

MORE BIG SHORTS

There's a short position and shorting a stock. We've covered the first. Now let's dive into the second: shorting a stock.

Here's how to think about it: Say you borrow my car, and as soon as you pull out of my driveway, you post the car on Craigslist and sell it. Rude, but I forgive you. For easy math, let's say you sell it for $10,000. That $10,000 is now in your pocket. Then, you wait. You wait because you're betting that the cost of the car will go down once a new model comes out. So, until the shiny new model comes out, you're sitting pretty.

Let's fast-forward. After a year, I'm about to come back into town after traveling the world and doing other awesome things, and by the time my plane lands, you need to have my car ready . . . or one that looks exactly like it. Let's say the value of my car (yep, the car you sold) goes down to $8,000. Well, this is the moment you've been waiting for. You buy that car, which is the very same make and model that you borrowed from me and sold at $10,000, but now you're buying it back at $8,000. Then, you give the car back to me, you thank me for letting you borrow it for a year, and you're able to pocket the $2,000 difference.

But there's a chance this move doesn't pan out. Say supply chain issues have led to a car shortage and the value of my car went up while I was away. Now I'm back and you owe me a car. If the price of the car has gone up to, say, $12,000, you will need to purchase the car at that higher price, meaning your nifty investment trick backfired and you are out $2,000. Ouch. That tricky maneuver? That's essentially what it means to short a stock.

With all the warnings in mind, here's how you short a stock:

STEP 1: HAVE A MARGIN ACCOUNT: To short sell, you need a margin account with your brokerage, not just a standard cash account. A margin account allows you to borrow money or stocks from the broker to make trades. You'll have to apply specifically for this. The brokerage reviews the application based on your trading experience and credit history. Approval usually takes a few days.

STEP 2: CHECK THE REQUIREMENTS AND AVAILABILITY: Short selling has specific requirements, including minimum account balances and margin thresholds. Also, not all stocks can be shorted. You need to make sure that your brokerage has shares of the stock available to borrow. This is known as "stock borrow" or "stock loan."

STEP 3: PLACE A SHORT SELL ORDER: Once you've picked a stock, place a short sell order through your brokerage platform. You specify the number of shares you want to short and at what price. The brokerage then borrows the shares and sells them on the market on your behalf.

STEP 4: MONITOR THE MARKET: After your short position is established, monitor the stock's performance closely. Remember, if the stock price goes up instead of down, you'll lose money. Short positions need careful monitoring. Be prepared to act quickly if the market moves against you to minimize losses.

STEP 5: BUY "INSURANCE," KNOWN AS A "COVER": If your bet pays off and the stock price falls, you buy the same number of shares at the lower price to cover your short position. "Buying cover" is extra credit and therefore not required. But you basically return the shares to your brokerage, and the difference between the selling price and the buying price is your profit, minus fees and interest.

Again, *this is an advanced investing move (which is why it is in the most advanced level of the "Advanced Markets" course) that involves extra risk.* I don't recommend it for inexperienced investors. So please be aware of the risks and understand the costs. There are costs associated with short selling, including interest on the borrowed shares and possible fees. These can eat into your profits or add to your losses. Not to mention when you buy a stock outright, the worst possible scenario is you lose 100 percent of your money. When you short a stock and it goes way up, there's no limit to how much you can lose.

Understanding derivatives is helpful for understanding the way a lot of traders and hedge funds make their money (Hi again, GameStop!). I promise you *can* understand how they work, but it's totally normal if they aren't intuitive for you. I'll let you in on a little secret. You can be very successful as an investor and never mess around with options at all. While they can be a great little tool to help protect your portfolio, they are a more advanced technique, so don't feel compelled to use them until you're comfortable with them.

Your Portfolio

YOUR PORTFOLIO 101
Funds

D o you like the good news or bad news first? I always like to take the bad first. So here goes . . .

Bad news: I could have spared you all the individual investment info and told you that my favorite (and the easiest) way to grow long-term wealth is by just investing in funds. But you wouldn't have truly appreciated that cheat code without knowing *why* the concept is so glorious. It's like eating a piece of fancy layer cake. It's delicious either way, but you appreciate the skill more if you've ever tried to make one from scratch yourself.

Good news: now you know how to make fancy investment layer cakes *and* are about to know where to buy the greatest ones done by the pros. In this lesson, we are going to dive into the world of funds: public and private.

PUBLIC FUNDS

When I say "public funds," I mean ones that anyone can go and purchase now through a brokerage, easy peasy, no connections required. Some public funds are passively managed, meaning they track something like an index or a smattering of securities and that's it. Actively managed funds are run by humans (managers).

Generally I have nicer things to say about passive funds than managed funds, though I can't guarantee that you will make more money in a passive fund than a managed fund or even that one is a better fit for you than the other. At the end of the day, either managed funds or passive funds will be good vehicles for you on your road to financial freedom; the key difference is that managed funds are constantly changing direction in order to attempt to get to the destination faster, while passive funds stick with the original route and will really only reroute if a road ahead is closed.

The main reason I'm hesitant about managed funds are the fees. As I hope I've illustrated here and at length in my other books, there are far, far too many fees in finance for my taste. It makes sense because we aren't dealing with charity here; we are dealing with financial companies, giving peak-capitalism energy so money has to be made. I just wish it could be distributed a little better, but that rant is for another book.

Some of the most common overall platform fees to look out for are:

Transaction Fees: Every time you buy or sell a stock, mutual fund, or other investment, you might pay a transaction fee or commission. Although many brokerages now offer commission-free trades, some still charge per transaction. These fees, while small individually, can add up over time, especially if you trade frequently.

Account Maintenance Fees: Some brokerage accounts charge annual or monthly account maintenance fees. These are especially egregious if your account balance is low.

Performance-Based Fees: Some investment accounts, particularly those managed by financial advisors or robo-advisors, might charge a performance fee. This means the fee is based on the account's performance and can vary year to year.

Knowing if you're paying investment fees requires a bit of diligence and understanding of where to look. Review your account statements; your brokerage or investment account statements should itemize any fees you're charged. Look for terms like *commission* or *sales charge*. These statements often come monthly or quarterly and should be reviewed regularly. Many brokerage firms provide detailed fee information on their websites once you log in to your account. Some even provide a fee summary or an expense calculator to help you understand the costs associated with your account. If you have a managed account, like one through a robo-advisor or a financial advisor, review your management agreement; it should outline the fee structure, including any performance-based fees.

As (I hope) I drove home in level one of this course when it came to funds, being aware of all kinds of fees is crucial because even small fees can compound and significantly impact your long-term investment returns. Here's what an initial investment of $50,000 looks like over time with seemingly insignificant differences in fees with 7 percent returns. Bottom line: paying just 2 percent more can erase almost two-thirds of your investment value!

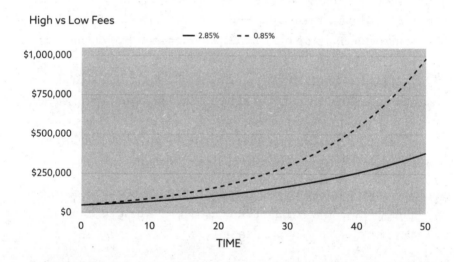

High vs Low Fees

The other reason I'm meh about them: managed funds, by definition, have humans involved. Humans, by definition, are imperfect. Don't get me wrong: some fund managers are brilliant and have made their clients oodles and oodles of money. But most don't.

They may be victims of their own success. As the fund gets larger, it becomes harder to move money around. Investing $100,000 in one company doesn't do much to the stock price. Investing millions absolutely will. Warren Buffett has complained about this very phenomenon saying that "anyone who says size does not hurt investment performance is selling. . . ."

With managed accounts, you have to trust that the people managing your account are going to act in your best interest. That is a lot of trust, and trust isn't cheap. With passive funds, you don't have to worry about whether or not you should trust the manager making investment decisions, because *there is no manager*. I generally recommend index funds to new investors because they are tried and true, and because the only person making the investment decisions is *you* (and emotionless computers).

INDEX FUNDS AND CHILL

As a quick refresh: an index is a collection of different stocks, grouped by a certain set of parameters. Analysts create indexes to help investors track changes in prices across these collections of stocks, so that they can decipher market trends. When you hear stock market reporters saying, "the Dow is at blah-blah," "the S&P 500 is at XYZ," and "the NASDAQ is at la-di-da level," they're talking about the three main indexes. Similarly, when reporters say things like "the market is down" or that it's "trending" in a certain direction, they're likely making those observations by tracking an index that they think represents the market as a whole.

While these three indexes track the heavy hitters and iconic brand names, the market is more than a few big names. There are other indexes, including the Russell 2000, Wilshire 5000, and the S&P SmallCap 600, that keep tabs on the smaller players. When you buy into an index fund, you are basically buying a little bit of all of the companies within that index, without buying shares in the individual companies. It probably goes without saying now, although I will just say it: like all other funds, there is diversification built in because you're buying a mishmash of different companies; this makes index funds less risky than stock picking because if one company fails within the index, you have all the others to prop it up. Not only that, but companies that no longer make the criteria get delisted from the index.

Here's the major pull of index funds: they don't need a Wall Street suit deciding who is in or out at the party. It's all passively managed, and anyone in the index makes the guest list here. Since you don't need nearly as much (wo)manpower behind the scenes, these funds are way more budget friendly. The result? Index funds offer an 80 percent discount in fees over actively managed mutual funds.

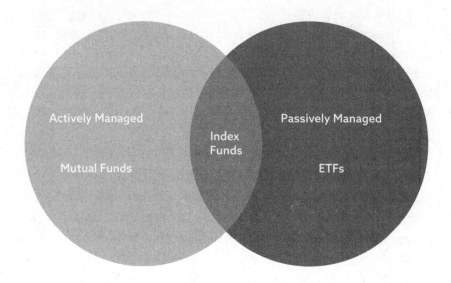

Here's where the distinction gets a little tricky. Index funds can be ETFs or mutual funds. But not all ETFs and mutual funds are index funds. There are some actively managed ETFs and a lot of actively managed mutual funds. If you want an index fund that is an ETF that tracks the S&P 500, you can take a look at ticker symbols SPY, IVV, or VOO, for example. If you want a mutual fund that tracks the S&P 500, you can look at VFAIX, FXAIX, or SWPPX. Each ticker has a slightly different fee, but basically they are all the same. The major difference between SPY and SWPPX, for example, is that you can buy SPY and other ETFs all day long but SWPPX and other mutual funds only once a day. Also, VFAIX is Vanguard's mutual fund that tracks the S&P 500, FXAIX is Fidelity's, and SWPPX is Schwab's. Usually you can buy those only on their respective platform; so if you trade on Schwab, it's SWPPX for you while you can buy SPY, IVV, or VOO on any platform.

These funds are all tracking the same group of shares and perform about the same over time.

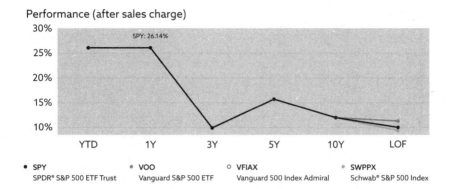

Performance (after sales charge)

If you really dig into their holdings, you can find teeny, tiny differences between the various funds.

SPY		VOO		VFIAX		SWPPX	
As of 12/31/2023		As of 12/31/2023		As of 12/31/2023		As of 12/31/2023	
30.77% of all holdings		30.81% of all holdings		30.81% of all holdings		30.60% of all holdings	
Apple Inc	7.01	Apple Inc	7.02	Apple Inc	7.02	Apple Inc	6.97
Microsoft Corp	6.96	Microsoft Corp	6.97	Microsoft Corp	6.97	Microsoft Corp	6.92
Amazon.com Inc	3.44	Amazon.com Inc	3.44	Amazon.com Inc	3.44	Amazon.com Inc	3.42
NVIDIA Corp	3.05	NVIDIA Corp	3.05	NVIDIA Corp	3.05	NVIDIA Corp	3.03
Alphabet Inc Class A	2.06	Alphabet Inc Class A	2.06	Alphabet Inc Class A	2.06	Alphabet Inc Class A	2.05
Meta Platforms Inc Class	1.96	Meta Platforms Inc Class	1.96	Meta Platforms Inc Class	1.96	Meta Platforms Inc Class	1.95
Alphabet Inc Class C	1.75	Alphabet Inc Class C	1.75	Alphabet Inc Class C	1.75	Alphabet Inc Class C	1.74

While the variation in assets owned is fairly small, the variation in the amount of assets invested under management is unimaginably large. Both Vanguard funds have $980 billion under management, but SWPPX only has $80 billion under management. Assets under management is a key figure to look at when researching a fund because it's a way of measuring the success of a fund since a higher number means more have trusted it with their money. It can also be used to calculate . . . fees. I know, it always goes back to fees. Mutual fund managers who grow their assets generally like to be rewarded with higher fees. So while a bigger number of assets under management can mean that a fund is successful, it can also mean that being part of that successful club can cost you some extra money.

Performance (before sales charge) -1Y

SPY
SPDR® S&P 500 ETF Trust

VOO
Vanguard S&P 500 ETF

VFIAX
Vanguard 500 Index Admiral

SWPPX
Schwab® S&P 500 Index

FYI — UNHUMAN ERROR

Even in the land of index funds, where human error takes a back seat, we're not completely error free. An index fund may not nail the perfect match for its underlying index and that's called a "tracking error." For example, a fund may invest only in a sampling of what's in the market index. Depending on how the stars align, this discrepancy can swing either way, a net positive or a net negative.

Generally speaking, few investors—even the most renowned fund managers—beat the market. Those who do beat the market put an awful lot more time into their investments than I would ever want to. (If I did, I wouldn't be able to write these books!) So, after my own cost-benefit analysis (cost being the time I spend managing my investments compared to the benefit of money I get from them), low-cost S&P index funds 500 are my go-to investments. I personally like to use a discount brokerage without having to put a ton of research into stocks all the time. I can automatically invest, month after month, by dollar-cost averaging, ignoring the ups and downs with the confidence that my investment will grow in step with the overall market, which has only gone up if you look at the data sets over long periods of time. My favorite kind of data sets.

Market Capitalization Funds

Another way to break down index funds is by market capitalization. There are four main buckets.

- Large-cap value funds invest in companies like those in the S&P 500 that have a total market value of $10 billion or more. The "value" part is more than a number; it's a trusted vibe. "Value companies" are ones with low price to earnings (PE) ratios, hinting that they're strong players trading below their "book value." Typically, these funds offer consistency and lower volatility.

- Large-cap growth funds focus on companies that are expected to grow rapidly. You guessed it: on Wall Street, the opposite of "value" would be "growth." Often, these companies don't pay dividends. It's not that these companies are in dire straits; rather they're go-getters, hungry for expansion. For them, growing means skipping the dividends for shareholders and socking that money right back into the company. The vision is that the investment will mean even more money in the pockets of investors in the future. For large-cap growth companies, we are talking about the heavyweights here like Meta, Apple, Amazon, Netflix, and Alphabet.

- Medium-cap funds are out here looking for those Goldilocks companies to invest in. By the way, medium-sized for Wall Street is still $2 to $10 billion. These funds see a lot of volatility because the companies in them are still hitting their stride, but there's also a potential for higher returns.

- Small-cap funds are made up of small companies, or companies with a market value of $250 million to $3 billion-ish.* Many of these companies are fresh faces when it comes to publicly offered shares, making investing in them a bit more of a gamble.

---

* These are general guidelines, and a fund's valuation may fluctuate.

Those are the main buckets, but of course, there are sub-buckets and sub-sub-buckets. For example, just like there are large-cap value and growth funds, there are medium-cap value funds and medium-cap growth funds. It's an endless nesting doll of funds, I know. Deciding which "cap" is better for you depends on your investing goals, and how much time you have to achieve them.

Bond Funds

Did you think index funds were just for stocks? Nope, bonds are invited to my favorite party too. The upside of bond funds is that you don't have to buy a whole bunch of different bonds. That's instant diversification across all the bonds the fund owns. Plus, when it comes to government bonds, they are super annoying to purchase directly at TreasuryDirect .gov. Trust me on this one or mosey on over there yourself to experience the horror of 1990s UX/UI firsthand.

The fund might own dozens or even hundreds of bonds, from which they pass on interest payments to investors, after they subtract expenses. Because the fund is a pool of a bunch of people's money, it allows you to get exposure to expensive bonds for much less than you would be able to on your own. Plot twist: There's no guarantee of a fixed return like with a lone bond. The fund's price fluctuates, so you get the price it happens to be when you sell it. Don't worry, you still get the benefit of those sweet interest payments, but unlike a solo bond it never fully comes to maturity. When you cash out, you get back whatever someone else is willing to pay for your share.

The biggest risk to these bond funds is interest rates. As you remember, the price and interest rate work like a seesaw. So, when interest rates go up, the price goes down. The funds with longer maturities tend to have more interest rate risk, which is also known as "market risk." As we've seen with that "just" 1 percent difference again and again, it will eat into your earnings big-time. The number you want to look at to get a sense of this is the "duration." Duration is different from maturity. There's a whole bunch of nonsense math to it, but all you need to know is that the longer the duration, the more volatile that bond fund is likely to be, and the shorter the duration, the less volatile it is likely to be. If you're getting serious about bonds, it's worth doing a deep dive on the math because it gauges the greatest risks you'd face.

When researching bond funds, I would first filter by fees. You're looking for a bargain here, ideally something below fifty basis points (which we now know is 0.5 percent). Say the fund earns an average of 6 percent, but the expense ratio is 1.5 percent, then the net yield to you is 4.5 percent; whereas with a 0.5 percent expense ratio, you'll get 5.5 percent. Over time we *know* how impactful that 1 percent can be. Next, I would consider:

- Thirty-day SEC yield, which is how much investors got in the last month (this is not fixed like it is when buying the bond itself)

- Types of bonds included (government, municipal, corporate, and so on)

- Credit quality of the bonds (remember, AAA is the best)

- The average term to maturity, or duration, of the bonds in the fund

ETFS

Not all ETFs track the S&P 500 or other indexes. There are ETFs that track just about everything. There are ones that track commodities (raw materials like gold and natural gas, and agricultural products like grains and beef and everything else we learned about in our lesson on commodities). It's not just traditional investments here; there are ETFs for everything from cannabis companies to crypto. If there's an area of the market that you think will go up, rather than delving into the deep details of each company in a specific sector, you can opt for an ETF in the industry and catch the wave of potential gains that way.

Some ETFs curate their assets based on their values and governance. So, if ethics are your investment guiding star, you can find an ETF for that too. Because of the proliferation of these funds, it's extra important to do your homework and study up to make sure that the ETF you're investing in is legit. Sure, it's funny to buy shares of TOKE or emotionally rewarding to invest in a fund that claims to support women. But be sure that you peek past the advertising materials at the actual holdings of these funds. Many of them hold shares of companies that may not have much to do with their stated mission.

ETFs are lower-cost fund options that let new investors get into the game, often for less than $100 per share (or even fractional shares), whereas there can be minimums of more than $1,000 to invest in mutual funds. Like stocks, ETFs trade all day long. This differs from mutual funds, which are bought at a set price at the end of each trading day. So, unlike mutual funds, you *could* buy an ETF at noon and sell it at 2:00 p.m. But don't. It's a strategy day traders use to gamble on potential rewards. It's not a strategy for the sustained, consistent growth that you need if you want to be Most Likely to Succeed at this school.

MUTUAL FUNDS

We need to double-click on one of the OGs of the fund world and even the investing world at large: mutual funds. When the modern version launched in 1924, they created whole new ways of investing. We're talking about the early days of the telephone, okay? Fewer than half the population had hot water; they weren't in the bath buying fractional shares with a tap of a screen. It was a whole process to buy a stock. But buying a mutual fund meant that regular folks could have access to an expert who would buy and sell stocks on their behalf.

It took a while for them to really catch on (the end of the 1920s were not a great time for investing), but by the '80s mutual funds were crushing it. They remained incredibly popular through the '90s. While they are no longer quite as dominant as they once were, they remain a large percentage of retirement accounts like 401(k)s and IRAs.

But what the heck are they, anyway? Well, mutual funds are named quite intuitively. If you opt into one, you are signing up to pool your money into one fund with many other investors who "mutually" buy into different investments like stocks or bonds. That money is then managed by investment professionals. The big appeal with mutual funds: we all want help managing our money, but it's pricey to have a big, fancy firm handle your portfolio. With mutual funds, you get your money managed, but because you participate with a larger group of investors, it's much more affordable. This model essentially allows investors to get a group discount on professional investment management.

I know this all sounds pretty great, but now I'm going to hit you with the catch: mutual funds are perhaps the biggest culprit of sneak-attack fees. Just like a magician, many mutual funds try to misdirect your attention to "something shiny over here" instead of what's actually happening—that is, them charging fees that eat into your return. You may think because your "expense ratio" is low and because you invest in "no load" mutual funds (meaning there is no sales fee or commission loaded on when you buy the fund) that you are a good bargain shopper. Well, wait a second. I'm not going to make you read a hundred pages of fine print to figure these fees out, but I will encourage you to go to sites like Bankrate.com to help you decode the fees on any mutual funds you have now as well as fees associated with additional investment vehicles you might be looking into for the future.

Of course, it's in the best interest of fund managers to make these fees look super small, even if they're not. Insiders call funds with excessive fees "fee factories," which, like the "farm factories" that value profits over the ethical treatment of animals, set you up for suffering before you even start. I mean, who actually calculates ahead of time to see how fees will impact their investments long-term? Students of The Money School do, that's who. Someone who makes $100,000 per year can end up paying about $300,000 in 401(k) fees in her lifetime[*] if she's not careful. Seriously. So I'm going to teach you to be careful but also take advantage of the type of fund if it makes sense for you and your goals. I'm not going to let you work the equivalent of three extra years in fees when you could retire in style.

Let's start by unpacking what those fees mean. Here's a cheat sheet of the five most common additional fees to look out for:

- Expense Ratio: This is a fee that investors are charged to cover the fund's marketing, distribution, and administrative costs. This fee usually costs investors between 0.5 percent and 1.5 percent of what they've invested, with an average of 1.3 percent. Like HOA fees, the fund's fees are due year in and year out and may be raised at any time.

---

[*] Assumptions: $1,000 initial investment; $2,000 annual contributions; 7 percent annual return; 4 percent fees.

- Transaction Costs: When fund managers buy and sell shares on behalf of the fund, there are costs involved with each trade. Some of these costs can come from listing the shares and other practical matters. But some of them are charged by the fund managers. Remember, mutual fund managers do a lot of trading, but not out of the goodness of their hearts. It's how they make a living. The size of the brokerage, market impact costs, and spread costs make the transaction costs the steepest fee in mutual funds (even more than expense ratios) at an average of 1.4 percent.

- Soft-Dollar Costs: This is like an expense account for fund managers to pay for extra stuff like research and reports. The fee is usually only tenths of a cent, if you have $50,000 under management for thirty years the cost may only be $150, but it is one more factor to consider when looking at a fund's pricing.

- Account Fees: These are maintenance fees just to keep an account open. Some funds also have exchange fees or redemption fees as part of your account.

- Sales Charge (Load): This charge is either paid when you purchase the fund or when you exit it. It's usually expressed as a percentage of your investment.

It would be one thing if mutual funds were the best investment on the planet. Maybe then, I wouldn't need to specifically shame them? Or just maybe then their fees would be worth it? Well, they are not. And far from it.

Nearly all (96 percent!) of actively managed mutual funds don't beat the market. That's right. Let that fact sink in. And then compare it to what happened when researchers used a computer program to simulate the results of monkeys throwing darts at the stock pages of a newspaper. While this sounds adorable—and somewhat dangerous—they found that your average monkey outperformed the index by almost 2 percent. Worse yet, when they (the researchers, not the monkeys) inverted traditional strategies, they found they often performed even better. To be clear, these are funds that are actively trying to *beat* the market, not passively managed funds, which are trying to *match* the market.

Now, I'm talking about the ones on Morningstar, the most popular service for evaluating mutual funds. Here you can read all about the track record of the dude (sadly, it's mostly dudes, only 26 percent of funds have any women on the management team at all) who acts as the fund's puppeteer, picking its investments. They spend a lot of time researching the perfect smorgasbord of offerings. But it's all a lot of hot air once you dig into the data. (Also, they should consider hiring monkeys. They probably charge fewer fees.)

The Morningstar rating, which is on a scale from 1 (worst) to 5 (best), is a make or break for mutual funds: just like most shoppers pick the best reviewed products, 75 percent of investments go to 4- and 5-star funds. A good rating is so important that mutual fund companies often do some magic tricks when one of their funds fails. They drop crappy ones and ride the track record of the good ones. It's not breaking news that many online reviews are fake. If the crummy little spot down the street can fake a Yelp review, you better believe that questionable mutual fund companies with millions or billions on the line are going to pull out all the smoke and mirrors to keep starry-eyed investors coming back for more.

Instead of getting caught up in the ratings, fees, and hoopla of actively managed mutual funds and their high fees, you could be putting your money into passively managed ones (à la a certain very special fund I'm going to tell you about next), which come out with the same if not better performance because they "track the market." The "market" is what most fund managers can't beat. Let's say another recession happens like back in the early 2000s, and you lose a decade of stock market gains seemingly overnight. Now, if you have a low-cost, low-fee setup, that will suck—but not as much as if you have, say, 3 percent in fees. If you put $100,000 in at the start of the decade and paid "just" 3 percent in fees, then at the end of the decade you would be down almost $30,000 in fees alone. Regardless of what happens to the market, the fund managers win.

I've already sounded the alarm bell on the hype around mutual funds as they relate to high fees, and also that most of them don't beat the market even though they are "professionally" managed. But that's not the only catch with mutual funds. You have to be careful that you are holding your mutual fund in the right type of account, or it could cost you money on top of the fees. Every quarter, mutual funds pay dividends that are taxed at the end of the year. Not only that, if the fund sells assets and realizes a gain, you could be taxed on your share of those profits as well. Since mutual funds are designed to set up and forget, my suggestion is to keep these long-term, dividend-paying investments growing inside tax-deferred accounts like a 401(k), IRA, defined-benefit plan, annuity, and so on, so that you're letting them compound in a tax-free environment (or a future tax-free environment in the case of Roths) to minimize the blow. "Prof, you sound like a broken record. I get it—check out the fees." Well, you're right—and I'm sorry I'm not sorry for drilling this into your head. Your future fee-free self will thank me.

You might be worried and think, *My work 401(k) only includes mutual funds. Should I go my own way?* Well, first compare all the offered funds. Some of them may have lower fees. If they are all high-fee funds, there's only one question to ask: Does your company match contributions? Because if they do, max out your matching contributions but nada more.

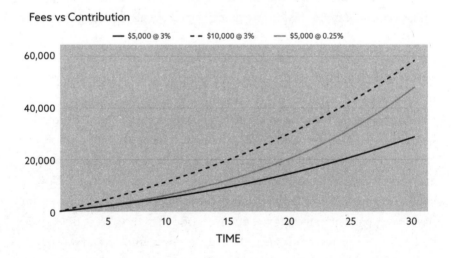

Fees vs Contribution

In this chart you can see what difference those extra "matching" contributions make. The bottom line is $5,000 a year in contributions with a return of 7 percent and 3 percent in fees. The middle line is $5,000 a year— same return but much smaller fees at 0.25 percent. And that juicy top line? That's your $5,000 a year, plus your company's $5,000 a year match even with those nasty fees of 3 percent. So don't pass up matching contributions just because of fees. But do you see the difference between the bottom and middle line? Do you see what I am talking about? Fees really, really matter. Okay, I'm done.

Alternative Mutual Funds

Alternative mutual funds follow the basic template of a traditional mutual fund: they pool the money of individual investors, a financial advisor picks the assets, and then they do all that SEC registration jazz. But unlike traditional mutual funds, which generally just stick to stocks and bonds, *alternative* mutual funds are looking for just that: alternatives. "Alt funds" can have a strategy built around options, or they can invest in companies that aren't publicly traded. Others may be focused on foreign currencies or commodities.

Now, fair warning, some of these exotic strategies might crank up the risk meter. If you are eyeing alternative investments, scout around for passively managed funds that have the same focus before committing to the actively managed mutual funds. If you're committed to the idea of investing in an alt mutual fund, be sure that you understand the strategy they employ, and that they have vetted the management team.

Target-Date Funds

The darlings and the fastest growing segment of the mutual fund community these days are target-date funds, sometimes called lifecycle funds. They're commonly found in retirement accounts, but you can also buy them as a more general investment tool. You'll know them when you see them because they always have a year in the name. They're named things like Vanguard Target Retirement 2045 Fund Investor Shares (VTIVX) or Lifecycle Index 2045 Fund Premier Class (TLMPX). Essentially, you give your brokerage a target date of when you want to take your money out, whether it's your retirement age or your honeymoon or some other date that you choose. Then the brokerage works to figure out the right balance of securities to go into that fund based on that date.

Target-date funds sound pretty perfect, but there are some hang-ups that many experts won't tell you about because they think you're not smart enough to understand more than the basics, or they believe target-date funds are better than either investing everything in your own company's stock or doing nothing. The number one thing that pisses me off about how the financial community educates people on this product is that they don't explicitly say that this is a target for a *date*, not for the *amount* you get on that date. According to a recent survey, about half of the people thought they wouldn't lose money in these funds and that they would magically get exactly what they wanted when they wanted it when their date arrived. I know, it sounds crazy when I put it that way, but it's true. There is absolutely no guarantee of what you will get on your target date. Additionally, not all rates of return are the same on all funds.

My second little annoyance with target-date funds is that they operate on the assumption that you need more bonds than stocks in the mix the closer you get to the target. Generally, bonds are a safer investment than stocks, so that makes sense on the surface. Think seesaw again. Bond prices tank when interest rates go up. The assumption with target-date funds is that the seesaw is stocks and bonds. That is not correct all of the time. For example, during the 2008 recession, *both* stocks and bonds fell, which means your fund would have been on the floor if that was your target date.

I get why someone telling you to "pick your date and we got the rest" is alluring, for sure. We all want an "easy" button, right? Just know that target-date funds can be more expensive than mutual funds and more volatile than some of the marketing makes you believe.

FYI — WTF IS A FOF?

A "fund of funds" is a real thing, and technically target-date funds are FOFs. It's what it sounds like. A fund that invests in other funds. Oh, Wall Street . . .

I know I sound like a mutual fund hater, but I'm not. It's like what I say to people who get a financial advisor who is not an RIA (Registered Investment Advisor): it's not ideal, and you can't lose sight of the fact that advisors from big banks and brokerages are hawking their own products and books, hard stop. But, for them, maybe it's better than having no financial person at all. Same situation here. If choice freaks you out or you honestly just don't want to deal with your own allocation over the years, then whatever variety of mutual fund your heart desires is a better choice than doing nothing at all. Just remember, they are basic. Their assumptions are for the "average" person. We are many things, but basic or average definitely isn't one of them.

REAL ESTATE FUNDS

If you're itching to start investing in real estate but your wallet's not quite there yet, or if you're still scouting for the perfect spot, don't fret. There is another, and IMHO sometimes a better, way to get those returns. Real estate investment trusts, or REITs, are a way to get into real estate without the hassle of property management or spending the next five years saving up for a down payment.

REITs are technically trusts, but traded publicly just like stocks. You can buy into a REIT mutual fund, index fund, or ETF. You can also buy individual REITs from bigger real estate companies like Simon Property Group (the folks behind a lot of malls) or Public Storage (the storage company is an REIT and traded on the S&P 500). You can get into them for as little as twenty-five dollars.

I know, I know. We all know someone who flipped a house or snagged a parking lot and made bank IRL and is stoked. I love that for them. But here's the deal—buying one building or one home is betting that that one particular property will increase in value. If it works out, ah-mazing. But if it doesn't, you've likely lost all your money. There's no diversification to mitigate the risk of that one lone parking lot. Not only do REITs offer a way to invest in multiple properties at once, they also offer some sweet perks. Many REITs offer fatty dividends giving you a steady stream of income. When they increase in value, and you want to cash out your investment, you can just sell them! No need to reno the kitchen or hire an inspector. As an extra bonus: unlike corporations (like the ones behind stocks), REITs don't pay corporate income tax, so you're pocketing more of that dough in dividends.*

So, what's the catch? Well, REITs track the overall real estate market and when that's bad, REITs are bad. Just think back to the 2007–2008 bubble: REIT investments took a nosedive and fell 20 to 40 percent. Ouch.

REITs can also take a beating when interest rates are low. That's because investors normally look for greater returns elsewhere in the market; when interest rates are high, investors gravitate more toward bonds or other fixed-income investments. REITs are not "bond substitutes" as some think—they are equities and carry that risk—but their movements more closely resemble the bond market. Because they tend to have a lower-than-average correlation with different areas of the market, they make a good hedge in your overall portfolio. And the best part? You don't need to worry about fixing a clogged toilet or hiring someone to handle tenant gripes.

PRIVATE FUNDS

Any of the funds we've talked about, whether passive or active, are open to anyone who wants to invest, so long as you have the money. Private funds, however, are not just taking orders online. The more chichi funds like venture capital funds and hedge funds don't just let anyone throw money at them. I know, it will never make sense to me that it's a privilege to be able to give your money to someone. But the more you get into the investing world, the more doors open for you so it's worth knowing what it might look like behind them.

VENTURE CAPITAL FUNDS

The most important question to ask before hanging with venture capitalists is: Do you like wearing fleece Patagonia vests? If your answer is yes, then let's delve deeper.

Seriously, though, there's a real draw to trying to find that unicorn, meaning a private company valued at more than a billion dollars. Start-up investing

---

* Post their fees, of course.

feels like panning for gold, and I'd be lying if I said I didn't feel a rush when I snag a seat at the cool kids' VC table, evaluating and guiding tech companies.

There's more than one way to invest in venture capital. Your involvement could entail nothing but being an LP (limited partner) in a VC fund who writes a check and waits for them to send back (hopefully) an even bigger check in a few years. Or you could be really involved in the companies the fund is invested in by getting regular updates and/or helping by making intros, because helping the fledgling companies succeed means a bigger payday for you.

It's also possible to invest in a company as an individual investor. These are traditionally known as "angel investors," but you've probably heard of them under another name—sharks. The crew over at *Shark Tank* are all angel investors. While the show pays them a salary, not all of their investments have paid off. Mark Cuban reports that one in four of his companies makes a profit, and Barbara Corcoran reports that she only gets a return on one in ten companies. This shows just how tricky it can be to turn a profit in the start-up biz.

Unless you have a TV show that funnels you investment opportunities, finding ideas and companies worth investing in can be tricky. That's where VC funds come in, if you can get into one. Minimum investment amounts vary, depending on the fund. And the minimums are definitely the minimums, due to the risk involved. You also need to be an accredited investor, which is basically a way of checking that you have enough money to afford taking on a big risk. To qualify as an accredited investor, you have to check off one box from these requirements although it's all done on the honor system.* It's worth noting that the personal income and net worth requirements were set in the '80s and have not been updated to reflect forces like inflation, but here they are:

---

* More people may soon be eligible. In 2023, a bill (H.R 2797) passed in the House that would allow people who passed an "accredited investor" exam to be able to access these more elite investments even if they didn't make the financial minimum. As of this publishing, it hasn't passed into law.

✓ OR ✗	YOU HAVE:
	$1 million in net worth, excluding a primary residence (as an individual, or pooled with a spouse)
	$200,000 in annual income for the last two years (as an individual, or $300,000 if pooled with a spouse)
	A Series 7 license, Series 65 license, or Series 82 license
	Certain professional certifications, designations, or credentials; or other credentials issued by an accredited educational institution
	An LLC with at least $5 million in assets

The biggest risk with venture investing is fairly obvious—there's a good chance you can tie up all your money for a long time and have no liquidity. No bueno. The start-up phase, before a company is profitable, or before it merges with another company, can be long. It may even be unending. One report from Harvard found that at least 75 percent of venture-backed start-up companies fail. If the companies you invest in fail, you could lose everything you put into them. So, if you're looking for stability, look elsewhere.

But the reasons so many people are fascinated by it is because when it works, it really works. This is what Uber's early "cap table," or list of investors, looked like. Needless to say, their return was insane:

INVESTOR	AMOUNT INVESTED	VALUE OF INVESTMENT AFTER TEN YEARS
Garrett Camp	$220,000	$1,092,412,800
Mitchell D. Kapor	$75,000	$372,412,800
Cyan and Scott Banister	$50,000	$248,275,800
Jason Calacanis	$25,000	$124,137,000

INVESTOR	AMOUNT INVESTED	VALUE OF INVESTMENT AFTER TEN YEARS
Shawn Fanning	$25,000	$124,137,000
Jason Port	$25,000	$124,137,000
Joshua Spear	$30,000	$148,968,400
Mike Walsh	$5,000	$24,827,400
Oren Michels	$5,000	$24,827,400

Venture capital fund owners, founders, or majority stakeholders are often called the general partners (GPs), and investors are referred to as limited partners. The general partners usually keep a portion of the money that limited partners put in as their investment. Once the investment starts paying off, general partners often charge a management fee and carried interest (carry) on a percentage of the profits made on fund investments. This is called a 2-and-20 model, meaning they collect 2 percent of the fund's total for operational/legal/Patagonia costs and a 20 percent carry on the profits the fund makes. And some of the biggest do a 3-and-30 model!

Only about 2 percent of VCs account for something like 95 percent of profit generated by more than a thousand firms out there. The top 25 percent of VC funds have an internal rate of return (IRR) of 25 percent. That's nothing to sneeze at when, over the same period of time, the S&P 500 returned about 12 percent.

So how do you get in if you're an accredited investor? Well, I got into a fund because I happened to end up on a hike with the firm's GP. But if you don't climb hills with anyone who's started a fund, you can look at accredited VC matchmaker sites, like FundersClub, Crowdfunder, iSelect, or EquityZen.

But what if you're not yet accredited? (Listen, you did just buy the book; give yourself some time—you'll get there!) There are also sites for you, such as AngelList, SeedInvest, and MicroVentures, or you could even buy into a publicly traded company like Hercules Capital (HTCG) or Horizon Technology Finance (HRZN).

The truth is: while you're less likely to do well in a VC fund than you are in the broader market, it can be an awful lot of fun, and that has its own merits. That's why I recommend you limit your investment to no more than 5 percent of your net worth. And by the way? If you want to rock one, I'm sure you'll look excellent in a vest.

PRIVATE EQUITY FUNDS

Some people want the ability to invest in private companies without having to go the whole tech founder route, and I get that. This is where private equity firms come in. These investment firms raise money from investors to form PE funds. These funds either take over publicly traded companies or buy out private ones and function as the majority shareholders. Sometimes they hold on to these companies and receive a dividend. More frequently, they increase a company's profitability and then sell it. In the last few years this market has exploded, and these funds have doubled since 2016.

But this isn't the only place that private firms are making big bucks. There's also the private credit market. This is like a top-secret bond market where nonbanks and investment firms, like private equity firms, can loan money to corporations at a rate they negotiate directly. During the last decade or so, when bonds were paying a very low rate of returns, this market exploded. It offered the diversification of bonds, with better returns—but yes, more risk.

To invest in a PE fund, you need to be an accredited investor and usually have a big chunk of cash on hand as the minimum buy-in. There's a big range here, but usually the absolute minimum is $250,000 and that's to buy into a feeder fund. Generally, $5 million for an individual is considered the starting amount.

Directly investing in these types of funds may not be available for you because, honestly, they are exclusive and weird. But let's put our "Think Like an Investor" hat on. Is there another way to invest in the companies running these funds? Yes, yes there is. A few of them are publicly traded, including Apollo Global Management (APO), Blackstone (BX), and KKR (KKR, but you could have guessed that). To take the guesswork out of picking one, there are also private equity ETFs like Invesco Global Listed Private Equity ETF (PSP),

ProShares Global Listed Private Equity ETF (PEX), and Complete Destiny Tech100 (DXYZ). This is where that fund of a fund thing comes into play. You may not be able to buy into the fund you would like to buy into directly, but you may be able to buy into a fund that will pool your money with other investors in order to be able to buy in that way.

It sucks that this sort of high-yield investment, between 10 percent and 15 percent for the last ten years, is so difficult to get into. It feels like you need money to make money, and when you're struggling the hardest it feels like you're shut out of the biggest returns. But now that you're serious about investing, I'm sure you'll be an accredited investor, hobnobbing with Henry Kravis and George Roberts* themselves soon enough.

HEDGE FUNDS

If you know me, you've probably heard me tell this story about a boyfriend I had from high school. He told me he wanted to be a hedge fund manager—and I thought the dude wanted to get into *gardening*.

Hedge funds are instead named after what hedge fund managers aim to do: hedge their bets. When these managers spot a market trend, they're not just diving all the way in. They're also throwing some cash in the opposite direction. By doing so, no matter what the market does, they should see some gains in the portfolio. For example, the overall trends of the stock market tend to be inversely related to the price of gold. In other words, gold and the stock market are on opposite ends of a balance beam: when the stock market is trending upward, the price of gold falls; and when the stock market dips, the price of gold bumps up. If hedge fund managers think that the stock market is going to swing up overall, they still will throw some money into gold, just in case.

Unlike mutual funds, hedge funds aren't confined to certain investment strategies. They can invest a wide array of assets, including stocks, bonds, commodities, and even more off-the-beaten-path investments like distressed securities. The aim is big returns. The biggest of the big. And they're not afraid to deepen their investments with a good bit of borrowed cash, which is a move known as leverage. Used in a sentence: "Jim's hedge fund is leveraged

---

* KKR was started by Jerome Kohlberg, Henry Kravis, and George Roberts. Kohlberg died in 2015.

up the wazoo with the debt they have for that alligator milk bet they made."
So, super high risk for super-duper high reward is their MO.

Hedge funds are to mutual funds what a private members-only pool with
$18 drinks is to the community pool. They're both pools, but the rules are
different and so are the costs. Like mutual funds, investors' money is pooled
together for hedge fund managers to, well, manage.

I know it may seem like hedge funds are the cool kids who are saying
"You can't sit with us" unless you have all the money. While that's part of it,
it's also for your own good. Hedge funds are much less regulated than other
funds and are the riskiest. Therefore, the SEC has set these qualifications for
hedge fund participants—essentially so that the only people who can invest
in hedge funds are people that have the money to lose and not be homeless.

There are a few questions you should have clearly answered before you
get into bed with a hedge fund:

- How are you getting your money back?

- When are you getting your money back?

- How is it being invested?

- Who is investing your money?

- Are they qualified to manage your money?

- Do they have any disciplinary history in the industry?

The last three questions should be easily answerable by looking up
the fund's information in the SEC's Investment Adviser Public Disclosure
(IAPD) database at adviserinfo.sec.gov or the Financial Industry Regulatory
Authority's (FINRA's) BrokerCheck database: brokercheck.finra.org. It's
important to check and double-check before wiring any money. Do it for
the victims of Bernie Madoff's $50 billion hedge fund Ponzi scheme who
wished they did.

CONFESSIONS OF A PROFESSOR

SUSSING OUT THE SUSPECT

It was 2:00 a.m. and I was on my way out the door to head to work the early morning shift when my phone lit up.

"Nicole, I have the biggest story of your career," the text read.

I was intrigued and I had a thirty-minute car ride to suss out what this was about.

"Who is this?" I wrote.

"I can't tell you in writing but I would like to meet you and potentially give you an exclusive interview."

Having my fair share of stalkers, I said, "Respectfully, I cannot meet someone in person I do not know. What else *can* you tell me?"

Then my phone rang from a blocked caller. I figured it was him and answered.

"This is Nicole—who is calling?"

A deep but shaky voice on the other end said, "Hello, Nicole. This is <so-and-so major disgraced hedge fund manager I sadly can't fully disclose because legal won't let me>."

"Oh," I said, knowing who it was immediately. His hedge fund had just collapsed and he was out on bond awaiting trial.

"I would like to tell my side of the story. I am innocent. I did not lose any investors' money. I am an honest man who worked up from nothing and just want the people who helped me do that to believe me. I have all the evidence and would like to show it to you," he said.

We arranged to meet.

Over the next few weeks, my producer and I met with this guy in a conference room filled with reams and reams of papers and stacks of binders. The research led to more questions than answers—this was not casual reading. What became clear is that regulations about what information hedge fund managers can and can't get from sources is hard to define. What is allowed and what isn't is nebulous at best. What's more is that law enforcement isn't—how could they be—well-versed with the intricacies of the financial regulations they are tasked with upholding.

After a few meetings, another 2:00 a.m. text: "With all the legal proceedings going on, I can't continue with our interview. Thank you for your time."

The next year, he was convicted by a jury and sentenced to over a decade in prison.

While there have definitely been some bad actors in the hedge fund world and practices that lie in the gray zone, there are also a lot of "rock star" fund managers with cult followings like Ray Dalio, the manager behind Bridgewater Associates. For some he's become a lifestyle and mindset guru outside of the investing space. Other funds are known for being far more quantitative and algorithmic, like Renaissance Technologies and Two Sigma.

But you don't need these big names, with their big fees, to make respectable returns. There are also passively managed index funds that are plodding along and matching the market. Whatever fund, or mix of funds, you pick, make sure you understand the way the fund is set up and what types of assets it includes. This will be important in our next lesson, which is all about how to pick and choose which assets to hold in your portfolio. Some of those strategies are straight out of hedge funds and from masters like Ray Dalio. So turn the page to learn how you can hedge your own fund.

YOUR PORTFOLIO 201
Asset Allocation

Think of your portfolio like your personal financial ecosystem. Just like a real ecosystem needs biodiversity to stay strong, your wealth creation thrives on diversification across different types of assets. This means spreading your investments around so if one thing goes south, the other parts can pick up the slack.

In this lesson, we will go over asset allocation recommended by some of the financial GOATs like Ray Dalio and Warren Buffett. You can take your cues from the greats or you can ignore those guys altogether. I'll also give you the "textbook" allocations, too, if that's more your speed.

We will also review your hopes and dreams. Remember, hopes and dreams have price tags. Hopes and dreams without plans are just wishes, and wishes are awesome, but they don't get you to the long-term, lasting, generational wealth you want. But the right asset allocation will.

PUT IT ALL TOGETHER

Let's take a beat here and define *portfolio*. This isn't a collection of the best paintings you've ever made. In the broadest sense this is everything you own with a measurable value. So your home, the treasury bond your grandmother bought you, and the value of your checking account could be considered part of your portfolio. However, here we're looking at all the assets you own for the purpose of building wealth. What that mix looks like is very personal. It could be your investment account, your life insurance policy, and your home. Or it could be your deferred compensation plan and an investment property. Some of this will be determined by external factors like your job's retirement plan, but you have a lot of agency here as well.

Constructing your own investment portfolio is all about you: your goals, your dreams, and your stomach for risk. To start, tell yourself what you want. And if you don't really know what that is—in a way you could clearly articulate it to others—try these questions:

1. What's my dream life?

Maybe you're aiming for early retirement, buying a mansion, or setting up your kiddo with a free ride through school. My dream life is not your dream life. We know by now that comparison is the thief of joy. The antidote to that is to clearly define what "having it all" means to you and stick to that definition. That way, when you're scrolling on social media and you see someone on a yacht and feel crummy about your life, ask yourself, "Self, was that really *my* goal?" If you look at what your goals are honestly (maybe you want to have a house fully paid for in Nashville decked out with rocking chairs from Cracker Barrel and juicy trusts set up for your kids and grandkids), maybe you'll realize a yacht isn't in your financial dreams, after all. Your life, your goals, your rules. The cool thing is that you get to write them, so you're destined to win if and only if you don't keep moving the goalposts on yourself midgame after Tiffany posted a picture of herself in Ibiza. Again.

2. How spicy am I?

Your tolerance for risk will influence the mix of assets in your portfolio. While there are hard factors like time and budget that may influence your risk level, some of it will simply come down to personality. If you can handle it hot, seriously investigate the more advanced lessons of The Money School. But there is a sweet spot for success: it doesn't mean to be too risky, and it also doesn't mean to play it too safe.

3. When do I want my dreams to come true?

The length of time you plan to invest can greatly affect your asset allocation. A longer investment horizon usually means you have time to take more risks. This extra time means you can be slightly riskier with what assets you pick for your portfolio. Conversely, a shorter horizon might mean picking safer assets, even if they have a lower return, just to avoid having to recover from any setbacks.

THE GOLDEN RULES OF INVESTING

Your portfolio management is an ongoing process. It's not a one-and-done deal. For it to be the most effective, it needs to be able to adapt to life's changing seasons and the shifts in the financial weather (aka short-term market moves). While your portfolio won't stay the same, the rules will. Here are the four golden rules you should keep in mind when balancing and rebalancing your portfolio:

Rule 1: Stay Disciplined—Don't let the weather mess with your head. Stick to the plan, and watch those investments grow at their own pace.

Rule 2: Keep Costs Low—Be the fee police of your own investments.

Rule 3: Be Tax Efficient—Protect yourself and your wealth by understanding the ways your investments will be taxed. With that knowledge you can develop sensible strategies that will lower your tax liability.

Rule 4: Avoid Overconcentration—Don't go all in on a single investment, type, or sector. Instead, spread out your investments. It lowers your risk by protecting you from disaster in one asset class.

In terms of how often to give your portfolio a shake-up, there's no strict rules here. Some say an annual or semiannual checkup is all your portfolio really needs, while others rebalance more or less frequently. I would recommend digging into your portfolio once a year to make sure you're still on track with your financial goals or maybe need to make some changes to get yourself back on track. There will be times when life throws you a curveball; that curveball could be a shift in your life or the entire market doing something weird. Being able to adjust to the world around you, while sticking to your plan, is the way to build a resilient portfolio.

CHEAT SHEET — INVESTING FOR INFLATION

Inflation happens. A little bit is a sign of a healthy, growing economy. But too much can really hurt your wallet day-to-day and likely cause some anxiety about what it means for your financial picture. To build inflation insulation into your portfolio, consider investing in these sectors:

1. **CONSUMER STAPLES:** Companies in this sector sell essential products like food, beverages, and household goods. These are products people need regardless of economic conditions, giving companies in this sector more power to raise prices without significantly reducing demand. Examples include Procter & Gamble, Unilever, and Coca-Cola.

2. **UTILITIES:** Utility companies often have regulated pricing, which can be adjusted for inflation. This makes their revenue streams relatively stable. Companies like Duke Energy, Southern Company, and NextEra Energy are examples of companies in this niche.

3. **HEALTH CARE PROVIDERS AND PHARMACEUTICALS:** Health care spending is often seen as nondiscretionary, so companies in this sector can maintain revenue even when consumer purchasing power declines. Big pharmaceutical companies with a strong lineup of essential drugs can be good picks, like Johnson & Johnson, Pfizer, and Merck.

4. **COMMODITIES PRODUCERS:** Companies that produce commodities like metals and agricultural products can benefit from rising commodity prices. Mining and agribusiness firms fall into this category, such as BHP, Rio Tinto, and Archer-Daniels-Midland.

5. **INFRASTRUCTURE AND CONSTRUCTION:** Inflation often leads to higher costs for raw materials, benefiting companies in the construction and infrastructure sector like Caterpillar and Vulcan Materials.

LET'S BUILD

At the most fundamental level, a mix of the securities we've covered here (mostly equity and debt securities) is key to a successful portfolio. If you have stocks and the market is up, you'll be raking in the gains. When the market is down, slow and steady bonds might save the day.

This is the same strategy that Warren Buffett, the guys who manage Yale's endowment, and almost all hedge fund bros employ. In the investment world, this is standard operating procedure. The question isn't if you should be doing this. The question is: How? Short answer: having a variety of asset types (everything is fair game including stocks, bonds, cash, real estate, and commodities) and a variety of risk.

A simple conservative portfolio might look like this: 15 percent cash, 15 percent stocks, 70 percent bonds

A moderate portfolio might look like this: 20 percent cash, 40 percent stocks, 40 percent bonds

An aggressive portfolio might look like this: 10 percent cash, 70 percent stocks, 20 percent bonds

THE 50/50

The 50/50 portfolio allocation is a classic move that's all about balance. You split your portfolio right down the middle: half in stocks with their risks and rewards and the other half in reliable old bonds. This is an old-school strategy from the early days of modern investing, when the value system was all about safety over gains. The foreparents of modern portfolio theory and value investing were all seriously shaped by the Great Depression. That trauma meant they all loved to play it safe. By allocating half of the portfolio to equities, investors could capture those stock market gains. But at the same time, the other half of the portfolio, invested in bonds, provided a passive income stream and helped them stay above water in times of market mayhem. The safety provided by being so heavily invested in bonds has made the 50/50 split the go-to move for decades.

Think about the roller coaster of the twentieth century: wars, booms, and recessions. It was a lot. But this strategy offered a simple approach that didn't require constantly keeping your eyes glued to the market monitoring trends and changes.

The 50/50 game plan is solid. Its biggest downfall is that it's so stinkin' conservative. When interest rates are low, bonds might not bring in the big returns. And when stocks are killing it, you might have FOMO. This portfolio could be leaving big gains on the table during a bull market by playing it so safe.

FYI

THE 60/40 PORTFOLIO

This is the "little black dress" of portfolio management—it's timeless, versatile, and has a knack for making people feel both comfortable and confident in their financial decisions. It's the classic 60 percent stocks and 40 percent bonds. After all, trends or "hot tips" die alone on Wall Street. Once upon a time, Amazon looked like a risky internet bookstore and Enron looked like a safe investment.

AGE PERCENTAGE PORTFOLIO

In recent years, with the Great Depression more in the rearview, a popular portfolio allocation strategy is to use your literal age as the percentage of your portfolio invested in bonds. The remaining sum, to add up to 100 percent, is the amount to invest in stocks. (I'm going to say funds here because that's my recommendation!) For example, if you're twenty-five years old, you'd invest 25 percent of your portfolio in bonds and 75 percent in equity funds. If you're sixty, you'd invest 60 percent of your portfolio in bonds and 40 percent of your portfolio in equity funds. Reason being, stocks are riskier than bonds but offer a higher potential payout. If you're younger, you have a longer runway to correct if one of your investments doesn't pan out. If you're older, mistakes matter more. One of the many joys of adulting.

MONEY TIP

THE B.I.G. PORTFOLIO

When you make your portfolio, think big. And when I say big, I mean B-I-G: Blue chip companies, Index funds, and Growth stocks.

THE PERMANENT PORTFOLIO

The brainchild of Harry Browne (politician and investment advisor) in the '80s, the permanent portfolio is structured to withstand economic ups and downs by diversifying across four distinct asset classes: 25 percent in stocks for growth, 25 percent in long-term government bonds for stability, 25 percent in cash for quick moves, and 25 percent in precious metals like gold as a hedge against inflation. This allocation is prepared for anything, no matter what the economic conditions are.

One way to set this up would be: snag a broad-based index fund for growth, government bonds (particularly long-term ones) for stability, a money market account or short-term Treasury bills (ensuring it's on hand when needed and still earning money) for quick moves, and a gold ETF serving as a hedge against inflation and currency devaluation.

Historically, the permanent portfolio has shown its strength in providing stable returns with lower volatility than more aggressive investment strategies. Its diversified approach has helped it stay relevant through many economic storms, from recessions to high inflation periods. This makes it a reliable option for investors seeking a long-term, careful, yet laid-back investment strategy that can handle pretty much all financial weather.

When the stock market is up, it grabs growth; when the stock market's down, the bonds are there to keep giving you returns. During inflation, gold will see its value go up. And if you need to rebalance, it's easy with cash on hand. Plus the cash comes in handy when interest rates rise. This strategy is best suited for conservative investors looking to swipe right on the perfect portfolio that reduces risk while still making gains. It's particularly attractive to those who aren't looking to constantly tweak and fuss over their investments.

THE ENDOWMENT PORTFOLIO

Big-name schools like Yale and Harvard manage massive funds or "endowments," and they don't hire dummies to do it. But there aren't any fixed percentages for this one. This is about mindset more than a set formula. It's about thinking beyond the traditional stock and bond mix with more alternative assets such as private equity, real estate, and hedge funds. The goal is to achieve long-term growth while lowering risk from the volatile stock market.

The financial whiz David Swensen of Yale's epic endowment gave some insight into the mix they use to consistently outperform other investment strategies. When Swensen first took over, the fund was mostly US stocks, bonds, and cash. Under his stewardship the Yale endowment has grown to the second largest in the country with a value of more than $40 billion. In largest to smallest percentage of the portfolio, it consists of:

- Absolute return assets (short-term investments like options that focus on generating profits)

- Venture capital

- Leveraged buyouts

- Foreign equity

- Real estate

- Cash and fixed-income-like bonds

- Natural resources

- US stocks

The endowment model has historically been successful for several reasons. But, namely, by being so diverse it's shielded against big losses. Even if you get an F in one class, as long as you get an A in the rest, after four years your GPA will recover. That's how this portfolio works too. By investing in asset classes with low correlation to one another, the portfolio can weather different economic conditions better than a traditional stock/bond portfolio might. For instance, during periods when the stock market is down, real estate or hedge funds might still do well, cushioning the portfolio against large swings.

THE RAY DALIO PORTFOLIO

Ah, behold the famous "all-weather portfolio." This model was first introduced by Ray Dalio. We've mentioned him before, but here are the highlights. He's the hedge fund manager behind Bridgewater Associates, the world's largest hedge fund. With billions under management, he is widely considered one of the most successful investors of our time. When Ray talks, investors listen. He keeps the recipe for his secret sauce hidden, and it isn't easily duplicated on a personal level. But here is a rough formula that Dalio says the individual investor could easily use to replicate his results. Here is the all-weather portfolio.

- 7.5 percent commodities

- 40 percent long-term bonds

- 7.5 percent gold

- 15 percent intermediate-term bonds

- 30 percent stocks

This mix is about covering all your bases to benefit from whatever economic conditions come your way, whether that's a bull market, a bear market, inflation, or deflation. The mix also needs to be rebalanced. If gold takes off and is suddenly 15 percent of the portfolio, all gold in excess of 7.5 percent must be sold to make sure that you stick to the game plan.

According to Ray, four things affect the value of assets:

1. Inflation

2. Deflation

3. Rising economic growth

4. Falling economic growth

Based on those factors, Ray says that we can expect four "seasons" of the economy:

1. Higher-than-expected inflation (rising prices)

2. Lower-than-expected inflation or deflation

3. Higher-than-expected growth

4. Lower-than-expected growth

This portfolio has actually "weathered" all of those seasons over time. When historically back-tested, this portfolio made money 85 percent of the time. It also would have lost "just" 20 percent during the Great Depression, while the S&P 500 lost 65 percent. In some of the other big market drops (1973 and 2002), Dalio's construction actually made money while the market suffered. Historically, this particular portfolio has made it through bull markets, bear markets, recessions, and everything in between.

One way to implement this strategy is to start with the equity portion, selecting a broad-market index fund or ETF to capture the growth potential of the stock market. For the bond components, ETFs or mutual funds that specialize in long-term and intermediate-term US Treasuries are ideal for their safety and stability. The gold and commodities allocations can be managed through ETFs that track the respective markets, providing a hedge against inflation and diversifying the portfolio further.

This approach is best suited for investors looking for a balanced, medium-maintenance portfolio that aims to reduce volatility and deliver steady returns over time. It's particularly appealing to those who want to diversify their investments extensively, beyond the conventional stock and bond mix, to include assets like commodities and gold that can provide protection against various economic risks. If you want to try an all-weather portfolio for yourself, don't be overwhelmed; you can do it using different ETFs that cover each of those asset classes like I just showed you. Beyond picking assets that fit this portfolio profile, it's important to stick to the balance. This means actively balancing and rebalancing your investments to ensure that they stay in line with the recommended mix. You can do this manually by regularly checking your account, or you can automate it by carefully setting the automatic buy/sell orders in your account. If you're just starting out, you can set up this strategy on your own, but if you are looking to transition substantial assets over to this portfolio setup (or any, really), you may want to employ a wealth manager* to help implement your plan in the most tax-savvy way. But it is absolutely possible to DIY this, with a collection of ETFs and a little discipline, all on your own in your retirement account. There's definitely no need to get a safe for your gold bars and buy individual bonds unless that's your thing.

---

* A wealth manager is a specialized type of financial advisor who deals with clients who have significant personal wealth. Usually in excess of a million dollars.

THE WARREN BUFFETT PORTFOLIO

Ah, him again. We just can't shake him . . . and we don't want to. They don't call him the Oracle of Omaha for nothing. He is the smartest but also the simplest. This portfolio only has two different assets!

Buffett reportedly outlined his target portfolio breakdown in instructions for his wife and their trust for when he dies: "Put 10 percent in short-term government bonds and 90 percent in a very low-cost S&P 500 index fund. (I suggest Vanguard's.) I believe the trust's long-term results from this policy will be superior to those attained by most investors—whether pension funds, institutions, or individuals—who employ high-fee managers."

Implementing Buffett's strategy is investing on "easy mode." It's also one of my favorites. You start by selecting a low-cost S&P 500 index fund, the Vanguard one he is recommending is VOO, but any of them will do. Then a little bit into short-term government bonds, either through Treasury bills themselves or a bond fund focusing on short-duration government bonds.

It sounds a little corny, but it's true—Buffett really believes in the US. He is confident that over the long haul the US economy will grow and thrive. By investing in an S&P 500 index fund, he's making a bet that his family will benefit from the growth, dividends, and stock buybacks of the top five hundred companies in the US. By investing in Treasuries, he's betting on the US government. This method has historically proven successful, as the S&P 500 has delivered an average annual return of around 10 percent* over the long term, despite some nasty weather along the way.

This investment strategy is for those looking for something super-duper low maintenance. It's particularly appealing to those who believe stocks mostly go up but want to avoid the headache and risks of picking individual stocks or timing the market. Buffett's allocation is designed for long-term investors who can ride out market volatility and are looking for a "buy and hold" strategy.

The historical success of the S&P 500, plus Buffett's blessing, offers a compelling case for picking this strategy. While no investment strategy is without risk, and past performance is not indicative of future results (read

* That's 7 percent after adjusting for inflation.

that again for the people in the back!), this approach has the backing of one of the most successful investors in history. It's a testimony to the power of simplicity in investing and the importance of patience, discipline, and confidence in the fundamentals of the US economy.

MARCH TO THE BEAT OF YOUR OWN DRUM

Dalio's and Buffett's portfolios are rough outlines. You can color inside or outside the lines depending on your particular assets, and ultimately the lines are drawn to your individual needs, time frames, and goals. It also comes down to your own preference, tolerance for risk, and time you want to spend on it. Ultimately, I want you to get a good night's sleep, so if you're scared now, honor that feeling. Forget about me, forget about Ray, forget about Warren. (Oh, Warren, I could never forget you.) Don't go skydiving if you're actually peeing in your pants; the people around you will thank you. There may come a day when you're just plain scared, not peeing-in-your-pants scared, and you zip into your flight suit and jump out of the damn plane—but if that's not today, that's okay. How you choose to create your portfolio today is up to you, and you have the complete right to change and re-create your investment mix whenever you want. You can always take on more or less risk as your circumstances change. And they will.

Investing isn't a onetime deal. This is a lifelong journey. It starts with buying a single share, and the plan will change and grow with you. There's no rush to balance a portfolio if you don't have one yet. If you have a bunch of random investments and no plan—this is your sign to try to come up with one. But if you're just starting out, don't get too caught up in building the perfect portfolio quite yet. Give yourself grace. You're exactly where you need to be. It takes time for assets and investors to mature.

YOUR PORTFOLIO 301
Revisit and Rebalance

Whether it's because of the market or because of your life, there will be times you'll want to rebalance your portfolio, which is basically rejiggering to accommodate for whatever happened. Rebalancing is pruning your prized rosebush. You got it to the perfect size and shape, but when it gets a little unruly, you have to trim it to get it back in balance.

In the case of maintaining any all-weather portfolio, I suggest you do timely reviews of what's happening. What's thriving? What's faltering? Do a quick assessment to determine what requires fertilizer or which blooms are spent and should be deadheaded.

If you've fallen out of that, say, 30 percent stocks / 40 percent bonds / 15 percent immediate term bonds / 7.5 percent gold / and 7.5 percent commodities that you decided to stick to, make an assessment as to what's changed. If your stocks went gangbusters (woo!), take the excess and channel it into the other categories so you stay in balance. Remember, your portfolio (and your landscaping) should work with the exact proportions *you* want. In this last lesson, I'll show you how to do that and protect yourself along the way.

REVISITING DAY

Revisiting your investment portfolio is a crucial aspect of maintaining a healthy financial plan. The timing and frequency of these reviews can vary based on different investment philosophies and personal circumstances. Here are some ways to think about reviews:

1. **REGULAR INTERVAL REVIEWS:** Many advisors and investors recommend scheduling checking your portfolio like any other checkup. You go to the doctor once a year, the dentist every six months; whatever it is, set a regular schedule and stick with it. This systematic approach ensures that you regularly peek under the hood at your investments' performance, asset allocation, and relevance to your current financial goals. But it also filters out the noise. If the market goes up or down, you're not racing to your portfolio to react. The idea is to provide a consistent opportunity to rebalance and make adjustments without overreacting to short-term market drama.

2. **PERFORMANCE-BASED REVIEWS:** Some investors prefer to check their portfolio based on its achievements. For instance, if an investment underperforms or outperforms its expected benchmark by a certain percentage, it may trigger a review.

3. **LIFE EVENT–TRIGGERED REVIEWS:** Significant life events such as marriage, the birth of a child, receiving an inheritance, changing jobs, or approaching retirement can send shock waves through your whole life. They also usually warrant a portfolio review. These events often alter your financial landscape, risk tolerance, and investment time horizon. That calls for adjusting your investment strategy to align with your new lifestyle.

4. **ECONOMIC AND MARKET CONDITION REVIEWS:** Some active investors closely follow economic indicators and market trends. They then might adjust their portfolios in response to big-time changes in the economic environment. These indicators include shifts in interest rates, inflation, or major geopolitical

events. This proactive approach aims to get out ahead of market movements and adjust the portfolio for peak performance under the new conditions.

5. **THRESHOLD-BASED REVIEWS:** This strict approach involves checking in on the portfolio when asset allocations start to go off track by a preset threshold (for example, 5 percent or 10 percent). This involves a deep commitment to the plan.

All of these review methods have their pluses. Choose a review strategy that aligns with your investment philosophy, lifestyle, and personal financial goals. Since most people aren't accounting robots, it is also common to combine these approaches, using regular intervals for routine checks and being open to additional reviews when significant life events or economic shifts occur. What works for you now may not be the right choice twenty years from now. Whichever strategy you choose, the goal is to maintain a portfolio that is responsive to change yet consistent with your North Star.

REBALANCING ACT

Just like you can schedule your reviews of your portfolio, you can also schedule rebalances when you actually go in and do the deed of buying and selling. If you are a calendar-invite devotee like yours truly, then you can set regular calendar reminders (annually, semiannually, or quarterly) to adjust your portfolio back to its target allocation. I like this method because it avoids making impulsive decisions. Imagine if it wasn't calendared: you could see the stock portion of your portfolio on a tear and just hold a little bit longer to see how high it can go based on emotion. But if you have too many calendar reminders already, here are some other ways to go about it:

- *Cash Flow Rebalancing:* Using the cash coming into your account (like dividends, interest payments, or new contributions) to purchase under-weighted assets. This does require a more hands-on approach but produces great results for the right investor. This method can minimize transaction costs and taxes.

- *Tax-Efficient Rebalancing:* Another hands-on approach that can seriously protect your gains. Consider the tax implications of selling assets. In taxable accounts, you might prioritize selling assets with losses to offset gains (tax-loss harvesting) or rebalance by making new purchases without selling.

- *Automatic Rebalancing:* On the other extreme is the most hands-off choice, automating everything. Many investment platforms offer automatic rebalancing services. This lets the algorithm take the wheel, and the account is automatically set back to a targeted spread of assets when appropriate. It does require more work on the front end to set everything up, but long term it requires less involvement.

Aside from the fact that rebalancing keeps your investment strategy on track, especially important as you approach milestones like retirement, it also puts the adage "buy low, sell high" into effect. By selling portions of assets that have gone up and buying more of those that have underpriced, you're taking profits and investing in areas with potential for growth. Ultimately, though, this is all about head over heart. By following a systematic rebalancing approach, you can avoid emotional decision-making based on market noise and unsettling economic weather. This discipline helps in avoiding the traps and pitfalls of impulsive investing and trying to time the market.

FYI

THINKING FAST AND SLOW

A study performed by Nobel Prize–winning psychologist Daniel Kahneman showed that we make financial decisions based 90 percent on emotion and only 10 percent on logic.

THE TAX MAN COMETH

I don't need to tell you that taxes are a big deal. They can make a huge difference in making or breaking your wealth. Let's say you made a million bucks last year. How much would you be left with after taxes? If your guess was "Not a million bucks?" Yep. That is definitely right. But what's your actual guess?

"Maybe $900,000?" Nice try! "$750,000?" Good guess but wrong-o.

If you had a 37 percent tax rate, the highest tax bracket in 2024, that would mean you would be left with about $675,000 after federal income taxes, and that doesn't even account for state taxes. If you live in a super tax-aggressive state like New York or California, that number would be way less, probably closer to $560,000. This is just an example, and not necessarily the case for those who made a million dollars in 2024, but it does get the point across: if you ignore taxes, your finances could take a major hit.

Of course, it's a privilege to pay more in taxes because that means you're making more money. Good things do come from taxpayer dollars, so pay your taxes, kids. I'm not advocating anything sketchy or illegal. I'm all for following the rules; but there are ways to maximize the money you see while keeping fully under the letter of the law.

Similar to the taxes you pay on the paycheck you earn from your job, as an investor, you also need to pay taxes on your winning investments. When you make money on an investment (yay!), you have to pay capital gains taxes (boo!). So . . . WTF are capital gains? Capital gains taxes are a particular genre of taxes that apply when you sell an asset—like a company, a house, and, yes, stocks. When it comes to investments, capital gains taxes apply to the difference between the price you paid for a stock and the price you sell the stock for.

When you sell an investment for more than you paid for it, you make a capital gain, which is taxable. If your investments pay dividends, these are also subject to taxes.* There are two types of capital gains taxes: short-term

---

* Look out for tax forms like 1099-DIV and 1099-B forms. These forms show the dividends earned and capital gains realized, which can give you an idea of the associated tax implications.

and long-term. The two have different rates of taxation, and which tax gets applied to your situation depends on *when* you sell the asset.

SHORT-TERM CAPITAL GAINS apply when you sell an investment within one year of purchase. Today the rates are currently the same as ordinary income tax. If you're already a high-income earner, the ordinary income tax rate adds up to, roughly, a lot. When it comes to taxes, remember that your income is taxed in brackets. So if you're single and making $150,000, the first $11,000 is taxed at 10 percent. The next chunk is taxed at 12 percent, when you hit $44,725, you're shelling out 22 percent in taxes on any income above that. Until you get to $95,735 and then for anything above that, the tax bill is 24 percent. The good news is that regular income gets taxed first. But short-term gains get taxed at the highest rate so in this case your short-term gains would be taxed at 24 percent. But if you had such a good year that you got pushed up to the next bracket? Then those short-term capital gains would be taxed at 32 percent. Any interest earned on investments like bonds is taxed this way too.

LONG-TERM CAPITAL GAINS, on the other hand, are taxes you pay on investments you hang on to for a year or longer. The tax rate for those gains is much lower than short-term capital gains; they are taxed at 20 percent for the highest earners and 0 percent for the lowest earners. Here's the biggest piece of advice to remember with capital gains: wherever possible, when you do sell investments, try to do so after a year so you are taxed at a much lower rate.

If you happen to lose money on your investments, then the short-term losses can be used to offset the short-term gains. And same-same, long-term losses can be used to offset the long-term gains. For example, if you lose $1,000 and earn $2,500 in the short term, you would be taxed on $1,500 because the $1,000 loss offsets the $2,500 gain. But if you're not careful, fees and taxes can be the enemy of all your good investment work.

FYI

HARVEST YOUR LOSSES

Some investors use strategies like tax-loss harvesting to offset capital gains taxes. This involves selling investments at a loss to offset the taxes on gains. While this can be effective, it requires careful management and understanding of tax laws, but if you have mega gains one year, this is something to look into.

PROTECT YOURSELF

Protecting your investment portfolio from potential legal issues or bankruptcy is more than just a financial strategy; it's a safeguard for you and your family's future. Long used by the rich, trusts and insurance play a key role in protecting what's yours. Together they not only offer a buffer against personal curveballs like surprise lawsuits but financial downturns as well.

TRUST YOURSELF

I know when we think of trust funds, we roll our eyes and think about trust fund babies. *Must be nice, right? Drinks had better be on them tonight.* But that's not all they refer to. Let's dig into how a trust can help you out and maybe even turn your kids into certified trust fund babies. Here are the general players involved in a trust:

- The *grantor*, sometimes known as the "trustor," is the one who creates and funds the trust.

- The *beneficiary* is, well, the trust fund baby or person who benefits from the trust.

- The *trustee* is the person or entity that is in control of operating the trust.

Trusts have a set legal framework. So, in order to be functional and recognizably a trust, they must use certain elements, but there are usually a couple of choices between types of elements.

The first question to ask is, "Is this a now or later trust?"

- *Living Trust:* This is the "now" choice. It is a trust set up while the creator or grantor is still alive. It also usually means they can dip into the trust if they need to.

- *Testamentary Trust:* This is the "later" choice. This is a way of protecting and passing on assets after the grantor has passed on.

Next big question: "Is this a forever trust or could things change?"

- *Revocable:* These can be revoked by the grantor. Say you set up a trust for your kids and then discover at forty-three that yes you could still get pregnant? This type of trust can be easily changed to meet whatever kinds of surprises life throws your way.

- *Irrevocable:* These cannot be easily changed, which can make them a great choice if you're setting up a trust to pass on your assets and you don't want your ex-husband to get his hands on your kids' money.

When you place assets in certain types of trusts, such as irrevocable trusts, those assets are effectively removed from your personal estate. This means they're locked out of the reach from creditors and legal judgments, providing a heavy-duty shield in high-liability scenarios. While everyone can benefit from this move, those who own businesses with a higher rate of lawsuits can seriously come out ahead here.

Overall, there are two big benefits of trusts: peace of mind and tax benefits. Because setting up trusts involves a lot of planning out various scenarios—like, what happens to your money when you die—they provide satisfaction. I know thinking about death is not exactly comforting. But hear me out. Do you want to use your estate to make sure your loved ones are taken care of? A trust can help you make sure that happens. Plus, having this plan will mean that your loved ones don't have to step in and make decisions on how your assets are used, which can add burden to an already difficult time.

There are two options when setting up a trust, and your circumstances will determine which one is right for you. If you are in a simple situation—your assets are all personal like a house and your brokerage account, and your benefactors are clear and uncontested, like two kids who get along—you can do the DIY route. This means picking your trust setup, doing the paperwork using templates from the internet, getting it notarized, and then funding the trust account. If this is a testamentary account, remember to change your will to reflect the new situation.

If the situation is more complex—a thriving business with an unrelated partner, your benefactors don't get along or one of them has an intellectual disability, or you suspect the trust will be contested for whatever reason—it is worth hiring an attorney to make sure that the trust is ironclad and your wishes are explicitly spelled out. This is true even if it's a living trust and you're there to say what you want. Once the trust is set up, the next step of funding it is the same no matter how it was created. Funding it is simply a matter of setting up an account for the trust and transferring the trust's assets there as well as putting any property or other physical assets into the trust's name.

Oof! Now that we've tackled the death subject, we can move on to a (marginally) better one: taxes. In some cases, trusts can also offer ways for grantors to minimize estate taxes or avoid them altogether. But this is not always the case, and estate-tax legislation is currently a hot-button topic in Washington. We're going to have to wait and see if, and how, estate taxes change. But in the meantime, if you want to use a trust as a way to soften a tax blow to your beneficiaries, you should talk with a lawyer about irrevocable trusts. That's the flavor of trust that will have the best chance at some tax love.

I know that this can get a little heavy, but we aren't just in this for ourselves. We're looking to build generational wealth here. Beyond just protection, trusts offer a jumping-off point for estate planning, allowing you to distribute your assets on your terms (and avoid dreaded probate).* This means that your wealth will be passed on according to your wishes, potentially protecting your heirs' inheritance from their creditors, divorce proceedings, or even their own financial mistakes. In the realm of bankruptcy, having assets in trusts or covered by certain insurance policies can be a lifeline, preserving a core of your wealth to help with rebuilding your financial foundation.

INSURE YOURSELF

We've been talking about hedges in your portfolio to mitigate risk. But what if you could hedge against risk for yourself, like your actual self? That's where insurance policies come in. They transfer the burden of financial loss from you to the insurer. To see this in action, look at life insurance, which secures the financial well-being of your dependents, or umbrella policies that provide an extra layer of liability protection, safeguarding your investments from substantial legal claims.

Life insurance comes in two main types: term and whole. *Term life insurance* is short term. For a very low price, a couple of hundred dollars a year, this type of life insurance will pay out a lump sum when the holder dies. But it's only intended to cover a few decades of life. Basically in exchange for the cost of dinner for one once a month for twenty or thirty years, your family can be paid out half a million in the case of your early death. But hopefully you live well past those twenty or thirty years, at which point the insurance expires.

Whole life or *universal life insurance* is far more expensive. But as the name suggests, it it for your whole life that means that your family will get what you paid for it. Beyond that, it also offers cash value. Part of the payments every month go toward building up a pot of money that can be used before the death of the holder. This money can be taken out as a loan or simply used by the holder. The cash value can also be invested to help build wealth that way. These plans also pay out a specific amount when the holder of the

---

* This is when the court system checks up on how things are given out after someone dies. The rules vary by state, but this almost always happens if there is property or a lot of money involved, which is part of why the rich favor trusts. The probate process is often slow and the legal fees can add up.

insurance dies. How much they pay out beyond that amount depends on if the cash value is still there, or has been invested.

All of these steps can be mixed and matched. So it's possible to create, say, a revocable, testamentary trust and then fund it with a term life insurance policy. Within the legal framework, there are many possibilities. For entrepreneurs, integrating trusts and insurance into your business framework is vital when it comes to passing on the family biz to the next generation. Instruments like buy-sell agreements, underpinned by life insurance, ensure that business operations can continue smoothly, even in the face of a partner's unexpected death.

FYI

HOW THE ROCKEFELLERS ROLL

The waterfall insurance strategy is rumored to have been invented by the Rockefellers. How it works: You buy a whole life insurance policy with the ability to roll it over, written right into the contract. You can then transfer the cash value of the policy to your kids or grandkids by rolling it over. This move can avoid a lot of inheritance tax.

This strategic use of trusts and insurance isn't just about asset protection. It's about creating a durable financial legacy. While the start-up costs may be steep, the long-term security and peace of mind they can offer may make them well worth it as a key part of financial planning. Part of getting (and staying) rich is thinking like the rich and protecting what you have for future generations.

Investment-Grade Insurance

Let's double-click on investment-grade insurance products, or ones that give you a return like certain life insurance policies and annuities. These financial tools are basically designed to let you double dip. Not only do they protect, they also offer a stable return component, making them attractive for conservative investors or those nearing retirement.

One of the key benefits of investment-grade insurance products is their ability to provide a death benefit or income stream. That can be particularly important in estate planning or as a means of securing a retirement income. For example, long-term or permanent life insurance policies (whole life or universal life) accumulate cash value over time. This cash stash can grow at a guaranteed minimum rate. Policyholders are able to borrow against this cash value or even make withdrawals, offering a flexible financial resource that can complement traditional investment accounts.

Annuities, another form of investment-grade insurance, bring a whole different set of perks to the table. With an annuity, you can convert a portion of your savings into a stream of payments for a set time or even the rest of your life. It's like a personal paycheck. This setup can really bring some peace of mind during retirement, giving you a steady income no matter what's happening in your world, the world at large, or the market. Fixed annuities, in particular, offer a guaranteed return, shielding investors from the volatility of the stock market.

Fair warning: these are complicated insurance products. So you can't go in willy-nilly. Have a clear understanding of their terms, costs, and features. Investment-grade insurance products often come with higher fees and more complex terms than traditional investment vehicles. Pulling out early from these plans can hit you with some serious surrender charges and tax headaches. With that said, incorporating investment-grade insurance products into your portfolio can provide a layer of protection and income stability, which is especially valuable in wild economic times. While they're not going to fit into everyone's vision board, they could make sense for those looking to fortify and level up their financial security.

GRADUATION DAY

I've not lied to you and I don't plan on starting now. The financial system is messed up. There are policies that are unfair. There are systems that suck.

Bad news first: we aren't going to change them, at least not quickly. This is not defeatist. This is realistic. I am certainly trying to bring more equality and justice into the way; others are trying too. But it's not going to be markedly different overnight even though it should be.

Good news: you can and should operate in an imperfect system. Cursing injustices will never make us more money. It will never make us feel more safe. Nor will it build us and our families financial security. The only thing that will is taking control of the only thing we can control . . . ourselves.

CONTROL YOURSELF

Here's the reality we live in: lots of people have jobs that they hate, or worse yet, jobs that they love but that they can't afford to do because the job pays them so little money. Yet we also live in a world where Elon Musk has so much money that no one in his family will have to work again for many generations. I'm not picking on Elon specifically, but we live in a time of stark economic inequality, and he's a good example.

The rich are getting much, much richer. To put it in perspective, if I gave you a million dollars and told you to spend $1,000 a day, it would take you a little under three years to spend all the money. So how long would it take you to spend a billion? Thirty years? Three hundred years? Nope. It would take almost three thousand years. To be exact: 2,739. Three thousand years ago, making stuff out of bronze was still considered cutting-edge technology. And that's to spend a single billion. Guys like Musk and Gates and Bezos have hundreds of billions. Instead of that wealth flowing through our economy, it's all one person's personal property.

At the same time, the poor are getting slightly poorer. Since 1999, average income has increased 76 percent, which sounds great until you realize that average rent has increased 134 percent. Everything from food to college has gotten more expensive, and wages, for most people, haven't kept up. CEOs are making more than ever. In 1968, CEOs made an average of twenty times what the average employee did. By 1989, that number had shot up to fifty-nine times. At this point, the gap is huge. The average CEO makes 399 times what the average employee at their company does. It can feel impossible to get ahead, especially if you're poor. And the middle class are screwed. There's a long list of macroeconomic factors for why the middle class just isn't thriving in the US. They range from policy issues to the legacy of past recessions. Collectively, we should all be working toward improving the situation. But communal action is slow. And none of us can control it. The only thing you *can* control is you—your own financial ecosystem, your personal microeconomy.

The best way to do that is to take control of your money—to recognize these realities for what they are and put your finger on the pulse of your own financial life. If anyone is promising to make you a millionaire overnight, they're lying to you. There's no getting-rich-quick secret life hack, other than crawling out of a wealthy woman's womb. And it's probably too late to get Elon to adopt you.

But it's not too late to change your circumstances. You don't have to work until you die, and you don't have to spend the end of your life in grinding poverty. With discipline and careful planning using the concepts you learned here at the prestigious institution The Money School, you can get to a place where your money is working as hard for you as you did for it. It's not quick. You can get to a place where you don't worry about money every hour of every day. If I did, I promise, you can too.

GETTING HELP

The last twelve lessons have been all about taking charge of your financial situation, avoiding fees, and DIYing your way to financial success. I believe you can do that. You believe you can do that, since you bought this book. But maybe you're not ready. Or maybe you got to this point and think, *Wow, not for me.* That's okay too.

For many investors, teaming up with a financial advisor can be a total game changer. We talked about this all the way back at the beginning of school. But if you're ready to have the conversation, I want to help jumpstart that.

CHEAT SHEET

HOW TO INTERVIEW A FINANCIAL ADVISOR

Here's a sample script highlighting some of the main points to touch on:

YOU: Thank you for meeting with me today. I have a few questions before we get started. First, can you please confirm if you are registered with the state or the SEC?

THEM: Of course! I am registered with the SEC. This means I follow strict rules to protect your money and give you the best advice.

YOU: That sounds good. Do you also have an investment advisor representative who works with you and follows the same rules?

THEM: Yes, I do. My investment advisor representative also abides by the same strict fiduciary practices to ensure we always act in your best interest.

YOU: Great! Now, can you explain how your compensation structure works? How do you get paid?

THEM: Sure thing! I charge a 1 percent fee of all the assets I manage for you. This means if I manage $100, I get $1 as my fee.

YOU: Okay, and do you take any extra fees for buying mutual funds or any 12b-1 marketing fees?

THEM: No, I do not. The 1 percent fee is the only fee I charge. I don't participate in any "pay-to-play" fees or take extra money for buying specific mutual funds.

YOU: That's good to know. Just to clarify, do you have your Series 7?

THEM: I do not.

> **YOU:** Thank you. So, to clarify, you don't get any compensation for trading stocks or bonds, right?
>
> **THEM:** That's correct. I don't get paid for trading any stocks or bonds. My compensation only comes from the 1 percent fee.
>
> **YOU:** Thank you. I have one more question. Do you have any affiliation with a broker-dealer or are regulated by FINRA?
>
> **THEM:** No, I don't. Some fiduciaries do sell products and get commissions, but I don't do business that way. I prefer to keep things simple and transparent.
>
> **YOU:** I appreciate that. And do you take my money directly?
>
> **THEM:** No, I don't handle your money directly. I work with third-party custodians like Charles Schwab and Fidelity. You can choose which one you prefer, and you will always have access to your money and accounts through them.
>
> **YOU:** Thank you so much for explaining everything. I feel much more confident now. I'm ready to talk about my specific goals and how you can help me with my investments!

If you do decide to get outside help, you need someone who has your back. Your personal back. Someone who can offer personalized advice based on your specific situation and help navigate complex financial decisions. You want to avoid anyone with their own agenda. So ask and make sure they are fiduciaries who are legally bound to put your interests first but don't also have a Series 7 license (broker's license).*

To find a financial advisor, start by checking letsmakeaplan.org for fee-based fiduciary, financial planners and NAPFA.org for registered financial advisors who are also fiduciaries. Then check adviserinfo.sec.gov to make

---

* And yes, thank you for asking, I am a fiduciary sans Series 7.

sure that their licensing and everything is up to date. If possible, meet with a few people. This is someone you are trusting with your future. You want to make sure that you are on the same page.

By the way, if you already have an advisor and they don't meet the criteria I talked about and you are looking for permission to break up with them—this is it. It's your money. Don't let anyone tell you differently.

FYI — TODAY IS AS GOOD A DAY AS ANY TO START

If you start investing in your twenties, and put $200 away a month, assuming a historical rate of 8 percent return, you'll have over $1 million by the time you retire.

But if you start investing at forty, and put $200 away a month, assuming that same return, you'll only have $210K for retirement. There are ways to catch up if you're starting later but you have to start.

KEEP CALM AND INVEST ON

Go into the investing world knowing that all assets—stocks, bonds, funds, home prices, and so on—go up and down. A lot. That's what markets do. Where we are today is not where we'll be (metaphorically) tomorrow, as we've seen in the wild swings of the past few years.

One of the most important things to remember as you go out into the investing world on your own: don't mistake volatility with risk. You haven't lost until you sell. You lose money only when you actually liquidate an investment, not when it looks lower on "paper."

Start getting into the habit early of not getting sad when something in your brokerage app looks like it's in the red. Unless a return is guaranteed, an investment is worth only as much as someone else will pay for it. You haven't gained until you sell. If you're like me, you may look at your account, see a massive number, and start googling five-star hotels in Tokyo. But just as you only lose money once you've sold, you gain money only once you've sold too. The market is ever shifting, and tomorrow that giant number could look very different. The most important day is the day you sell. The rest is noise.

Never forget the best chief investment officer of your life *is the one you see in the mirror.* No one will ever care more about your money than *you!* With the lessons you learned in *The Money School,* there is nothing a professional investor can do that you can't. And when you choose the investment mix that works best for you, you're investing big in yourself—and that's definitely the best investment you'll ever make.

Congratulations, Class of The Money School. Good luck out there.

DICTIONARY

50/50 PORTFOLIO: An investment strategy that equally divides assets between stocks and bonds, providing a careful approach to balancing growth potential against risk.

60/40 PORTFOLIO: An old-school investment strategy that allocates 60 percent of a portfolio to stocks (for growth) and 40 percent to bonds (for income and stability), aiming for a balance between risk and return.

ACTIVELY MANAGED FUNDS: Funds managed by professionals who make the investment decisions. Almost always come with high fees.

ADD-ON CD: A certificate of deposit that permits the bearer to add additional deposits to the initial investment during the term of the CD.

ALL-WEATHER PORTFOLIO: A Ray Dalio portfolio strategy that includes a mix of asset classes designed to perform well across different economic environments, including both growth and inflationary periods.

ALTERNATIVE INVESTMENTS: Investments in nontraditional assets beyond stocks, bonds, and cash. Examples include memorabilia, collectible sneakers, and horses. These assets often involve hobbies and can provide diversification in a portfolio but require specialized knowledge to profit.

AMEX (NYSE AMERICAN): A stock exchange focused on trading shares of smaller, emerging companies and exchange-traded funds (ETFs).

ARBITRAGE: The buying and selling of an asset in different markets to profit from differences in the price.

ASK: An options trading term, the ask price is the price per share paid to buy the option or contract to purchase the shares at the strike price on the expiration date.

ASSET ALLOCATION: How assets like stocks, bonds, and real estate are distributed in an investor's portfolio.

BANK CREDIT RATINGS: Grades given to banks by agencies like Standard & Poor's, Moody's, and Fitch Ratings, rating their financial health and ability to meet financial obligations.

BASIS POINT: One-hundredth of a percent (0.01 percent), commonly used to quote interest rates and rates of return in the financial markets.

BEAR MARKET: Bad news bears! A moment in the market when prices are falling, people are selling, and everyone is down. Often defined by a fall of 20 percent or more in broad stock indices.

BETA: A measure of risk, expressed as volatility, of a single security compared to the entire market as a whole.

BOND FUNDS: Investment funds, such as ETFs or mutual funds, that focus on investments in various types of bonds and other debt instruments.

BONDS: Debt securities, essentially IOUs, almost always from a corporation or government. Considered safer investments than stocks, but the resale price and opportunity cost are sensitive to Federal Reserve interest rate changes.

BROKER: A person or entity with a license to trade assets on an exchange on behalf of regular people. They can simply execute trades, or they may offer advice.

BROKERAGE: A company that plays matchmaker between those buying and those selling financial securities like stocks and bonds.

BROKERED CD: Certificates of deposit (CD) from a brokerage firm, not a bank, offering a variety of terms and rates from different banks.

BULL MARKET: A financial market in which prices are rising like a bull's horns. The term is typically used in reference to the stock market but can be applied to any market from bonds to Bitcoin.

BUMP-UP CD: A type of certificate of deposit (CD) that allows the investor to raise the interest rate if the bank's rates for new CDs go up during the term of the CD.

CALL OPTIONS: A type of option or contract that gives the bearer the right to buy an asset at a set price before a specific date.

CALLABLE CD: A CD where the issuing bank has the right to terminate the CD early, typically when interest rates fall.

CAPITAL GAINS: The profit from the sale of an asset, such as stocks or real estate, when you've made or gained money. Capital gains are often subject to taxes.

CBOE (CHICAGO BOARD OPTIONS EXCHANGE): An exchange for options and futures contracts on stocks, indices, and interest rates.

CENTURY BOND: A bond with long maturity, usually a hundred years, sometimes longer, typically issued by governments or corporations.

CERTIFICATE OF DEPOSIT (CD): A financial instrument offered by banks and credit unions with a fixed interest rate in return for loaning the bank a lump sum for a set period of time.

CME (CHICAGO MERCANTILE EXCHANGE): A derivative exchange trading various assets, including futures and options—mostly on commodities.

COMMODITIES: Basic goods that are interchangeable with other goods of the same type.

COMMODITY FUTURES TRADING COMMISSION (CFTC): A US federal regulatory agency that manages all manner of derivatives including the futures and options markets.

COMMODITY STOCKS: Shares in companies involved in the processing or production of commodities.

CONSUMER PRICE INDEX (CPI): An index that looks at the weighted average of prices of a set of consumer goods and services, used as an indicator of inflation.

COST-PUSH INFLATION: Inflation caused by rising production costs, resulting in higher prices for consumers.

CREDIT RATING: An evaluation of the creditworthiness of a borrower in broad terms or with regard to a particular debt or financial obligation.

CREDIT UNION: A member-owned financial institution that acts as a cooperative, providing its members with financial services, usually at favorable rates.

CRYPTOCURRENCY: Digital currency using cryptography rather than a central bank for security.

CURRENCY TRADING (FOREX): The act of buying and selling different currencies in the foreign exchange market for the purposes of making money.

DEBT SECURITIES: A type of tradable financial asset that represents borrowed money that must be repaid, with terms for loan size, interest rate, and maturity/renewal date.

DEMAND-PULL INFLATION: Inflation that occurs when the demand for goods and services is greater than their supply.

DERIVATIVE: A financial security whose value is derived or based on an underlying asset like stocks, bonds, commodities, or currencies.

DISCOUNT RATE: The interest rate paid by banks and depository institutions for loans from the Federal Reserve's discount window.

DIVERSIFICATION: A risk management strategy that utilizes a wide variety of investments within a portfolio to minimize the impact of any single asset's poor performance.

DIVIDEND: A portion of a company's earnings paid out to shareholders, usually as cash but sometimes as additional shares.

DIVIDEND REINVESTMENT PLAN (DRIP): A plan where shareholders automatically reinvest their cash dividends in additional shares of the company's stock.

DOLLAR-COST AVERAGING: Investing a set amount of money on a fixed schedule; this can result in the best price over time.

DOT-COM CRASH: When the market crashed in 2000–2002, primarily affecting internet-based companies whose stock values tanked.

ENDOWMENT MODEL: A portfolio strategy used by large institutional investors that goes beyond traditional stocks and bonds into alternative assets like private equity and real estate for long-term growth.

EQUITY SECURITIES: A type of asset that gives you ownership of an entity—basically a fancy way of saying *stock*.

EXCHANGE-TRADED FUND (ETF): A type of investment fund that is publicly traded on an exchange, with shares that can be bought and sold during the trading day.

EXERCISE (OF AN OPTION): The act of using the right to buy or sell the underlying asset of an options contract.

EXPIRATION DATE: The "use by" date on an option contract.

FEDERAL DEPOSIT INSURANCE CORPORATION (FDIC): A US government agency that makes available deposit insurance, protecting depositors' accounts in qualifying banks up to $250,000.

FINANCIAL INDUSTRY REGULATORY AUTHORITY (FINRA): A nongovernmental organization that supervises brokerage firms and exchange markets.

FINANCIAL LITERACY: The ability to understand and use a number of financial skills, such as budgeting, saving, understanding debt, and investing.

FISCAL POLICY: Government policies covering all things financial, used to control inflation, reduce unemployment, and influence economic growth.

FOREX (FOREIGN EXCHANGE MARKET): A global market exclusively for trading currencies; this is where you swap one currency for another.

FRACTIONAL RESERVE BANKING SYSTEM: A banking system under which banks hold a fraction of their depositors' money in reserve and lend out the remainder.

FUND MANAGERS: Professionals responsible for making investment decisions in a fund, aiming to achieve the fund's investment objectives.

FUNDS: Pooled investment vehicles allowing investment in many companies at once, contrasted with stock picking.

FUTURES CONTRACTS: Contracts to buy or sell a set quantity of a commodity or financial instrument at a future date at a fixed and predetermined price.

GOVERNMENT BOND: A debt-based financial asset created by a national government, generally promising to pay regular interest payments and to repay the face value at the maturity date.

GROWTH STOCKS: Companies anticipated to grow at an above-average rate compared to others in the market.

HARD COMMODITIES: Physical substances—commodities you can touch—that are mined or extracted, like minerals and oil.

HEDGE: Investments or strategies used to reduce the risk of adverse price movements in an asset.

HEDGE FUND: An investment fund that is structured to get the maximum return for a given level of risk, usually limited to high–net worth individuals and institutional investors.

IN THE MONEY (CALL OPTIONS): A situation where the market price of the underlying asset is higher than the strike price of a call option.

INDEX FUND: A type of mutual fund or exchange-traded fund with a portfolio constructed to match or track the components of a financial market index, such as the S&P 500. Index funds provide broad market exposure, low operating expenses, and low portfolio turnover.

INFLATION: The rate at which the average price for goods and services is increasing and purchasing power is falling.

INTEREST RATE RISK: The risk to bond prices on the secondary market from a change in interest rates. It does not change the yield of already purchased bonds held to maturity.

INVESTING: The act of purchasing assets such as stocks, bonds, or derivatives with the expectation of generating income or profit.

INVESTMENT HORIZON: The expected time period over which an investment is anticipated to be held before being liquidated for a profit.

IPO (INITIAL PUBLIC OFFERING): When a private company makes shares of itself available to the public for the very first time.

IRREVOCABLE TRUSTS: Trusts that cannot be modified or terminated without the permission of the beneficiary.

JUMBO CD: A CD requiring a large minimum deposit, usually $100,000 or more, generally offering more competitive interest rates than standard CDs.

LARGE-CAP GROWTH FUND: A fund that invests in large public companies, targeting ones that are projected to grow faster than the economy in general.

LARGE-CAP VALUE FUND: A fund that prioritizes stability over growth and invests in large public companies with relatively low-priced shares.

LEADING INDICATOR: An economic statistic that gives a hint about where the market is going.

LEVERAGE: The use of borrowed money (debt) to amplify investment returns. While it can increase profit potential, it also comes with a higher risk of losses.

LIBERTY BOND: US bonds sold to support the Allied cause in World War I.

LIQUID CD: Also known as a "no-penalty" CD, it permits partial or total withdrawal of funds without any penalties but generally offers a lower interest rate.

LIVING TRUST: A trust established between two living persons, such as a parent and a child.

MARGIN LOAN: A loan that allows the borrower to buy and sell financial assets, usually backed by the assets in their brokerage account. Considered risky because if the assets purchased go down, the borrower will still have to come up with the money to pay back the loan, and if the assets used as collateral go down, the borrower will have to come up with more money to back the loan.

MARKET CAPITALIZATION (MARKET CAP): The total value of a company's outstanding shares of stock. It is calculated by multiplying a company's shares outstanding by the current market price of one share.

MATURATION VALUE: The amount paid to the bondholder at the time of maturity.

MATURITY DATE: The end of a bond's term when the initial investment is returned to the investor.

MEDIUM-CAP FUND: A fund that invests in the stock of medium-sized public companies.

MONETARY POLICY: Actions by a central bank or regulatory committee that determine the size of the money supply, interest rates, and banking reserve requirements.

MUNICIPAL BOND (MUNI): A debt-based security issued by a state, municipality, or county to fund its big projects.

MUTUAL FUND: An investment vehicle that pools investors' funds to enable a professional manager to purchase securities such as stocks, bonds, and other assets; traded only after the market has closed and may require a minimum investment.

NASDAQ: A global electronic marketplace for buying and selling securities, known for technology and internet-related stocks.

NATIONAL FUTURES ASSOCIATION (NFA): The regulatory association for the US derivatives industry, financed by members.

NYSE (NEW YORK STOCK EXCHANGE): The world's largest stock exchange, trading shares of large, established companies.

OPTIONS: A financial contract that gives the holder the right to purchase or sell an asset at a predetermined price and date. The holder can choose to do so or not based on market conditions.

OTC MARKETS GROUP: A special marketplace for over-the-counter securities. These are not listed on other exchanges and are often small and foreign stocks.

OUT OF THE MONEY (CALL OPTIONS): In this situation the spot or market price is lower than the strike price of a call option.

PAPER: Short for commercial paper, super short-term loans used by companies for large payments.

PAR VALUE: A bond's face value; the amount of money that the bearer of the bond will receive upon maturity.

PASSIVELY MANAGED FUNDS: Low-fee funds that aim to mirror the performance of a specific index, with minimal buying and selling.

PAYMENT FOR ORDER FLOW (PFOF): Payment a brokerage earns when they buy and sell orders to a specific market maker.

PERMANENT PORTFOLIO: A strategy that divides investments equally among four asset classes—gold, bonds, stocks, and cash—to perform under various economic conditions.

PIIGS: An acronym of Portugal, Italy, Ireland, Greece, and Spain, all countries facing financial hardships during the European debt crisis. The term is considered derogatory.

PORTFOLIO: A collection of investments held by a person or organization, including stocks, securities, and other financial assets.

POSITION: The dollar amount an investor has in an investment. Measures the size of the investment.

PREMIUM: Paid by the buyer, this is the fee for acquiring the rights granted by an option.

PRICE-TO-EARNINGS RATIO (P/E RATIO): A ratio that solves for the value of a company's current share price compared to its per-share earnings. It is a moment-in-time number, not one that shows change.

PRIMARY MARKET: The first market in which brand-new securities are issued.

PRODUCER PRICE INDEX (PPI): An index tracking the average change in selling prices domestic producers are able to charge for their output.

PUBLIC COMPANY: A company with shares available for purchase on a stock exchange.

PUT OPTIONS: A type of option giving the holder the right to sell an asset at a set price before a specific date.

RAY DALIO: Founder of Bridgewater Associates, known for his All-Weather Portfolio.

REAL ESTATE INVESTMENT TRUST (REIT): A fund that invests in income-generating real estate.

REBALANCING: The process of realigning by selling and buying assets to maintain the proportions in a portfolio.

REGISTERED INVESTMENT ADVISOR (RIA): Someone who gives investment advice and is registered with the SEC.

RETURN ON INVESTMENT (ROI): A calculation of the profit found by dividing the profit by the cost.

REVOCABLE TRUSTS: Trusts that can be altered or terminated by the grantor during their lifetime.

RIA FIRM: RIA stands for Registered Investment Advisor, a type of financial advisor or investment management firm, usually with a fee-based structure. They are registered, regulated, and sworn to adhere to their fiduciary duty, meaning they must act in the best interest of their clients.

RISK MANAGEMENT: The practice of identifying and classifying risks and analyzing their impact on an investment, then making decisions to control the impact of that risk on the investment.

RISK TOLERANCE: An investor's capacity to endure loss in their investment value without freaking out.

SECONDARY MARKET: The market where investors trade securities or assets with other investors rather than with the issuing companies themselves in the primary market.

SECURITIES: A broad term for financial assets such as equity securities, debt securities, and derivatives.

SECURITIES AND EXCHANGE COMMISSION (SEC): An independent US agency formed by the federal government for the purpose of regulating the securities industry.

SECURITIES-BASED LINE OF CREDIT: A personal loan offered by brokerages that allows individuals to borrow under favorable conditions using securities in their account as collateral. This enables the borrower to access the value of their account without having to sell their assets.

SERIES I BOND: A US government savings bond that earns both a fixed interest and variable inflation rate, adjusted semiannually.

SHARE: An ownership unit of a corporation, representing a proportion of the company's capital.

SHAREHOLDER: An owner of shares in a company can be an individual or an entity, thus holding a portion of the company's stock.

SHORT POSITION: Attempting to profit from an asset's decline in price by selling options, generally transferring decision-making power to another investor.

SHORT-TERM INVESTMENTS: Assets that can be turned into cash or sold within a year. These are highly liquid and are often used by firms to manage their cash flow.

SMALL-CAP FUND: A fund that invests in the stock of smaller public companies.

SOFT COMMODITIES: Agricultural products and livestock—goods that need to be nurtured—subject to price fluctuations but easily exchangeable.

SPREAD: The yield/rate/price difference between two different debt instruments, sometimes used to measure the risk or credit quality of a bond.

STEP-UP CD: A certificate of deposit with an interest rate that goes up at regular intervals throughout the term.

STOCK: A financial security signifying ownership in a corporation. Sometimes this also gives the holder a claim to part of the corporation's earnings in the form of dividends.

STOCK EXCHANGE: A marketplace where brokers purchase or sell stocks and other securities.

STOCK MARKET: The collection of exchanges where buyers and sellers exchange stocks.

STOCK PICKING: Selecting, or picking, individual stocks for investment based on an understanding of their potential growth, value, or other criteria.

STOCK SPLIT: A corporate action splitting or dividing a company's shares in circulation into multiple shares, reducing the price per share while maintaining overall value of shares traded.

STOP-LOSS ORDER: An order placed by an investor with a broker to buy or sell a stock once it reaches a certain price point, designed to limit an investor's loss on a security position.

STRIKE PRICE: The specified price for buying or selling the underlying asset in an options contract.

STRUCTURED NOTE: A combination financial instrument with a debt obligation and a derivative component.

TARGET-DATE FUNDS: Mutual funds that adjust their asset allocation toward more conservative investments as a target date approaches.

TESTAMENTARY TRUSTS: Trusts created as part of a will that go into effect upon the death of the creator.

TICKER SYMBOL: A short but unique set of letters assigned to a publicly traded company for identification.

TREASURY BILL (T-BILL): A short-term US Treasury that matures in one year or less.

TREASURY BOND (T-BOND): An interest-bearing, long-term bond backed by the US Treasury.

TREASURY INFLATION-PROTECTED SECURITIES (TIPS): A Treasury security where the interest rate goes up or down with inflation to protect investors from the impact of rising prices.

TREASURY NOTE (T-NOTE): A midrange (two to ten years) US government debt security with a fixed interest rate.

TRUSTS: Legal arrangements that transfer assets to a trustee to hold and manage for beneficiaries.

UNCOVERED OPTION / NAKED OPTION: Selling an option without owning the underlying shares.

VALUE STOCKS: Well-known, established companies known for dependable investment returns, often trading at a lower price relative to their fundamentals.

VENTURE CAPITAL FUNDS: Investment funds, with strict rules for membership, that provide capital to start-ups and small businesses with long-term growth potential.

VOLATILITY: The degree of price variation, usually rapid and unpredictable, in a financial instrument over time.

WARREN BUFFETT: Renowned investor and chairman of Berkshire Hathaway, known for his value-investing philosophy.

WARREN BUFFETT PORTFOLIO: An investment approach suggested by Warren Buffett, predominantly invested in a low-cost S&P 500 index fund with a side of short-term US Treasuries.

WHOLE LIFE INSURANCE: A forever life insurance policy that pays out upon the death of the holder but also has a cash value that can be invested and borrowed against.

YIELD: The income return on an investment, such as the interest or dividends earned from holding a security. Yield is generally measured annually as a percentage based on the investment's cost, current market value, or face value.

YIELD CURVE: A line that plots the rate of change over time. Often used to refer to the change in the interest rates of bonds, which are then compared. These bonds have equal credit quality but differing maturity dates.

STUDY GUIDE

THE STOCK MARKET

This is money school and this means studying. Learning requires repetition and thinking about the lessons in a critical way. Use the study guide below to help probe the material a little deeper. You can work through it with a friend who also read the book or you can work through it on your own by writing down the answers.

STOCKS 101
WALK WITH ME DOWN WALL STREET

Initial Perceptions of the Stock Market: Before reading *The Money School*, what was your image of the stock market? How does this compare to what you've learned?

Early Exposure to the Stock Market: Reflect on your first encounter with the concept of the stock market. How did this shape your current understanding?

Emotional Responses to Investing: What emotions are triggered by the thought of investing in the stock market? Are these influenced by specific experiences?

Understanding Stock Exchanges: After learning about various stock exchanges, how do you perceive their roles? Were there any surprising aspects?

The Concept of Shares and Ownership: How would you explain the concept of share ownership to a novice? What does being a shareholder mean to you?

Importance of Investor Education: Why is it important to understand the basics of the stock market? How can ignorance affect investment decisions?

Investment Anxieties and Excitement: What aspects of investing cause worry or excitement for you? How do you plan to handle these emotions?

ROI (Return on Investment) Perspectives: How do you view ROI in your financial planning? How does it aid in assessing investment opportunities?

Investing Versus Quick Gains: Consider the metaphor of climbing a mountain versus a quick elevator ride. How does this relate to your investment outlook?

Understanding Over-Shortcutting: Have "get rich quick" schemes ever tempted you? How does prioritizing understanding over shortcuts alter your perspective?

Learning from Mistakes: Can you recall a learning shortcut that backfired? How does this relate to understanding the stock market?

Real-Life Applications of Financial Knowledge: Discuss the practicality of your formal education, like calculus, versus understanding the stock market.

The Role of Experts and Social Media: How do you differentiate between sound advice and misinformation, particularly in today's social media landscape?

Investment Options and Decision-Making: With numerous investment options available, how do you make decisions? What are your key considerations?

The Mental Shift in Investing: If you are new to investing, what mental barriers do you face? How can you overcome them with your new knowledge?

Accessibility of Investing: Discuss how accessible the stock market is today compared to the past. How do modern platforms affect your participation?

Investment Language and Learning: Assess your comfort with investment terminology and concepts. Are there areas or terms that challenge you?

Personal Investment Goals: What are your personal goals for investing? Do you prioritize long-term growth, stability, or quick gains?

STOCKS 201
BLOCKING AND TACKLING

Foundation of Your Financial House: Reflect on the metaphor of the stock market as the foundation of your financial house. How does this perspective change your view of investing?

Types of Stocks—Solid Versus Potential: Differentiate between stocks that are "solid and dependable" and those "full of potential and promise." How would you balance these in your portfolio?

Hands-On Versus Hands-Off Investing: Consider your personal preference: Would you prefer being a hands-on or hands-off investor? Why?

Discount Versus Full-Service Brokerages: Discuss the differences between discount and full-service brokerages. Which type aligns more with your investment style?

Trust Issues in Financial Guidance: How do you feel about relying on financial advisors or stockbrokers? Discuss the importance of being actively involved in your financial decisions.

Broker Versus Financial Advisor (Fiduciary): Compare the roles, duties, compensation, and objectives of brokers and financial advisors. How would each affect your investment strategy?

Investment Allocation—the Three Es: Analyze the Three Es budgeting method (Essentials, Extras, Endgame). How would you apply this to your current financial planning?

Assessing Investment Needs and Goals: What are your primary goals for investing (retirement, funding a project, and so on)? How does this influence your choice between value and growth stocks?

Understanding Dividends and Shares: Explain the concept of dividends and how they contribute to investment earnings. What types of dividends are you most interested in?

Risk Tolerance Assessment: Based on the provided quiz, evaluate your risk tolerance. How does this understanding shape your investment strategy?

Investment Strategies: Discuss the principle of "buy low, sell high." How would you implement this in your investment decisions?

Dollar-Cost Averaging and Diversification: Explain dollar-cost averaging and diversification. How can these strategies mitigate investment risks?

Index Funds and Market Indexes: Identify the main indexes (Dow, S&P 500, NASDAQ) and the concept of index funds. How do index funds fit into your investment plan?

Short Selling Stocks: Describe the process and risks of short selling stocks. Would you consider short selling as part of your strategy?

Capital Gains and Tax Implications: Discuss the impact of capital gains taxes on investment returns. How important is tax planning in your investment decisions?

Fees and Investment Costs: Evaluate the different types of fees associated with investing. How would you minimize these costs?

Emotional Management in Investing: How do you plan to manage emotions when investing? Share any anxieties or excitement you have about starting to invest.

The Role of Stock Simulators: Consider using a stock simulator as a learning tool. How might this help you understand the stock market better?

The Future-Oriented Nature of the Stock Market: Reflect on the idea that the stock market is based on the hope of a better future. How does this align with your personal financial philosophy?

BUYING A STOCK
STEP-BY-STEP

STEP 1: Search for the ticker symbol for the stock you are thinking of buying. On your brokerage portal or app, the first thing you will see is the research and stock information like the price over time, 52-week average, and current market sentiment. Let's take a look at Apple, AAPL:

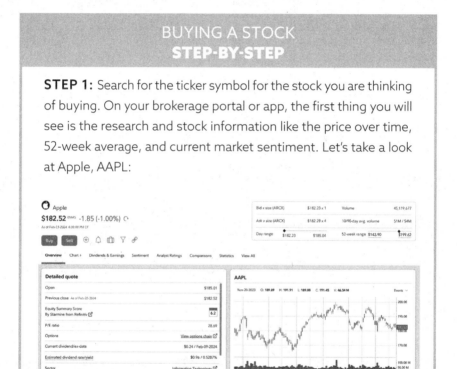

STEP 2: From that page, you can click "Buy" or "Sell." Here you can select the number of shares you want to buy and the price. You can choose to use the market order, which will fulfill it at the current

price, or set your own with a limit order.* You will then be taken to a preview page. It's only after confirming your order that you'll be able to purchase the shares.

* There are three types of orders when it comes to buying and selling a stock. **Market Order:** buying or selling at the current market price; **Limit order:** You set a price limit when buying or selling. A max price for buying and a minimum for selling; **Stop orders:** These stop a stock's price movement. If you're worried about a price drop, you set a sell order that triggers if the price drops below a set amount. If you're trying to catch a rising stock, you set a buy order above a certain amount.

POP QUIZ

WHAT'S YOUR RISK TOLERANCE?

Whether you want to go for a slow-and-steady strategy or a high-risk, high-reward strategy is up to you, your goals, and your risk tolerance. Your risk tolerance is the extent to which you're willing to risk a bust for a boom. And typically, the risk that you are able to stomach in your everyday life translates into the heat you can handle in the investment world. Like a Scoville scale, only for risk. Are you bell pepper or cayenne? To help you figure out what your risk tolerance is, I've put together a little two-part pop quiz (where there are no wrong answers!) to help you find out how spicy your investment strategy really is.

1. Your friends would typically describe you as . . .
    a.   the designated driver.
    b.   usually down to hang.
    c.   the thrill-seeking party animal.

2. You win $100 at a friendly game of poker and . . .
    a.   put it in your savings account.
    b.   use the money to go out for the rest of the night.
    c.   insist on playing another game so you can try to double your money.

3. Your dream vacation would be . . .
    a.   having a nice, well-planned staycation.
    b.   saving up to go somewhere you've always wanted to visit.
    c.   splurging on a far-off adventure or the buzziest exotic hot spot.

4. The most important position on the field is the . . .
    a. defense.
    b. coach.
    c. offense.

5. The thought of investing in the stock market makes you feel . . .
    a. sick to your stomach. Obviously you are going to lose everything.
    b. intrigued and excited to learn more.
    c. awesome! You're going to make a killing, duh.

If you answered all or mostly As, you are not the daredevil of the bunch. You're likely to be a more conservative investor, and your priority is minimizing your chances of losing money, even if it means you'll make less money in the market.

If you answered all or mostly Bs, you'll likely be a middle-of-the-road investor with a healthy attitude to assess risk and reward.

If you answered all or mostly Cs, you'll likely be an aggressive investor, seeking the highest possible reward without flinching at the possibility of losing money.

Now, you might consider yourself a thrillist, but should you act that way in the market? Maybe . . . but maybe not. For some basic guidelines for the level of risk you *should* take on, here's part two of the quiz:

1. How old are you?
    a. 45+ (but you look way younger)
    b. 35–44
    c. 18–34

2. What is the next big purchase you are focused on?
    a. Living a sweet retirement
    b. My kids' college education

    c.   Nothing on the horizon, but a second house or car would be nice!

3.   When is your next big purchase?

    a.   5 or so years

    b.   10–15 years

    c.   15+ years

4.   I expect my income to:

    a.   Decline in the next few years; unfortunately, my job is on shaky ground.

    b.   Stay the same. I'm tenured and have no worries that my salary will change significantly in the next few years.

    c.   Increase! I am getting a raise or jumping to another job with a higher salary.

If you answered all or mostly As on part two, you should be a more conservative investor because you are older, have more of an urgent need for the money, or have uncertainties with your future income. If you answered all or mostly Bs, you should be a more moderate investor because you don't need the money too soon or you have a steady income stream. If you answered all or mostly Cs, you should be a more aggressive investor because you have a long time horizon for your investments or are flush with cash to play with.

If you found you answered mostly As on both quizzes or strongly on the second one, you are positioned to be a conservative investor. If you answered mostly Cs on both, then you are set to be an aggressive investor. But if you answered mostly Bs on both or As on the first and Cs on the second, then you are a more moderate investor.

As we well know, the stock market is risky. But whether that fact sits well with you . . . or whether your stomach just did back-flips at the mere thought of possibly losing money . . . *that's* your risk tolerance. And knowing that about yourself will put you on track to the investment strategy that works best for you.

STOCKS 301
FUNDAMENTAL AND TECHNICAL ANALYSIS

The Fundamentals

Fundamental Versus Technical Analysis: Compare and contrast fundamental analysis and technical analysis in terms of their focus, key elements, time horizon, and types of analysis. How do these approaches influence investment decisions?

Understanding Financial Statements: Explain the importance of financial statements (P&L, balance sheets) in fundamental analysis. How do they provide insights into a company's financial health?

Evaluating Company Performance: Discuss how to use a company's P&L statement and balance sheet to evaluate its performance. What key indicators should you focus on?

The Significance of R&D Expenses: Analyze the role of research and development (R&D) expenses in assessing a company's potential for growth and innovation.

Interpreting Balance Sheets: Explain how to read a balance sheet and understand its components (assets, liabilities, equity). How does this information influence investment choices?

Assessing Company Net Worth: Discuss the calculation and significance of a company's net worth or equity. How does this factor into investment decisions?

Understanding 10-K and 10-Q Reports: Describe the importance of 10-K and 10-Q reports in fundamental analysis. How do these reports differ from other financial statements?

Impact of Company News on Stock Performance: Evaluate how company-specific news (product launches, leadership changes) and general economic news can affect stock performance.

Analyzing Economic Indicators: Discuss the role of key economic indicators (GDP, unemployment rate, CPI) in influencing stock market trends and investment decisions.

The Technicals

Reading Stock Market Data: Explain how to interpret stock market data (price, P/E ratio, volume, market cap). What insights do these metrics provide?

Understanding Stock Tickers and Symbols: Discuss the significance of stock tickers and symbols in technical analysis.

Deciphering Price and Volume Data: Analyze how price and volume data can be used to gauge market sentiment and stock performance.

Evaluating Market Capitalization: Explain the concept of market capitalization and its relevance in assessing a company's size and investment risk.

Dividends and Dividend Yield Analysis: Discuss the importance of dividends and dividend yield in evaluating a stock's investment potential.

Understanding Stock Volatility (Beta): Explain the concept of beta in stock analysis. How does it help in understanding a stock's volatility compared to the overall market?

Earnings Per Share (EPS) and Its Significance: Describe the earnings per share metric and its role in evaluating a company's profitability.

Interpreting P/E Ratios: Analyze the price-to-earnings ratio and its importance in stock valuation. How can it be used to compare stocks within an industry?

Importance of Ongoing Technical Analysis: Discuss the necessity of regularly revisiting technical analysis metrics to maintain an accurate understanding of stock performance.

Handling Investment Losses: How should an investor approach losses in the stock market? Discuss the importance of distinguishing between market trends and individual stock performance.

Beyond Stocks: Diversifying Investments: Explain why a successful investment strategy involves more than just picking individual stocks. What other types of securities should be considered for a balanced portfolio?

COURSE II
THE FIXED-INCOME MARKET

FIXED INCOME 101
WHEN DEBT IS A GOOD THING

Initial Perceptions of Fixed Income: Before reading *The Money School*, how did you perceive fixed-income investments like CDs and bonds? Has your view changed after learning about them?

Discovering Fixed-Income Investments: Reflect on when you first heard about fixed-income investments. How did that initial exposure shape your current understanding?

Emotions Around Fixed Income: What feelings arise when you think about investing in fixed-income products? Are these feelings influenced by past experiences or societal perceptions?

Understanding Certificates of Deposit (CDs): How would you explain the concept of a CD to a friend? What key aspects of CDs surprised you the most?

FDIC Insurance and Bank Reliability: Discuss the role of FDIC insurance and its importance. How has your perception of bank reliability changed after learning about bank failures?

Different Types of CDs and Their Features: Can you differentiate between traditional, jumbo, and brokered CDs? Which type appeals to you most and why?

Inflation and Its Impact on Fixed Income: How does inflation affect fixed-income investments like CDs? How would you use this knowledge in your investment decisions?

Strategies to Combat Inflation Risk: Considering tools like CD ladders and TIPS, how would you plan to mitigate inflation risk in your fixed-income investments?

Risk Tolerance in Fixed-Income Investing: Evaluate your risk tolerance when it comes to fixed-income products. Which types of CDs align with your risk profile?

Learning from Financial History: Reflect on historical banking crises like those in 2008 and 2023. What lessons can be learned regarding fixed-income investments?

Understanding Structured Notes: How do you perceive structured notes as an investment option? Discuss their risks and potential benefits.

Credit Ratings of Banks: Discuss the importance of understanding a bank's credit rating when choosing fixed-income products. How would you assess a bank's stability?

Decisions in Fixed-Income Investments: With the variety of fixed-income options available, how would you approach making decisions? What factors would you consider?

Practical Applications of Fixed-Income Knowledge: How do you see the knowledge of fixed-income investments being practically applied in your financial life?

Fixed-Income Versus Other Investment Options: Compare your interest in fixed-income investments with other investment types. What role do fixed-income products play in your overall portfolio?

Accessibility and Convenience of Fixed-Income Investing: Discuss the accessibility of fixed-income investments today. How do online platforms and brokers influence your participation?

Comfort with Fixed-Income Terminology: Assess your comfort level with fixed-income terms and concepts. Which terms or concepts do you find challenging?

Personal Goals with Fixed Income: What are your personal goals for investing in fixed income? Are you seeking stability, regular income, or diversification?

FIXED INCOME 201
GOVERNMENT BONDS

Understanding Government Bonds: How would you describe a government bond to someone unfamiliar with investing? Why might someone choose to invest in government bonds?

Historical Perspective: Reflect on the role of bonds in funding significant historical events, like the World Wars. How do you think the concept of bonds as a patriotic duty influenced their popularity?

Evaluating Bond Types: What are the key differences between Treasury bills, Treasury notes, Treasury bonds, and TIPS? How does the maturity period of these bonds affect their use and attractiveness to investors?

Inflation and Bonds: How do TIPS protect investors against inflation? Can you think of a scenario where TIPS would be particularly beneficial?

Series I Bonds in High-Inflation Environments: Discuss why Series I bonds became an attractive investment option during high-inflation periods between 2021 and 2023.

Municipal Bonds: What are municipal bonds, and what makes them unique compared to federal government bonds? Discuss their pros and cons.

Debt Ceiling and Bond Investments: How does the debate over the debt ceiling affect government bond yields, and how can investors potentially benefit from this situation?

Credit Ratings and Bond Risks: Explain the importance of credit ratings in bond investments. How does the credit rating of a bond issuer influence the bond's yield and risk?

Primary Versus Secondary Bond Markets: Distinguish between the primary and secondary markets in bond trading. How do the dynamics of these markets affect bond prices?

Yield Curve Insights: How can the shape of the yield curve provide insights into economic expectations? Discuss the significance of a normal versus an inverted yield curve.

Investment Strategies: Considering the different types of government bonds, what strategies might an investor use to balance risk and returns?

Tax Implications of Bonds: Explore the tax implications of investing in different types of government bonds. How might this affect an investor's decision?

Bond Market as an Economic Indicator: Discuss why the bond market is considered a leading indicator for the economy. How can changes in bond market trends guide your investment decisions?

Personal Connection to Bonds: Have you or your family ever invested in government bonds? If so, what motivated the decision, and what was the experience like?

Selling Bonds in the Secondary Market: What factors should you consider when selling bonds in the secondary market? How do market conditions affect the sale price?

FIXED INCOME 301
CORPORATE AND INTERNATIONAL BONDS

Initial Thoughts on Corporate Bonds: How did you view corporate bonds before this chapter, and what has changed now?

First Impressions of "Junk Bonds": When you first heard about junk bonds, what was your reaction? How has your understanding of them evolved?

Emotional Response to High-Risk Bonds: What are your feelings toward investing in high-risk bonds, like high-yield or junk bonds?

Impact of Michael Milken on Bonds: How would you describe Michael Milken's influence on the corporate bond market?

Corporate Bond Maturities and Credit Ratings: Discuss the significance of maturity periods and credit ratings in corporate bonds.

Interest Rate Dynamics in Corporate Bonds: How do market conditions affect the interest rates of corporate bonds?

Balancing Risk and Reward in Bond Investments: Reflect on your approach to balancing risk and reward when choosing between different types of corporate bonds.

Insights from Real-World Corporate Bonds: What lessons can be learned from the bond issuance strategies of companies like Apple or AT&T?

Perceiving International Bonds: How has this chapter influenced your views on the risks and opportunities in international bonds?

The Role of Sovereign Credit Ratings: Discuss how sovereign credit ratings affect your approach to international bond investments.

Analyzing Argentina's Century Bond: Share your thoughts on Argentina's hundred-year bond and its implications for risk management in bond investing.

Integrating Chapter Concepts into Investment Strategies: How do you plan to incorporate the insights from this chapter into your future investment strategies?

ADVANCED MARKETS 101 & 201
COMMODITIES AND CURRENCIES

Perceptions of Commodities Before and After: How has your understanding of commodities, such as gold and oil, evolved after reading this chapter? Were there any misconceptions or surprises?

Gold's Role in Investment: Reflecting on gold as a "safe haven," how do you see its place in your own investment strategy or portfolio?

Oil Price Dynamics: How do you now understand the factors that influence oil prices, especially in relation to the US dollar and global events?

The Significance of Soft Commodities: In what ways do you think soft commodities like wheat or coffee affect the market and daily life?

Understanding Futures Contracts: How has your perception of futures contracts changed? Do you see them as a viable investment option for your portfolio?

Diversity in Commodity Stocks: After learning about commodity stocks, how do you view their role in diversification of an investment portfolio?

Insights into Forex Trading: Reflect on your newfound knowledge of forex trading. How do you perceive its risks and potential rewards in the world of investing?

Changing Views on Cryptocurrency: How has your perspective on cryptocurrency as an investment option changed? What are the key risks and benefits you now recognize?

Commodities Versus Stocks and Bonds: How do commodities as an investment differ from stocks and bonds, based on your understanding?

The Importance of Commodity Markets: Why are commodity markets important in the global economy, and how do they affect everyday consumers?

Gold and Economic Crises: How do you think gold behaves during economic crises, and why might it be considered a "safe haven"?

Role of Geopolitics in Oil Prices: How do geopolitics and global events influence oil prices, and why is this significant for investors?

The Concept of Currency Trading: How would you explain the concept of currency trading to someone new to this topic?

Personal Risk Tolerance in Forex and Crypto: Given the volatility in forex and crypto markets, how do you assess your own risk tolerance in these areas?

Learning from Commodity and Currency Markets: What are the most important lessons or insights you have gained from this chapter about advanced markets?

ADVANCED MARKETS 301
DERIVATIVES

Understanding Derivatives: How would you explain derivatives to someone unfamiliar with them? What makes them different from direct investments like stocks and bonds?

Risk Assessment of Derivatives: Reflect on the risks associated with derivatives. How do they compare to other investment classes you are familiar with?

2008 Financial Crisis and Derivatives: How did your perception of derivatives change after learning about their role in the 2008 financial crisis?

Appropriateness of Derivatives for Different Investors: Based on your financial situation and investment experience, do you think derivatives are a suitable investment for you? Why or why not?

Options in Derivatives: Explain the difference between call options and put options. How can each be used in an investment strategy?

Deciding to Exercise Options: What factors would you consider when deciding whether to exercise a call or put option?

Real-Life Applications of Options: Can you think of a real-life scenario where buying an option (either call or put) would be advantageous?

The Role of Expiration Dates in Options: How does the expiration date of an option affect your decision-making process in option trading?

Premiums in Option Trading: Discuss the significance of the premium paid for an option. What does it represent, and how does it impact your investment?

Market Price Versus Strike Price: How does the relationship between the market price and the strike price of a stock affect your decision to exercise an option?

Long Positions Versus Short Positions in Options: Compare and contrast long and short positions in options trading. Which do you think involves more risk?

The Concepts of "In the Money" and "Out of the Money": Explain what it means for an option to be in the money or out of the money. How does this status influence investment decisions?

Naked Options and Their Risks: What are naked options, and why are they considered risky? Would you consider using them in your investment strategy?

YOUR PORTFOLIO 101
FUNDS

Funds as a Wealth Growth Strategy: Reflect on why investing in funds might be considered an "easy" way to grow long-term wealth. How does understanding individual investments enhance appreciation for funds?

Public Versus Private Funds: Distinguish between public and private funds. What makes public funds more accessible to the average investor?

Passive Versus Active Management: Compare and contrast passive and actively managed funds. What are the benefits and drawbacks of each?

The Impact of Fees on Fund Investments: Discuss how fees can affect the profitability of managed funds over time. Why might lower-fee funds be more appealing to investors?

Index Fund Basics: What is an index fund, and how does it work? How do index funds provide diversification?

Differences Between ETFs and Mutual Funds: Explain the key differences between ETFs and mutual funds that track indexes. What are the implications for investors?

Large-Cap Versus Small-Cap Funds: Describe the differences between large-cap and small-cap funds. How might an investor decide which is more suitable for their portfolio?

Growth Versus Value Funds: What distinguishes growth funds from value funds? Provide examples of what types of companies might be included in each.

Advantages and Risks of Bond Index Funds: What are the benefits of investing in bond index funds, and what risks do they carry, especially in relation to interest rates?

Understanding Duration in Bond Funds: Explain the concept of duration in bond funds and its significance in assessing risk.

Alternative Mutual Funds: Explore the concept of alternative mutual funds. What might these include, and how do they differ from standard mutual funds?

Target-Date Funds: Discuss the purpose and structure of target-date funds. What are the potential misconceptions and risks associated with them?

Introduction to REITs: What are Real Estate Investment Trusts (REITs), and how do they allow investors to engage in real estate markets without owning physical properties?

Venture Capital and Hedge Funds: Contrast venture capital funds with hedge funds in terms of investment goals, risk levels, and accessibility for the average investor.

Personal Investment Strategy: Based on the information about funds, how would you adjust or reaffirm your personal investment strategy?

The Role of Funds in Diversification: How do different types of funds contribute to portfolio diversification, and why is this important for long-term investment success?

YOUR PORTFOLIO 201
ASSET ALLOCATION

Investment Portfolio as a Financial Ecosystem: Reflect on the analogy of an investment portfolio as a personal financial ecosystem. How does diversification contribute to the resilience of this ecosystem?

Defining Investment Goals: Why is it important to define your investment goals before constructing a portfolio?

Assessing Risk Tolerance: How does understanding your risk tolerance influence the composition of your investment portfolio?

Determining Investment Horizon: Discuss the impact of your investment horizon on asset allocation within your portfolio.

Importance of Diversification: Why is diversification across different asset classes crucial for managing investment risk?

Choosing Investments: What factors should you consider when selecting specific investments for your portfolio?

Staying Disciplined in Investing: How can staying disciplined help you maintain your investment strategy during market fluctuations?

Keeping Costs Low: Why are low costs important in investment choices, and how can they affect your long-term returns?

Tax Efficiency in Investing: Discuss the role of tax efficiency in investment strategy and portfolio construction.

Avoiding Overconcentration: Explain the risks of overconcentration in a single investment, sector, or country.

Portfolio Adjustments and Market Changes: How often should a portfolio be reviewed and adjusted in response to market changes or personal circumstances?

Balanced Portfolio Approach: Describe the benefits of a balanced portfolio and how to achieve it through a mix of equities and debt securities.

Age Percentage Rule in Portfolio Allocation: How does the age percentage rule guide the allocation between bonds and stocks/funds in a portfolio?

Venture Capital Funds: Discuss the appeal and risks associated with investing in venture capital funds.

Hedge Funds: What are hedge funds, and what unique risks and opportunities do they present to investors?

The 60/40 Allocation Strategy: Explain the rationale behind the classic 60/40 allocation between stocks and bonds.

The 50/50 Portfolio Allocation: Discuss the advantages and potential drawbacks of a 50/50 allocation between stocks and bonds.

Permanent Portfolio Strategy: Describe the Permanent Portfolio strategy and its intended benefits across different economic conditions.

The Endowment Model: What is the endowment model, and how does it diversify investments beyond traditional stocks and bonds?

Ray Dalio's All-Weather Portfolio: Explain the composition and philosophy behind Ray Dalio's All-Weather Portfolio.

Warren Buffett's Investment Strategy: Summarize Warren Buffett's recommended portfolio allocation and its underlying principles.

Personalizing Your Portfolio: How can individual preferences and risk tolerance influence the customization of your investment portfolio?

YOUR PORTFOLIO 301
REVISIT AND REBALANCE

Concept of Rebalancing: What does rebalancing your investment portfolio involve, and why is it compared to tending a flowering bush?

Importance of Revisiting Day: Discuss the significance of setting aside a day to revisit your investment portfolio. What factors might prompt this review?

Strategies for Rebalancing: What are some effective strategies for rebalancing your investment portfolio, and how do they help maintain your desired asset allocation?

Calendar-Based Rebalancing: Explain how calendar-based rebalancing works and its benefits in maintaining investment discipline.

Threshold-Based Rebalancing: Describe threshold-based rebalancing and how it ensures your portfolio remains aligned with your investment strategy.

Cash Flow Rebalancing: How does cash flow rebalancing minimize transaction costs and taxes while maintaining portfolio balance?

Tax-Efficient Rebalancing: Discuss the role of tax efficiency in rebalancing and strategies to minimize tax liabilities.

Automatic Rebalancing Services: What are automatic rebalancing services, and how can they simplify portfolio management?

Risk Management Through Rebalancing: How does rebalancing help in managing the risk profile of your investment portfolio?

Maintaining Investment Goals with Rebalancing: Explain how rebalancing keeps your investment strategy on track with your goals.

Buy Low, Sell High Principle in Rebalancing: How does rebalancing naturally incorporate the principle of buying low and selling high?

Adapting to Life Changes: How does rebalancing allow your portfolio to adapt to changes in life circumstances and financial goals?

Emotional Discipline in Investing: Discuss the importance of emotional discipline in the rebalancing process and avoiding market timing mistakes.

Protecting Your Portfolio: What measures can you take to protect your investment portfolio from legal issues or bankruptcy?

Role of Trusts and Insurance: How do trusts and insurance play a role in protecting your investments and ensuring financial security?

Investment-Grade Insurance Products: Describe investment-grade insurance products and their role in a comprehensive investment strategy.

Mixing and Matching Trust Characteristics: Explain the flexibility in trust structures, such as revocable versus irrevocable and living versus testamentary trusts.

Benefits of Trusts: Discuss the peace of mind and potential tax benefits provided by setting up trusts.

Seeking Professional Advice: When might it be beneficial to seek professional advice for protecting and managing your investment portfolio?

Volatility Versus Risk: How does understanding the difference between volatility and risk influence your investment decisions?

The Role of Self-Advising: Reflect on the importance of becoming your own investment advisor and the benefits of investing in yourself.

SOURCES

ARTICLES AND INFOGRAPHICS

"1867: First Stock Ticker Debuts," This Day in History, History.com, n.d., https://www.history.com/this-day-in-history/first-stock-ticker-debuts.

"7 U.S. Code § 13–1 - Violations, Prohibition Against Dealings in Motion Picture Box Office Receipts or Onion Futures; Punishment," Legal Information Institute, Cornell Law School, n.d., https://www.law.cornell.edu/uscode/text/7/13-1.

Adams, Riley. "What Is My Tax Bracket?" Intuit Turbotax, updated December 19, 2023, https://turbotax.intuit.com/tax-tips/irs-tax-return/what-is-my-tax-bracket/L3Dtkab8G.

"Advantages and Disadvantages of Future Contracts," Upcounsel, updated February 1, 2023, https://www.upcounsel.com/advantages-and-disadvantages-of-future-contracts.

Aguirre, Jessica Camille. "'It's Like a Burning Theater, and Everyone Is Trying to Get to the Door': Oil Traders on the Day Prices Went Negative," *Vanity Fair*, May 27, 2020, https://www.vanityfair.com/news/2020/05/oil-traders-on-the-day-prices-went-negative.

Alladi, Amrutha, and Neelotpal Shukla. "The Percentage of Female Fund Managers Is Almost Exactly Where It Was 20 Years Ago," Morningstar, March 7, 2023, https://www.morningstar.com/funds/percentage-female-fund-managers-is-almost-exactly-where-it-was-20-years-ago.

Alvarez, David. "July 13, 1977: New York City Blackout Adjourns Mets-Cubs Game for Two Months," Society for American Baseball Research, December 2020, https://sabr.org/gamesproj/game/july-13-1977-nyc-blackout-adjourns-mets-cubs-game-for-two-months.

Amadeo, Kimberly. "Securities and Their Effect on the U.S. Economy," The Balance, April 11, 2021, https://www.thebalance.com/securities-definition-and-effect-on-the-u-s-economy-3305961.

"American Stock Exchange: Historical Timeline," New York Stock Exchange, https://www.nyse.com/publicdocs/American_Stock_Exchange_Historical_Timeline.pdf.

"The Apology, Plato," SparkNotes, n.d., https://www.sparknotes.com/philosophy/apology/section3/.

Arezki, Rabah, and Ha Nguyen. "Coping with a Dual Shock: COVID-19 and Oil Prices," World Bank Group, April 14, 2020, https://www.worldbank.org/en/region/mena/brief/coping-with-a-dual-shock-coronavirus-covid-19-and-oil-prices.

Arnott, Rob, Jason Hsu, Vitali Kalesnik, and Phil Tindall. "The Surprising Alpha from Malkiel's Monkey and Upside-Down Strategies," Research Affiliates, August 2013, https://www.researchaffiliates.com/publications/journal-papers/p_2013_aug_surprising_alpha.

Bajpal, Prableen. "What Is the Nasdaq Composite, and What Companies Are in It?" Nasdaq, May 12, 2021, https://www.nasdaq.com/articles/what-is-the-nasdaq-composite-and-what-companies-are-in-it-2021-05-12.

Baldridge, Rebecca. "Why Hedge Funds Love Investing in Distressed Debt," Investopedia, updated June 16, 2023, https://www.investopedia.com/articles/bonds/08/distressed-debt-hedge-fund.asp.

Baldwin, James Garrett. "How to Become an Accredited Investor," Investopedia, updated March 17, 2024, https://www.investopedia.com/articles/investing/092815/how-become-accredited-investor.asp.

Barber, Felix, and Michael Goold. "The Strategic Secret of Private Equity," *Harvard Business Review*, September 2007, https://hbr.org/2007/09/the-strategic-secret-of-private-equity.

"The Basics of Outstanding Shares and the Float," Investopedia, updated July 23, 2023, https://www.investopedia.com/articles/basics/03/030703.asp.

Beattie, Andrew. "The SEC: A Brief History of Regulation," Investopedia, updated September 23, 2021, https://www.investopedia.com/articles/07/secbeginning.asp.

Benson, Alana. "Betterment Review 2024: Fees, Service & Features to Know," NerdWallet, January 2, 2024, https://www.nerdwallet.com/reviews/investing/advisors/betterment.

Benson, Alana, and Arielle O'Shea. "12 Best Robo-Advisors: Top Low-Cost & Free Options," NerdWallet, July 1, 2024, https://www.nerdwallet.com/best/investing/robo-advisors.

Berger, Rob, and Benjamin Curry. "How to Understand the P/E Ratio," *Forbes*, October 25, 2023, https://www.forbes.com/advisor/investing/what-is-pe-price-earnings-ratio/.

"Bernie Madoff and Wife Ruth Attempted Suicide," ABC News, October 26, 2011, https://abcnews.go.com/Blotter/bernie-madoff-wife-ruth-attempted-suicide/story?id=14821587.

Birger, Jon. "What Onions Teach Us About Oil Prices," CNN Money, June 30, 2008, https://anewscafe.com/2008/06/29/redding/what-onions-teach-us-about-oil-prices/.

Bivens, Josh, and Jori Kandra. "CEO Pay Has Skyrocketed 1,460% Since 1978," Economic Policy Institute, October 4, 2022, https://www.epi.org/publication/ceo-pay-in-2021/.

Bolton, Noah. "Best Dividend Stocks for July 2024," Investopedia, updated July 1, 2024, https://www.investopedia.com/best-dividend-stocks-4774650.

Boocker, Sam, and David Wessel. "What Is Private Credit? Does It Pose Financial Stability Risks?" Brookings Institution, February 2, 2024, https://www.brookings.edu/articles/what-is-private-credit-does-it-pose-financial-stability-risks/.

"Breaking Down Venture Capital's Out Performance of Public Markets: Perspective from Alumni Ventures," Yahoo!Finance, January 18, 2023, https://finance.yahoo.com/news/breaking-down-venture-capital-performance-153000397.html.

Brewer, Preston. "ANALYSIS: Three Decades of IPO Deals (1990–2019)," Bloomberg Law, January 9, 2020, https://news.bloomberglaw.com/bloomberg-law-analysis/analysis-three-decades-of-ipo-deals-1990-2019.

Browning, Lynnley. "The Loneliest Woman in New York," *New York Times*, June 12, 2009, https://www.nytimes.com/2009/06/14/fashion/14ruth.html.

"California Income Tax Calculator, 2023–2024," https://www.forbes.com/advisor/income-tax-calculator/california/?deductions=0&filing=single&income=1000000&ira=0&k401=0.

Caplinger, Dan. "How to Invest in Bonds: A Beginner's Guide to Buying Bonds," The Motley Fool, updated March 7, 2024, https://www.fool.com/investing/how-to-invest/bonds/.

Cardwell, Matt. "Capital Gains vs. Ordinary Income Tax," Rocket Money, updated December 15, 2023, https://www.rocketmoney.com/learn/personal-finance/capital-gains-vs-ordinary-income-tax.

Champlin, Robert. "'When I Buy Stock Where Does My Money Go?' & Other Questions," Invest Some Money, updated February 3, 2024, https://investsomemoney.com/when-i-buy-stock-where-does-my-money-go-other-questions/.

Chen, James. "Cash Management Bill (CMB): Meaning, Examples and Use Cases," Investopedia, updated August 19, 2022, https://www.investopedia.com/terms/c/cmb.asp.

Chen, James. "Day Trader: Definition, Techniques, Strategies, and Risks," Investopedia, updated June 13, 2022, https://www.investopedia.com/terms/d/daytrader.asp.

Chen, James. "Earnings Call," Investopedia, updated June 20, 2021, https://www
.investopedia.com/terms/e/earnings-call.asp.

Chen, James. "Outstanding Shares Definition and How to Locate the Number," Investopedia,
updated April 10, 2024, https://www.investopedia.com/terms/o/outstandingshares
.asp.

Chen, James. "Yields in Finance: Formula, Types, and What It Tells You," Investopedia,
updated May 31, 2024, https://www.investopedia.com/terms/y/yield.asp.

Christian, Rachel. "What Is a Treasury Bond?" Bankrate, April 10, 2024, https://www
.bankrate.com/investing/treasury-bonds/.

Click, Kelli. "Amended SEC Accredited Investor Definition Opens New
Doors for Some Investors," Forbes, November 25, 2020, https://www
.forbes.com/sites/kelliclick/2020/11/24/amended-sec-accredited-investor
-definition-opens-new-doors-for-some-investors/.

Cohen, Lauren, Christopher J. Malloy, and Quoc Nguyen. "Lazy Prices," Academic
Research Colloquium for Financial Planning and Related Disciplines, March 7,
2019, https://ssrn.com/abstract=1658471.

Cote, Catherine. "3 Key Types of Private Equity Strategies," Harvard Business School,
July 13, 2021, https://online.hbs.edu/blog/post/types-of-private-equity.

Cummans, Jared. "A Brief History of Bond Investing," BondFunds, October 1, 2014,
http://bondfunds.com/education/a-brief-history-of-bond-investing/.

Curwen, Lesley. "The Collapse of Enron and the Dark Side of Business," BBC, August 3,
2021, https://www.bbc.com/news/business-58026162.

de Chesare, Bryan. "Traders and Brokers: Bud Fox vs. Gordon Gekko?" Mergers and
Acquisitions, November 15, 2016, https://www.mergersandinquisitions.com
/traders-vs-brokers/.

Deichmann, Jake. "Wealthfront," The PMF Chronicles, August 31, 2021, https://pmf
chronicles.substack.com/p/wealthfront.

Deter, Amber. "3 Types of Securities Investments Explained," Investment U, January 23,
2020, https://investmentu.com/types-of-securities-investments-explained/.

Edwards, John. "The 9 Biggest Hedge Fund Failures," Investopedia, updated May 29,
2023, https://www.investopedia.com/articles/investing/101515/3-biggest-hedge
-fund-scandals.asp#citation-12.

"ETFs 101," Fidelity, n.d., https://www.fidelity.com/learning-center/investment
-products/etf/what-are-etfs.

"Evolution of OTC Derivatives Markets Since the Financial Crisis," ISDA, January 12,
2021, https://www.isda.org/2021/01/12/evolution-of-otc-derivatives-markets-since
-the-financial-crisis/.

Farley, Alan. "How to Set Up Your Trading Screens," Investopedia, updated June 30, 2024, https://www.investopedia.com/articles/active-trading/081215/how-set-your -trading-screens.asp.

Feinzeig, Leslie. "Why It's Incredibly Rare for Companies Led and Founded by Women to IPO," *Fast Company*, July 16, 2021, https://www.fastcompany.com/90655295 /why-arent-more-women-starting-vc-funds.

Fernando, Jason. "Bonds: How They Work and How to Invest," Investopedia, updated May 3, 2024, https://www.investopedia.com/terms/b/bond.asp.

Fernando, Jason. "Market Capitalization: What It Means for Investors," Investopedia, updated March 5, 2024, https://www.investopedia.com/terms/m/marketcapital ization.asp.

Ferri, Rick. "Any Monkey Can Beat the Market," *Forbes*, April 14, 2022, https:// www.forbes.com/sites/rickferri/2012/12/20/any-monkey-can-beat-the-market /?sh=5fa32c9e630a.

Fink, Ronald. "Why Active Managers Have Trouble Keeping Up with the Pack," Chicago Booth Review, July 3, 2014, https://www.chicagobooth.edu/review /why-active-managers-have-trouble-keeping-up-with-the-pack.

Fisher, Ken. "November 1867: The Invention of the Stock Ticker," kenfisher .com, November 20, 2019, https://www.kenfisher.com/market-history /november-1867-the-invention-of-the-stock-ticker.

Fontinelle, Amy. "Companies That Pay Dividends—and Those That Don't," Investope- dia, updated November 30, 2021, https://www.investopedia.com/ask/answers/12 /why-do-some-companies-pay-a-dividend.asp.

Fontinelle, Eric. "4 Basic Things to Know About Bonds," Investopedia, updated June 14, 2024, https://www.investopedia.com/articles/bonds/08/bond-market-basics.asp.

Franck, Thomas. "Build America Bonds May Be Key to Financing Biden's Infrastructure Plans," CNBC, March 26, 2021, https://www.cnbc.com/2021/03/26/build-america -bonds-may-be-key-to-financing-bidens-infrastructure-plans.html.

Frankel, Matthew. "Stock vs. Share: What's the Difference?" The Motley Fool, updated November 20, 2023, https://www.fool.com/investing/how-to-invest/stocks /stock-v-share/.

Frankel, Matthew. "When to Sell Stocks—for Profit or Loss," The Motley Fool, updated November 13, 2023, https://www.fool.com/investing/how-to-invest/stocks /when-to-sell-stocks/.

"Fraudster Bernard Madoff and Wife 'Attempted Suicide,'" BBC News, October 26, 2011, https://www.bbc.com/news/world-us-canada-15471683.

Fries, Tim. "Brokers vs. Traders," The Tokenist, updated January 24, 2023, https://tokenist.com/investing/brokers-vs-traders/.

Furhmann, Ryan. "How to Invest in Private Companies," Investopedia, updated January 7, 2024, https://www.investopedia.com/articles/basics/11/investing-in-private-companies.asp.

"Futures and Commodities," Finra, n.d., https://www.finra.org/investors/learn-to-invest/types-investments/security-futures.

Gad, Sham. "What Is a Hedge Fund?" Investopedia, updated February 2, 2024, https://www.investopedia.com/articles/investing/102113/what-are-hedge-funds.asp.

Ganti, Akhilesh. "What Is a Trust Fund and How Does It Work?" Investopedia, updated February 26, 2024, https://www.investopedia.com/terms/t/trust-fund.asp.

Glode, Vincent. "Why Mutual Funds 'Underperform,'" *Journal of Financial Economics*, October 2010, https://finance.wharton.upenn.edu/~vglode/WMFU.pdf.

Goodkind, Nicole. "America Has Lost Half Its Public Companies Since the 1990s. Here's Why," CNN Business, June 9, 2023, https://www.cnn.com/2023/06/09/investing/premarket-stocks-trading/index.html.

"A Guide to the Capital Gains Tax Rate: Short-Term vs. Long-Term Capital Gains Taxes," Intuit Turbotax, updated December 22, 2023, https://turbotax.intuit.com/tax-tips/investments-and-taxes/guide-to-short-term-vs-long-term-capital-gains-taxes-brokerage-accounts-etc/L7KCu9etn.

Hansen, Sarah. "Here's What Negative Oil Prices Really Mean," *Forbes*, April 21, 2020, https://www.forbes.com/sites/sarahhansen/2020/04/21/heres-what-negative-oil-prices-really-mean/?sh=783fbc535a85.

Hawkins, Ken. "The Art of Cutting Your Losses," Investopedia, updated June 30, 2024, https://www.investopedia.com/articles/stocks/08/capital-losses.asp.

Hayes, Adam. "Bernie Madoff: Who He Was and How His Ponzi Scheme Worked," Investopedia, updated June 23, 2024, https://www.investopedia.com/terms/b/bernard-madoff.asp.

Hayes, Adam. "The Bond Market and Debt Securities: An Overview," Investopedia, updated October 25, 2023, https://www.investopedia.com/terms/b/bondmarket.asp.

Hayes, Adam. "Listing Requirements: Definition and Criteria for Stock Exchanges," Investopedia, updated April 19, 2023, https://www.investopedia.com/terms/l/listingrequirements.asp.

Hayes, Adam. "Mezzanine Financing: What Mezzanine Debt Is and How It's Used," Investopedia, updated June 13, 2024, https://www.investopedia.com/terms/m/mezzaninefinancing.asp.

Hayes, Adam. "The NYSE and Nasdaq: How They Work," Investopedia, updated March 14, 2024, https://www.investopedia.com/articles/basics/03/103103.asp.

Hayes, Adam. "REIT vs. Real Estate Fund: What's the Difference?," Investopedia, updated July 16, 2023, https://www.investopedia.com/ask/answers/012015/what -difference-between-reit-and-real-estate-fund.asp.

Hayes, Adam. "Understanding Liquidity and How to Measure It," Investopedia, updated May 18, 2024, https://www.investopedia.com/terms/l/liquidity.asp.

Hayes, Adam. "What Is a Stock Ticker? Definition, How It Works, and Origins," Investo-pedia, updated May 3, 2024, https://www.investopedia.com/ask/answers/12/what -is-a-stock-ticker.asp.

Hayward, Clarissa. "Why Does the U.S. Use Public Revenue to Support Pri-vate Home Ownership?" *Washington Post*, April 15, 2015, https://www .washingtonpost.com/news/monkey-cage/wp/2015/04/15/why-does-the-u-s -use-public-revenue-to-support-private-home-ownership/.

"Hedge Fund: Definition, Examples, Types, and Strategies," Investopedia, updated April 12, 2024, https://www.investopedia.com/terms/h/hedgefund.asp.

Hertig, Alyssa. "Bitcoin Halving, Explained," CoinDesk, October 4, 2022, https://www .coindesk.com/learn/bitcoin-halving-explained/.

Hirtzer, Michael. "Flashy Jackets of Chicago Traders May Soon Exist Only on the Silver Screen," Reuters, February 25, 2015, https://www.reuters.com/article/cme-group -closure-jackets/rpt-flashy-jackets-of-chicago-traders-may-soon-exist-only-on-the -silver-screen-idUSL1N0VF3AB20150206.

Hollingsworth, David, and Emily Liner. "The Bond Market: How It Works, or How It Doesn't," Third Way, February 27, 2015, https://www.thirdway.org/report /the-bond-market-how-it-works-or-how-it-doesnt.

Horowitz, Juliana Menasce, Ruth Igielnik, and Rakesh Kochhar. "Trends in Income and Wealth Inequality," Pew Research Center, January 9, 2020, https://www.pew research.org/social-trends/2020/01/09/trends-in-income-and-wealth-inequality/.

"How to Get a Company's Prospectus," Investopedia, updated April 12, 2024, https:// www.investopedia.com/ask/answers/04/022104.asp.

"How to List on a Stock Exchange," Chron., n.d., https://smallbusiness.chron.com /list-stock-exchange-43211.html.

Huang, Eustace, and Pippa Stevens. "An Oil Futures Contract Expiring Tuesday Went Negative in Bizarre Move Showing a Demand Collapse," CNBC, April 20, 2020, https://www.cnbc.com/2020/04/20/oil-markets-us-crude-futures-in-focus-as -coronavirus-dents-demand.html.

Jarzebowski, Martin. "Will ESG Prevent the Next Enron?" *Forbes*, August 4, 2021, https://www.forbes.com/sites/forbesfinancecouncil/2021/08/04/will-esg-prevent-the-next-enron/?sh=320c21f45cd7.

Kagan, Julia. "What Is FINRA's Central Registration Depository (CRD)?" Investopedia, updated November 29, 2020, https://www.investopedia.com/terms/c/crd.asp.

Kaiser-Schatzlein, Robin. "Bernie Madoff Lives," *New Republic*, April 15, 2021, https://newrepublic.com/article/162053/bernie-madoff-dead-hedge-fund-regulation.

Kaplan, Michael. "How the Macho NYSE Trader Became an Endangered Species," *New York Post*, February 15, 2020, https://nypost.com/2020/02/15/how-the-macho-nyse-trader-became-an-endangered-species/.

Karma, Rogé. "The Secretive Industry Devouring the U.S. Economy," *The Atlantic*, October 30, 2023, https://www.theatlantic.com/ideas/archive/2023/10/private-equity-publicly-traded-companies/675788/.

Kenton, Will. "Derivatives Time Bomb: Definition and Warren Buffett's Warnings," Investopedia, updated September 19, 2023, https://www.investopedia.com/terms/d/derivativestimebomb.asp.

Kenton, Will. "Order Imbalance: Definition, Causes, and Trading Strategies," Investopedia, updated March 17, 2022, https://www.investopedia.com/terms/o/order-imbalance.asp.

Kenton, Will. "What Are Financial Securities? Examples, Types, Regulation, and Importance," Investopedia, updated May 31, 2024, https://www.investopedia.com/terms/s/security.asp.

Kenton, Will. "What Beta Means for Investors," Investopedia, updated May 31, 2024, https://www.investopedia.com/terms/b/beta.asp.

Klempner, Geoffrey. "Socrates and the Oracle of Delphi," Ask a Philosopher, September 9, 2011, https://askaphilosopher.org/2011/09/09/socrates-and-the-oracle-of-delphi/.

Kolhatkar, Sheela. "Poor Ruth," *New York*, July 2, 2009, https://nymag.com/news/features/57772/.

Kramer, Leslie. "How Are a Company's Stock Price and Market Cap Determined?" Investopedia, updated September 11, 2022, https://www.investopedia.com/articles/basics/04/100804.asp.

Kuepper, Justin. "Black Wednesday: George Soros's Bet Against Britain," The Balance, May 8, 2022, https://www.thebalance.com/black-wednesday-george-soros-bet-against-britain-1978944.

La Roche, Julia. "A Day in the Life of a New York Stock Exchange Floor Broker," *Business Insider*, March 21, 2013, https://www.businessinsider.com/what-a-nyse-floor-broker-does-2013-3?op=1.

Lee, Juhohn. "How Negative Oil Prices Revealed the Dangers of the Futures Market," CNBC, June 16, 2020, https://www.cnbc.com/2020/06/16/how-negative-oil-prices-revealed-the-dangers-of-futures-trading.html.

Light, Joe, and Scott Thurm. "Disney, Walton, Ford, Gates: Tales of When Legends Leave," *Wall Street Journal*, August 26, 2011, https://www.wsj.com/articles/SB10001424053111904875404576530864214225444.

Lioudis, Nick. "How Does an Investor Make Money on Bonds?" Investopedia, updated September 17, 2022, https://www.investopedia.com/ask/answers/how-does-investor-make-money-on-bonds/.

Liu, Evie. "AMC and GameStop Are Taking Over These Small-Cap ETFs," *Barron's*, June 3, 2021, https://www.barrons.com/articles/amc-and-gamestop-are-taking-over-these-small-cap-etfs-51622756046.

Long, Heather. "Ultimate Office Decoration: Stock Certificate," CNN Business, September 10, 2014.

Lutz, James D. "Lest We Forget, a Short History of Housing in the United States," American Council for an Energy-Efficient Economy, Summer Study on Energy Efficiency in Buildings, August 2004, https://www.aceee.org/files/proceedings/2004/data/papers/SS04_Panel1_Paper17.pdf.

Marples, Alice. "The South Sea Bubble of 1720," The National Archives (UK), September 18, 2020, https://blog.nationalarchives.gov.uk/the-south-sea-bubble-of-1720/.

McFarlane, Greg. "What Beta Means for Investors," Investopedia, updated March 4, 2021, https://www.investopedia.com/articles/active-trading/040615/introduction-trading-oil-futures.asp.

"The Men Behind the Curtain: Who Are Market Makers?" Scanz, n.d., https://scanz.com/the-man-behind-the-curtain-who-is-the-market-maker/.

Michayluk, David. "The Rise and Fall of Single-Letter Ticker Symbols," *Business History* 50, no. 3 (2008), 368–385, https://doi.org/10.1080/00076790801968947.

Microsoft Corporation (MSFT) chart, Yahoo!Finance, https://finance.yahoo.com/quote/MSFT/chart.

"Microsoft Stock Certificate," RR Auction, ended March 17, 2022, https://www.rrauction.com/auctions/lot-detail/345341806328064-microsoft-stock-certificate.

"MicroStrategy Announces Fourth Quarter 2023 Financial Results; Now Holds 190,000 BTC," press release, MicroStrategy, February 6, 2024, https://www.microstrategy

.com/press/microstrategy-announces-fourth-quarter-2023-financial-results-now
-holds-190000-btc_02-06-2024.

Mitchell, Cory. "How to Use Stock Volume to Improve Your Trading," Investopedia, updated February 23, 2024, https://www.investopedia.com/articles/technical
/02/010702.asp.

Morah, Chizoba. "What Happens When Options Expire?" Investopedia, updated June 5,
2024, https://www.investopedia.com/ask/answers/09/option-expiration-date
-profits.asp.

Nagarajan, Shalini. "A Day Trader Who Bought Hundreds of Oil Contracts Was Told
He Owed $9 Million After a Trading-Platform Issue Meant It Failed to Show Oil's
Historic Plunge Below $0," Business Insider, May 13, 2020, https://markets.business
insider.com/news/commodities/oil-trader-loses-millions-on-brokerage-glitch-2020-5.

Nagarajan, Shalini. "Oil's Record-Setting Plunge Spreads as June Contracts Fall 36%,"
Business Insider, April 21, 2020, https://markets.businessinsider.com/news/stocks
/oil-price-wti-positive-after-historic-negative-prices-2020-4.

Nguyen, Joseph. "5 Reasons Why Investors Trade Bonds," Investopedia, updated August 1,
2022, https://www.investopedia.com/articles/bonds/11/5-reasons-to-trade-bonds
.asp.

"The Onion Ringer," Wall Street Journal, July 8, 2008, https://www.wsj.com/articles
/SB121547293036933987?mod=todays_asia_opinion.

"Opening Price: Definition, Example, Trading Strategies," Investopedia, updated January 16, 2024, https://www.investopedia.com/terms/o/openingprice.asp.

"Organ Futures," Wikipedia, updated October 14, 2022, https://en.wikipedia.org/wiki
/Organ_futures.

Palmer, Barclay. "Broker or Trader: Which Career Is Right for You?" Investopedia,
updated December 24, 2023, https://www.investopedia.com/articles/financial
careers/07/broker_trader.asp.

Palmer, Barclay. "Broker vs. Market Maker: What's the Difference?" Investopedia, updated March 30, 2022, https://www.investopedia.com/ask/answers/06
/brokerandmarketmaker.asp.

Pareto, Cathy. "Pick the Perfect Trust," Investopedia, updated December 14, 2023,
https://www.investopedia.com/articles/pf/08/trust-basics.asp.

Peck, Emily. "America's Growing Rent Burden," Axios, May 22, 2023, https://www.axios
.com/2023/05/22/americas-growing-rent-burden.

"Penny Stock," Wikipedia, updated June 4, 2024, https://en.wikipedia.org/wiki
/Penny_stock.

Petroff, Eric. "The Fed's Tools for Influencing the Economy," Investopedia, updated May 22, 2024, https://www.investopedia.com/articles/economics/08/monetary -policy-recession.asp.

Pisani, Joseph. "Disney Stops Issuing Paper Stock Certificates," *USA Today*, October 9, 2013, https://www.usatoday.com/story/money/business/2013/10/09 /disney-stock-certificates-head-to-never-never-land/2956765/.

Plaehn, Tim. "What Happens to a Stock Option If It Is Expired and You Don't Exercise It?" The Nest, updated April 24, 2019, https://budgeting.thenest.com/happens -stock-option-expired-dont-exercise-it-32350.html.

Pollman, Elizabeth. "Startup Failure," Harvard Law School Forum on Corporate Governance, September 29, 2023, https://corpgov.law.harvard.edu/2023/09/29 /startup-failure/.

"Primary and Secondary Markets for U.S. Treasury Securities," ThisMatter, n.d., https:// thismatter.com/money/bonds/types/government/treasury-markets.htm.

Rao, Dileep. "20 VCs Capture 95% of VC Profits: Implications for Entrepreneurs & Venture Ecosystems," *Forbes*, April 14, 2023, https://www.forbes.com/sites /dileeprao/2023/04/14/20-vcs-capture-95-of-vc-profits-implications-for -entrepreneurs--venture-ecosystems/?sh=7e440a534bf2.

Robbins, Tony. "Tony Robbins: Ray Dalio's 'All Weather' Portfolio," Yahoo!Finance, November 18, 2014, https://finance.yahoo.com/news/tony-robbins--ray-dalio-s --all-weather--portfolio-161619133.html.

"Role of Derivatives in Causing the Global Financial Crisis," Management Study Guide, n.d., https://www.managementstudyguide.com/role-of-derivatives-in-causing -global-financial-crisis.htm.

Romer, Keith. "The Great Onion Corner and the Futures Market," *Morning Edition*, NPR, October 22, 2015, https://www.npr.org/2015/10/22/450769853 /the-great-onion-corner-and-the-futures-market.

Roque, Hugo. "'I Think I Could Make 50% a Year:' Warren Buffett," Yahoo!Finance, December 5, 2018, https://finance.yahoo.com/news/think-could-50-warren -buffett-180028441.html.

Saefong, Myra P. "Oil Prices Went Negative a Year Ago: Here's What Traders Have Learned Since," MarketWatch, April 19, 2021, https://www.marketwatch.com /story/oil-prices-went-negative-a-year-ago-heres-what-traders-have-learned -since-11618863839.

Saito-Chung, David. "Still the No. 1 Rule for Stock Market Investors: Always Cut Your Losses Short," *Investor's Business Daily*, September 15, 2022, https://www .investors.com/how-to-invest/investors-corner/still-the-no-1-rule-for-stock -investors-always-cut-your-losses-short/.

Sauer, Megan. "Barbara Corcoran Says 90% of Her 'Shark Tank' Investments Don't Make Her Money—Here's Why She Doesn't Regret Any of Them," CNBC, May 9, 2023, https://www.cnbc.com/2023/05/09/barbara-corcoran-most-of-my-shark-tank-investments-dont-make-me-money.html.

Schonfeld, Erick. "SEC Gives Social Investing Site kaChing Green Light to Take On Mutual Funds," TechCrunch, December 15, 2008, https://techcrunch.com/2008/12/15/sec-gives-social-investing-site-kaching-green-light-to-take-on-mutual-funds/.

"SEC Charges Bernard L. Madoff for Multi-Billion Dollar Ponzi Scheme," press release, Securities and Exchange Commission, December 11, 2008, https://www.sec.gov/news/press/2008/2008-293.htm.

"Secondary Bond Market Trading," Overbond, n.d., https://www.overbond.com/academy/bond-investors/secondary-market-trading.

"Securities," Napkin Finance, n.d., https://napkinfinance.com/napkin/finance-securities/.

Segal, Troy. "The Art of Selling a Losing Position," Investopedia, updated June 1, 2022, https://www.investopedia.com/investing/selling-a-losing-stock/.

Segal, Troy. "Enron Scandal and Accounting Fraud: What Happened?" Investopedia, updated June 3, 2024, https://www.investopedia.com/updates/enron-scandal-summary/.

Seth, Shobhit. "10 of the Most Famous Public Companies That Went Private," Investopedia, updated April 30, 2023, https://www.investopedia.com/articles/active-trading/073015/10-most-famous-public-companies-went-private.asp.

Shaw, Richard. "Relationship Between Stock Price Direction and Gold, Silver and Copper," Seeking Alpha, May 16, 2011, https://seekingalpha.com/article/270029-relationship-between-stock-price-direction-and-gold-silver-and-copper.

Shiller, Robert J. Portfolio Investor Insurance and Other Investor Fashions as Factors in the 1987 Stock Market Crash, NBER Macroeconomics Annual 1988, Volume 3 (MIT Press, 1988), https://www.nber.org/system/files/chapters/c10958/c10958.pdf.

Shontell, Alyson. "Hundreds of Startups Go Public Every Year. Only 20 Are Founded and Led by Women," Business Insider, January 5, 2021, https://www.businessinsider.com/female-entrepreneurs-face-obstacles-taking-companies-public-2020-12.

Sraders, Anne. "What Is a Trust? Different Types & Their Uses," The Street, updated April 8, 2023, https://www.thestreet.com/personal-finance/what-is-a-trust-14644964.

Stewart, Terry. "The South Sea Bubble," Historic UK, n.d., https://www.historic-uk.com/HistoryUK/HistoryofEngland/South-Sea-Bubble/.

"Stock Market Crash Timeline," PBS, n.d., https://www.pbs.org/fmc/timeline/estock mktcrash.htm.

Stock Ticker, National Museum of American History, n.d, https://americanhistory .si.edu/collections/search/object/nmah_703474.

"Stocks Then and Now: The 1950s and 1970s," Investopedia, updated January 26, 2021, https://www.investopedia.com/articles/stocks/09/stocks-1950s-1970s.asp.

Streissguth, Tom. "Is a Negative Beta Coefficient More Risky Than a Positive in the Stock Market?" Zacks, March 31, 2019, https://finance.zacks.com/negative-beta -coefficient-risky-positive-stock-market-7596.html.

Taft, John. "Let's Not Forget—Bernie Madoff Was a Fiduciary," Financial Planning, November 12, 2018, https://www.financial-planning.com/opinion /lets-not-forget-bernie-madoff-was-a-fiduciary.

Teng, May, and Alyson Shontell. "Meet 22 Women Who Launched and Led Startups to an IPO, an Accomplishment Few Female Founders Have Ever Reached," Business Insider, February 9, 2021, https://www.businessinsider.com/female-founders -startup-fundraising-ipo-data#casey-lynch-co-founded-biopharmaceutical -company-cortexyme-and-took-it-public-in-may-2019-16.

Thompson, Cedric. "Payment for Order Flow (PFOF): Definition and How It Works," Investopedia, updated March 24, 2024, https://www.investopedia.com/terms/p /paymentoforderflow.asp.

"TIL Onions are the only commodity banned from futures trading in the United States. The Onion Futures Act was passed in 1958 after two traders cornered the onion market in Chicago controlling 98% of all available onions," Reddit, December 26, 2015, https://www.reddit.com/r/todayilearned/comments/3yc2jm /til_onions_are_the_only_commodity_banned_from/.

"Trading Jacket," Wikipedia, updated July 3, 2024, https://en.wikipedia.org/wiki /Trading_jacket.

"Types of Security," Corporate Finance Institute, n.d., https://corporatefinanceinstitute .com/resources/knowledge/trading-investing/types-of-security/.

"Using Beta to Understand a Stock's Risk," Investopedia, updated May 31, 2024, https:// www.investopedia.com/investing/beta-gauging-price-fluctuations/.

Vipond, Tim. "IPO Process," Corporate Finance Institute, n.d., https://corporatefinance institute.com/resources/knowledge/finance/ipo-process/.

"Wall Street Timeline," History.com, January 3, 2019, https://www.history.com/topics /us-states/wall-street-timeline.

"What Are Convertible Bonds?" Fidelity, n.d., https://www.fidelity.com/insights /investing-ideas/glossary-convertible-bonds.

"What Are Hedge Funds?" Syndicate Room, n.d., https://www.syndicateroom.com
  /alternative-investments/hedge-funds.

"What Are Small-Cap Stocks, and Are They a Good Investment?" Investopedia, updated
  June 27, 2024, https://www.investopedia.com/terms/s/small-cap.asp.

"What Causes Stock Prices to Change," Desjardins Online Brokerage, n.d., https://
  www.disnat.com/en/learning/trading-basics/stock-basics/what-causes-stock
  -prices-to-change.

"What Do Onion Prices Tell Us About Oil Prices?" *TIME*, July 9, 2008, https://business
  .time.com/2008/07/09/what_do_onions_tell_us_about_o/.

"What Does a Stockbroker Do?" Master of Finance, n.d., https://www.master-of-finance
  .org/faq/what-does-a-stockbroker-do.

Wile, Rob. "A Timeline of Elon Musk's Takeover of Twitter," NBC News, November 17, 2022, https://www.nbcnews.com/business/business-news/twitter-elon
  -musk-timeline-what-happened-so-far-rcna57532.

Young, Julie. "Special Purpose Acquisition Company (SPAC) Explained: Examples and
  Risks," Investopedia, updated December 16, 2023, https://www.investopedia.com
  /terms/s/spac.asp.

VIDEOS

"A Guide to Open Outcry Arbitrage Hand Signals," WBEZ Chicago, YouTube, July 2,
  2015, https://www.youtube.com/watch?v=yd3reEEWOoc.

"ICAP - Day in the Life of a Broker," ICAP Media Centre, October 29, 2010, YouTube,
  https://www.youtube.com/watch?v=ATlRemuKN_0.

Jordaan, Hannes. "How Trading on the New York Stock Exchange Actually Works," You-
  Tube, August 4, 2017, https://www.youtube.com/watch?v=eL1c11K5DmA&t=774s.

Piercy, Tony. "The Wall Street Stock Exchange - Top Documentary Film," YouTube,
  February 4, 2016, https://www.youtube.com/watch?v=90t-FBO8WNo.

taub .., "Open Outcry (PBS) - Part 2," YouTube, April 19, 2013, https://www.youtube
  .com/watch?v=mvx3xMo2iUs.

"Where Does the Money Go When You Buy a Stock?," Intelligent Stock Investing,
  YouTube, September 2, 2020, https://www.youtube.com/watch?v=h2kNYtbfiKw.

GOVERNMENT DOCUMENTS

"Alternative Mutual Funds," Investor.gov, U.S. Securities and Exchange Commission, n.d., https://www.investor.gov/introduction-investing/investing-basics
  /investment-products/mutual-funds-and-exchange-traded-funds.

Bernhardt, Donald, and Marshall Eckblad. "Stock Market Crash of 1987," Federal Reserve History, November 22, 2013, https://www.federalreservehistory.org/essays /stock-market-crash-of-1987.

"Bonds," Investor.gov, U.S. Securities and Exchange Commission, n.d., https://www .investor.gov/introduction-investing/investing-basics/investment-products /bonds-or-fixed-income-products/bonds.

"Dow Jones Industrial Average First Published," This Month in Business History, Library of Congress, n.d., https://guides.loc.gov/this-month-in-business-history /may/djia-first-published.

Engen, Eric M., and Andreas Lehnert. "Mutual Funds and the U.S. Equity Market," *Federal Reserve Bulletin*, December 2000, https://www.federalreserve.gov/pubs /bulletin/2000/1200lead.pdf.

Featured Stories, U.S. Department of the Treasury, https://home.treasury.gov/news /featured-stories.

"The History of U.S. Savings Bonds," Treasury Direct, Bureau of the Public Debt, n.d., https://www.treasurydirect.gov/timeline.htm.

"A History of the United States Savings Bond Program, 50th Anniversary Edition," Treasury Direct, Bureau of the Public Debt, January 1991, https://www.treasurydirect .gov/files/research-center/history-of-savings-bond/history-sb.pdf.

"H.R.2797 - Equal Opportunity for All Investors Act of 2023," 118th Congress (2023– 2024), https://www.congress.gov/bill/118th-congress/house-bill/2797.

"Interest Rate Risk—When Interest Rates Go Up, Prices of Fixed-Rate Bonds Fall," Office of Investor Education and Advocacy, Securities and Exchange Commission, n.d., https://www.sec.gov/files/ib_interestraterisk.pdf.

"Mutual Funds," Investor.gov, U.S. Securities and Exchange Commission, n.d., https:// www.investor.gov/introduction-investing/investing-basics/investment-products /mutual-funds-and-exchange-traded-1.

National Register of Historic Places nomination form for New York Stock Exchange, March 1977, https://npgallery.nps.gov/GetAsset/a7592662-8c96 -46be-af44-ebf03e828d13/.

"New York Stock Exchange Building Description and Analysis," Landmarks Preservation Commission, July 9, 1985, http://s-media.nyc.gov/agencies/lpc/lp/1529.pdf.

"Reserve Requirements," Board of Governors of the Federal Reserve System, March 15, 2020, https://www.federalreserve.gov/monetarypolicy/reservereq.htm.

"Savings Bonds," Investor.gov, U.S. Securities and Exchange Commission, n.d., https:// www.investor.gov/introduction-investing/investing-basics/investment-products /bonds-or-fixed-income-products/savings.

"SEC Modernizes the Accredited Investor Definition," press release, U.S. Securities and Exchange Commission, August 26, 2020, https://www.sec.gov/news/press-release/2020-191.

Sutch, Richard. "Liberty Bonds," Federal Reserve History, December 4, 2015, https://www.federalreservehistory.org/essays/liberty-bonds.

Treasury Direct, FAQ, opening an account, directory of services, https://www.treasurydirect.gov/indiv/help/tdhelp/faq.htm.

"What Is Risk," Investor.gov, U.S. Securities and Exchange Commission, n.d., https://www.investor.gov/introduction-investing/investing-basics/what-risk.

DATA REPOSITORIES

The Destiny Tech 100, https://destiny.xyz/tech100.

"Document Archives," Center for Research in Security Prices, n.d., http://www.crsp.org/resources/data.

Dow Jones Industrial Average, Google Finance, https://www.google.com/finance/quote/.DJI:INDEXDJX?sa=X&ved=2ahUKEwigyLOIi4DzAhWLRzABHYF1BCEQ3ecFegQITRAS&window=YTD.

National Association of Securities Dealers Automatic Quotation System (Nasdaq), https://www.nasdaq.com/glossary/n/national-association-of-securities-dealers-automatic-quotation-system.

"New York Stock Exchange: Company Listings," ADVFN, https://www.advfn.com/nyse/newyorkstockexchange.asp.

Ritter, Jay R. "Initial Public Offerings: Updated Statistics," Warrington College of Business, University of Florida, May 10, 2024, https://site.warrington.ufl.edu/ritter/files/IPO-Statistics.pdf.

"Wall Street and the Stock Exchanges: Historical Resources," Library of Congress, n.d., https://guides.loc.gov/wall-street-history/exchanges.

ACKNOWLEDGMENTS

I've long ranted that we should have learned about money in school. But ranting about and creating a solution for it are two very different things. The former is a solo sport (running my mouth is one of my favorite forms of cardio) and the latter is very much a team endeavor. So thank you to:

My brilliant business partner, Morgan Lavoie, for not only finishing my sentences but making them infinitely better.

My chief of staff for The Money School, Emily Holmes, for making all the trains run on time and for turning my gobbledygook into gold.

My web and social wizard, Sabrina Andersen, who has stuck with me for nearly twenty(!) years, for translating my nerdiness into—dare I say—fun online content.

My longtime book agent, Steve Troha, for giving me the best epidurals during all of my book births. And look at our five beautiful book babies now!

The entire HarperCollins Leadership team, Tim Burgard, Sicily Axton, Hannah Harless, Kevin Smith, and Lauren Kingsley, for not only helping to get *The Money School* out in the world but in the hands of those who need it most.

My fabulous beta team readers Jane Stoller, Alana Hart, Tabitha Cooper, Greg Cirillo, Mallory Pearce Foss, Jennifer Sunday, David Silversmith, Leah Graden, Kayla Wales, Rebecca Knows the Ground, Kelly Courington, Hannah Kliger, Julie Griggs, Heather Holland, Brie Johnson, Valerie Floyd, Rachael Paskvan, Andrew Goodman, and Patrick Grandinetti, for your hard work and insights that helped improve and elevate the final manuscript exponentially.

My personal squad, my cheerleaders, Tracy DiNunzio and Sarah Zurell, for always being there to hype me up. When the finish line for this book seemed impossibly far away, you were there to cheer me on . . . or lovingly drag me across it kicking and screaming.

My new Feldman family, for always proudly spreading the word about my work. We have the strongest and mightiest Bradenton, Florida, fan base because of it.

And to my husband, Jared Feldman, my home. I would set fire to and walk barefoot across the broken road a thousand times and again if I knew it would lead me straight to you. You are precisely and perfectly everything I had no reason to believe could exist but did anyway.

INDEX

Treasury notes (T-notes), 100, 101, 241
Trump, Donald, 110
trustees, 216, 242
trustors. *see* grantors
trusts
    inflation and, 102
    insurance for, 218–19, 220
    irrevocable, 217–18, 235
    living, 236
    protection from, 216
    real estate investment (REIT), 187–88, 238
    revocable, 217–18, 239
    testamentary, 217, 230, 241
Two Sigma, 196
Tyson Foods, Inc. (TSN), 137

UBS, 23
uncovered options, 167, 242
unemployment rate, 47, 93
universal life insurance, 219
Upwork, 149
US dollar (USD), 139
utilities, 27, 32, 137, 200

value stocks, 31–33, 59, 62, 242
Vanguard (VFAIX), 12, 22, 175, 208
Vanguard Target Retirement 2045 Fund
    Investor Shares (VTIVX), 185
venture capital, 188–89, 191, 205
venture capital funds, 188–92, 242
Verizon (VZ), 10, 59
VFAIX, 174
Visa (V), 10
VIX (volatility index), 57–59
VOL (volume of shares traded), 56
volatility
    of all-weather portfolios, 207–8
    in Argentina, 121
    beta as measure of, 59, 230
    definition of, 242
    and dollar-cost averaging, 37

insurance against, 221
of large-cap value funds, 177
negative EPS as cause of, 68
of permanent portfolios, 204
pros and cons of, 58
risk vs., 226
of soft commodities, 129
stress over, 40
VOO, 174, 208

Wachovia, 75
Wall Street (film), 110
Wall Street: Money Never Sleeps (film), 110
Wall Street Journal, xiii, 19, 54
Warren Buffett portfolio, 208–9, 242. *see also* Buffett, Warren
Washington Mutual, 75
waterfall insurance strategy, 220
Wealthfront, 22
wealth managers, 207
Webull, 22
Wells Fargo, 23
Wheaton Precious Metals Corp. (WPM), 135
whole life insurance, 219–20, 242
Wilshire 5000, 173
Wong, Stanford, 6

XOM (Exxon Mobil Corporation), 32

Yale University, 201, 204
yield curve, 93–95, 242
yields
    of CDs, 77, 86
    definition of, 242
    dividend, 60
    of savings accounts, xiv, 3, 37, 89
    of stock market, xvi

Zoe Financial, 26

ABOUT THE AUTHOR

NICOLE LAPIN is the *New York Times* and *Wall Street Journal* bestselling author of *Rich Bitch, Boss Bitch, Becoming Super Woman,* and *Miss Independent.* Her books have become instant hits with audiences looking to take charge of their money and careers. Lapin has been an anchor on CNN, CNBC, and Bloomberg, as well as the host of the network business reality competition show *Hatched.* She is the founder of Money News Network, a pioneer business- and finance-focused podcast network, which is the home of her daily show *Money Rehab*—consistently number one on Apple's business charts—as well as *Help Wanted,* which she cohosts with the editor-in-chief of *Entrepreneur* magazine Jason Feifer, among other top shows on MNN's slate.

Lapin teaches a series of online masterclasses also called The Money School. She has been a finance professor at the Jack Welch School of Business at Strayer University. Lapin was named GOBankingRates' Money Expert of the Year for the second year in a row and is the first female winner. Lapin earned the Accredited Investment Fiduciary (AIF®) certification and graduated *summa cum laude* and valedictorian of her class at Northwestern University's Medill School of Journalism, also earning honors in political science.

NEW YORK TIMES BESTSELLING AUTHOR OF
RICH BITCH AND RENOWNED MONEY EXPERT

NICOLE LAPIN

makes investing accessible and fun so
women can make bank and become

Miss Independent

"What I love about Nicole is that you don't
need a dictionary to understand her advice.
It's crystal clear, straight-up, and spot-on."

—ALYSSA MILANO, actress, activist,
and founder of Touch by Alyssa Milano

"A financial diet is like a regular diet:
if you allow yourself small indulgences,
you won't binge later on. Nicole offers
you a plan you can stick to."

—SANJAY GUPTA,
CNN chief medical correspondent